MACAU
In Black and White

A Photographic Exploration

Scott Shaw

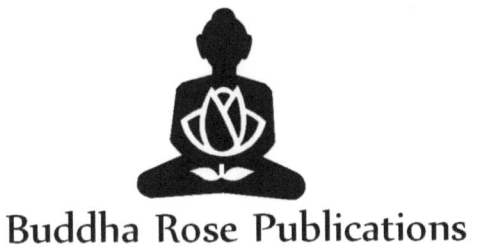

Buddha Rose Publications

Macau in Black and White: A Photographic Exploration
Copyright © 2015 by Scott Shaw
www.scottshaw.com
All Rights Reserved

No part of this book may be reproduced in any manner without the expressed written permission of the author or the publishing company.

ISBN 10: 1-877792-86-1
ISBN 13: 978-1-877792-86-1

Printed in the United States of America
By Buddha Rose Publications

10 9 8 7 6 5 4 3 2 1

MACAU
In Black and White

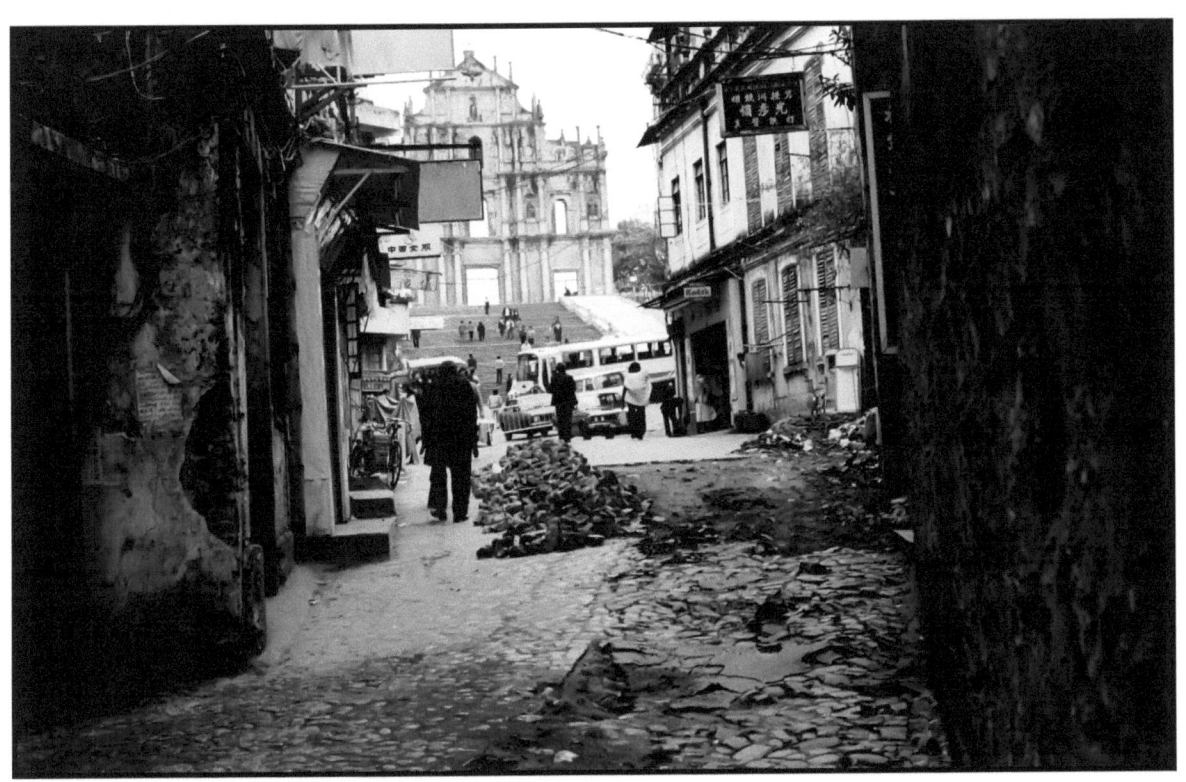

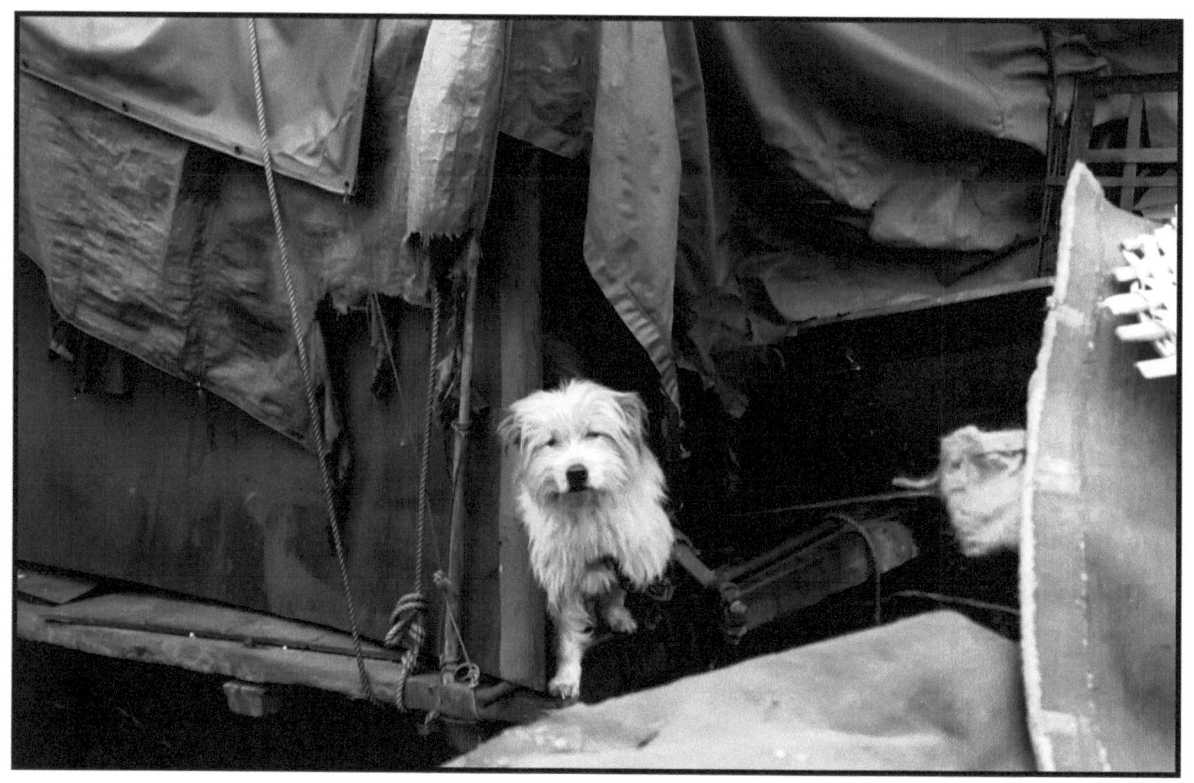

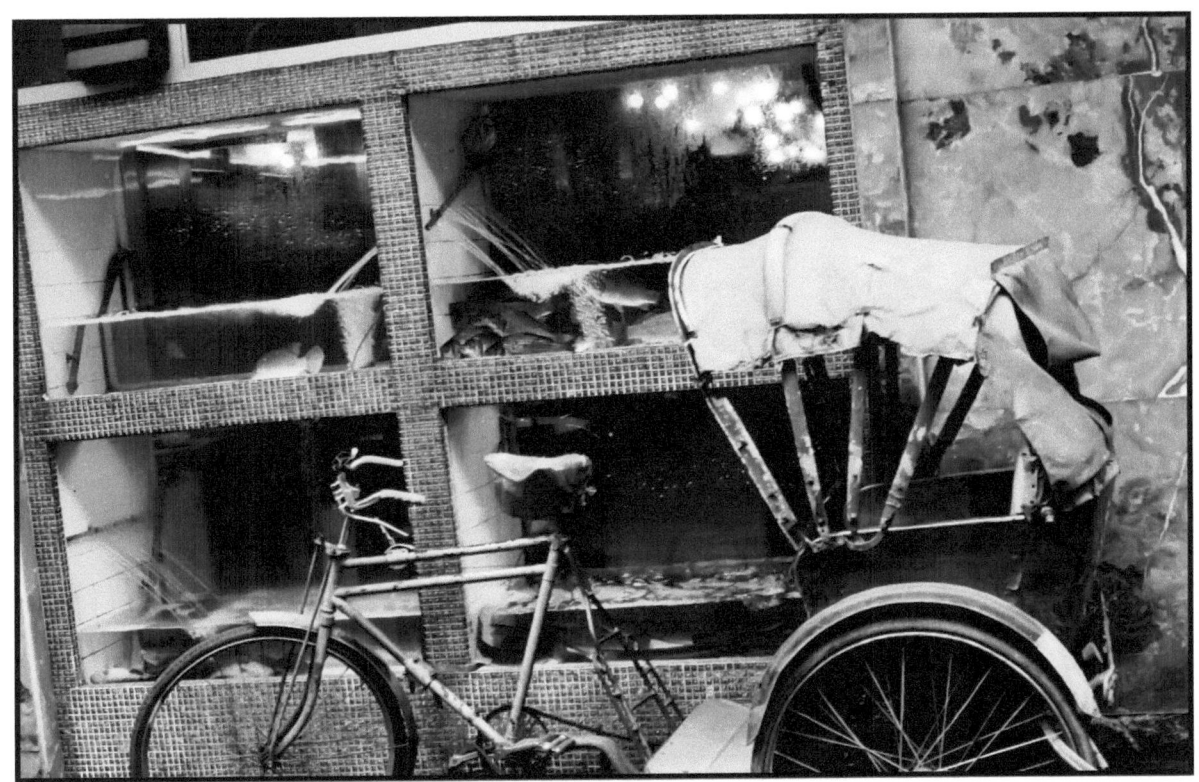

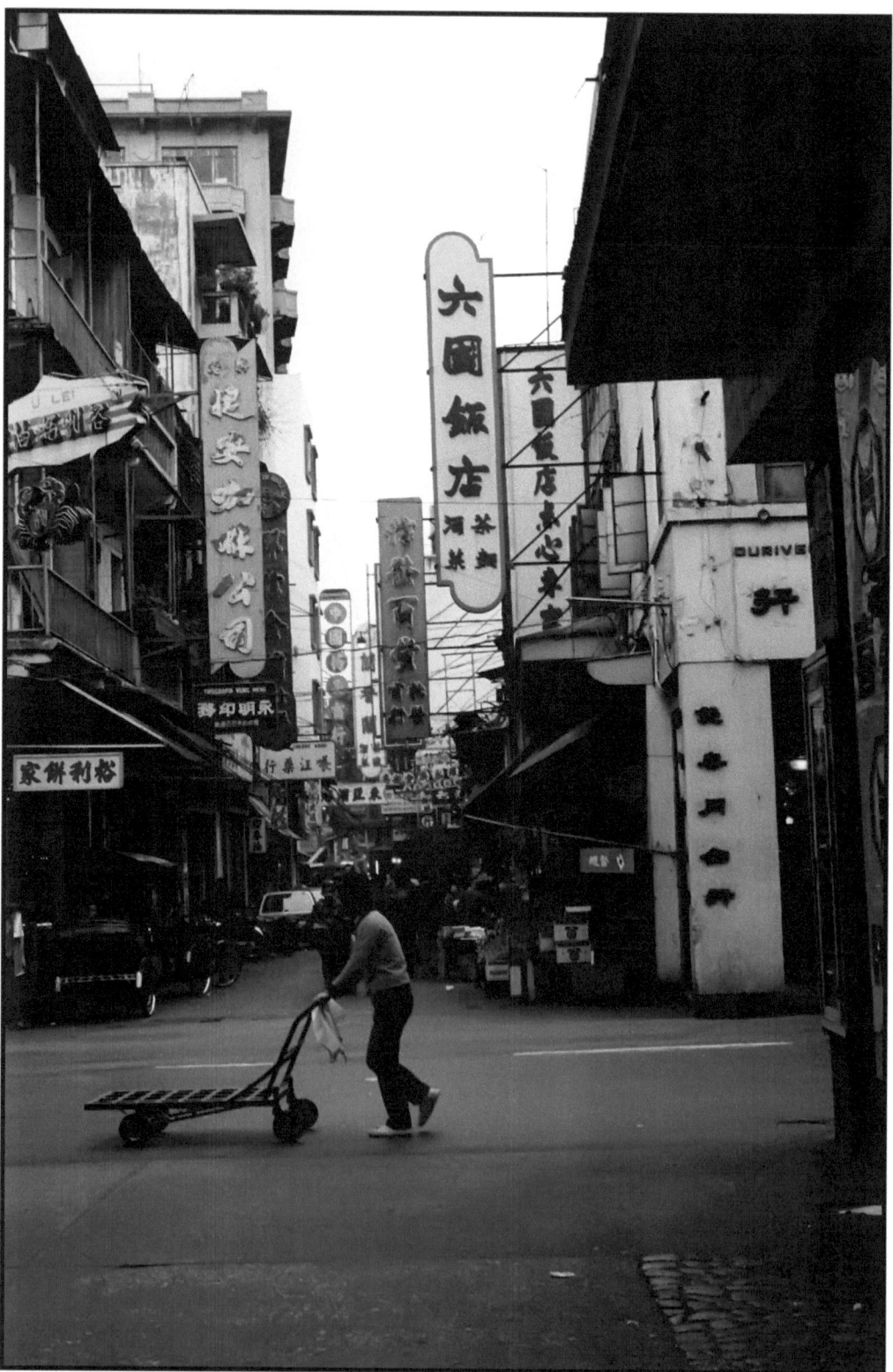

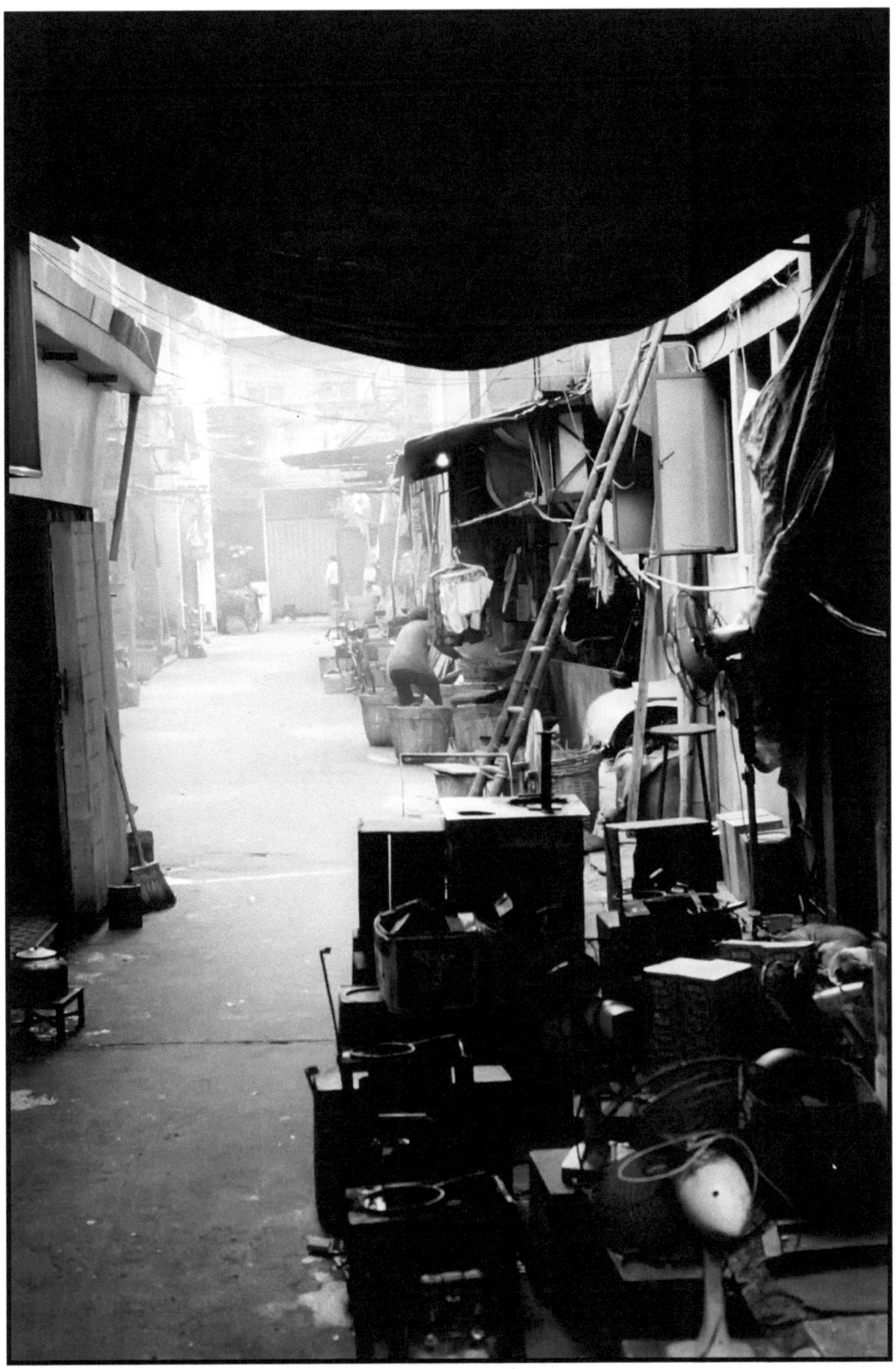

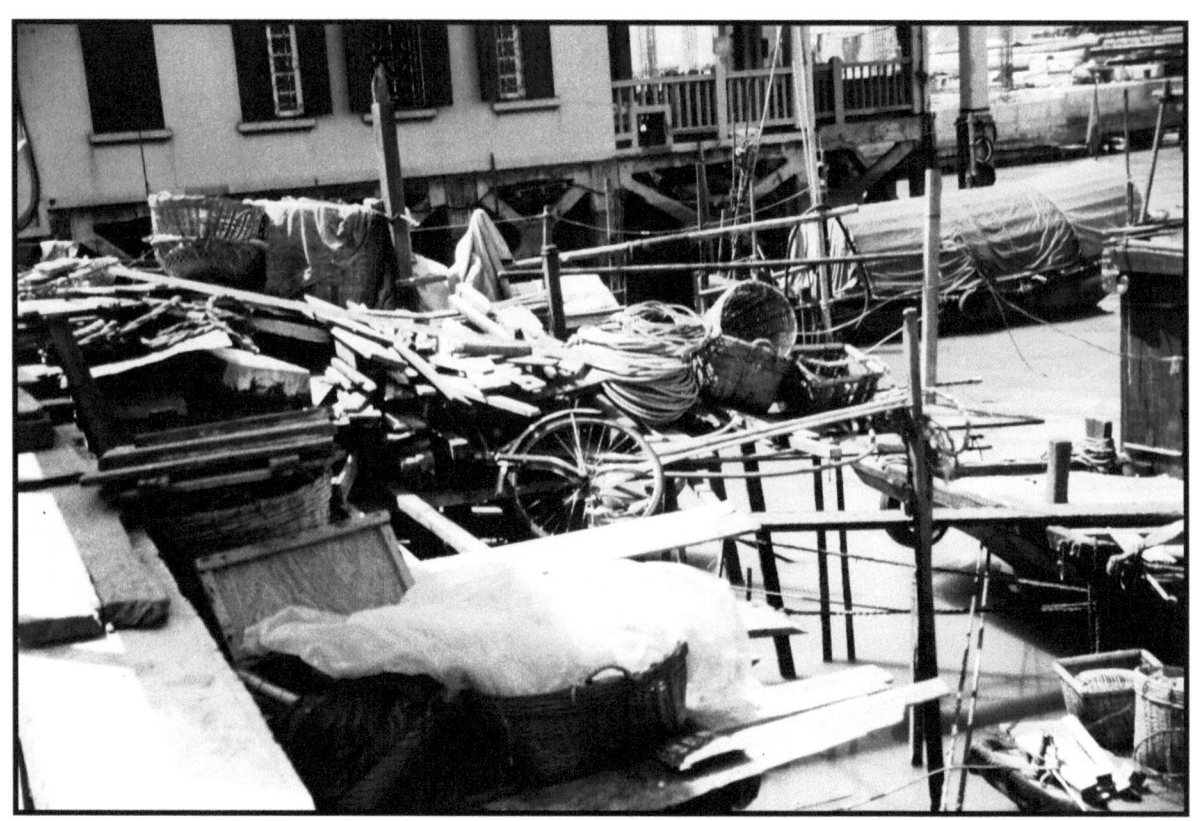

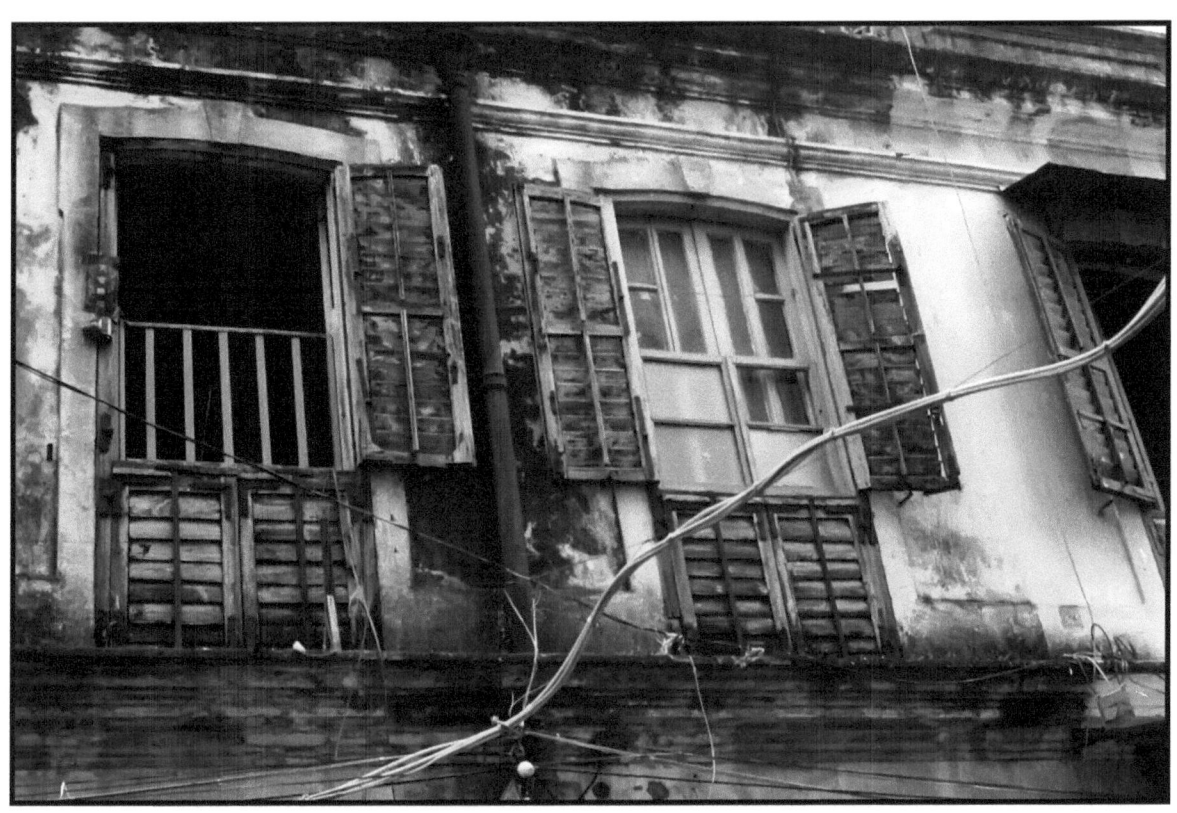

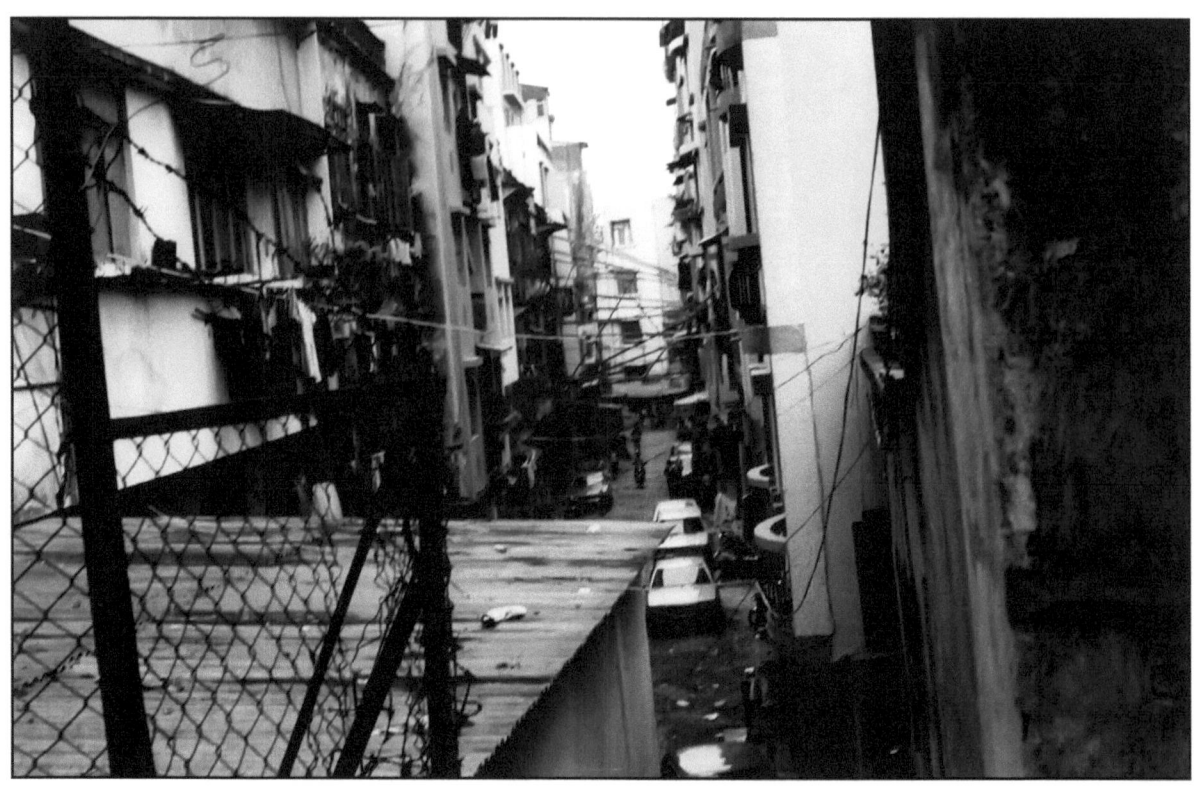

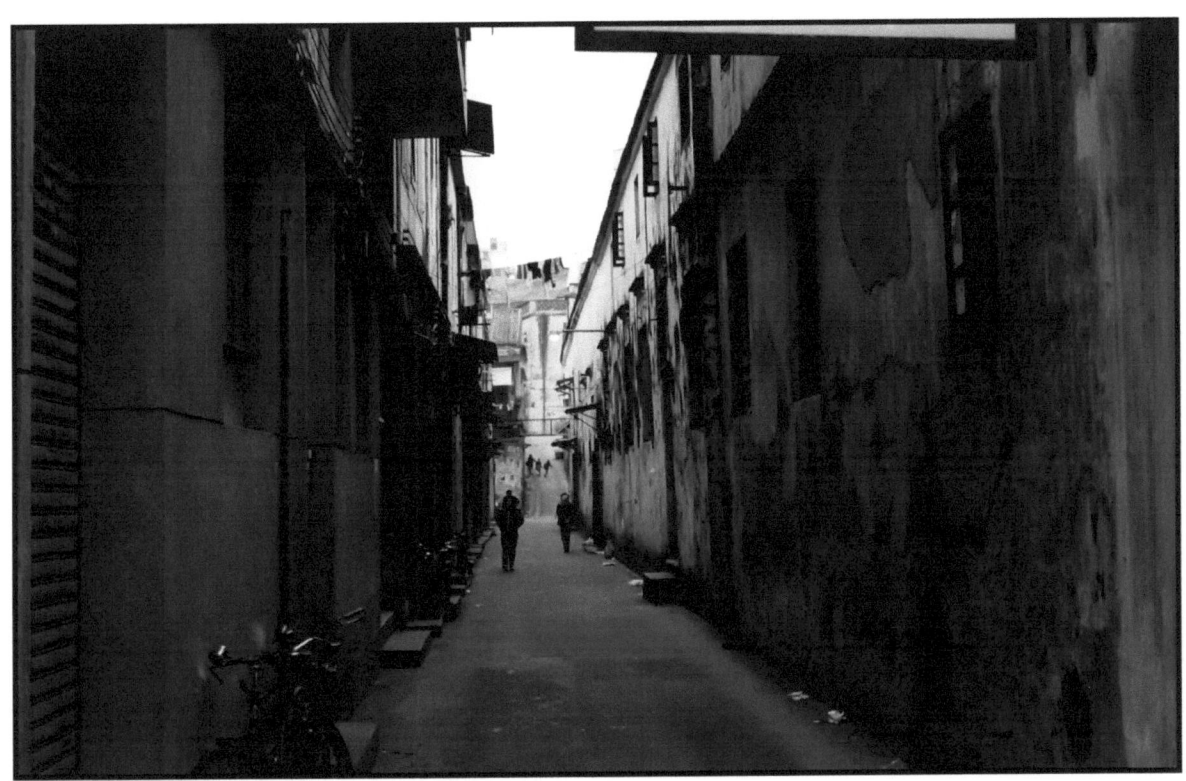

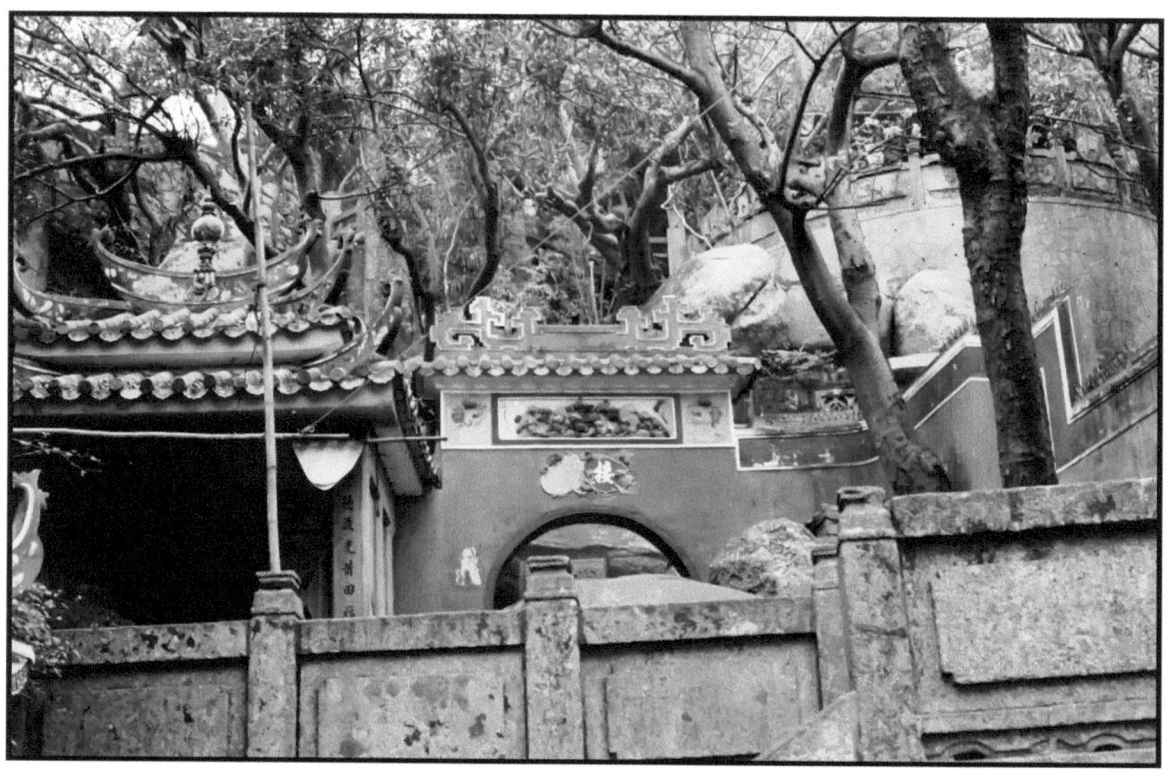

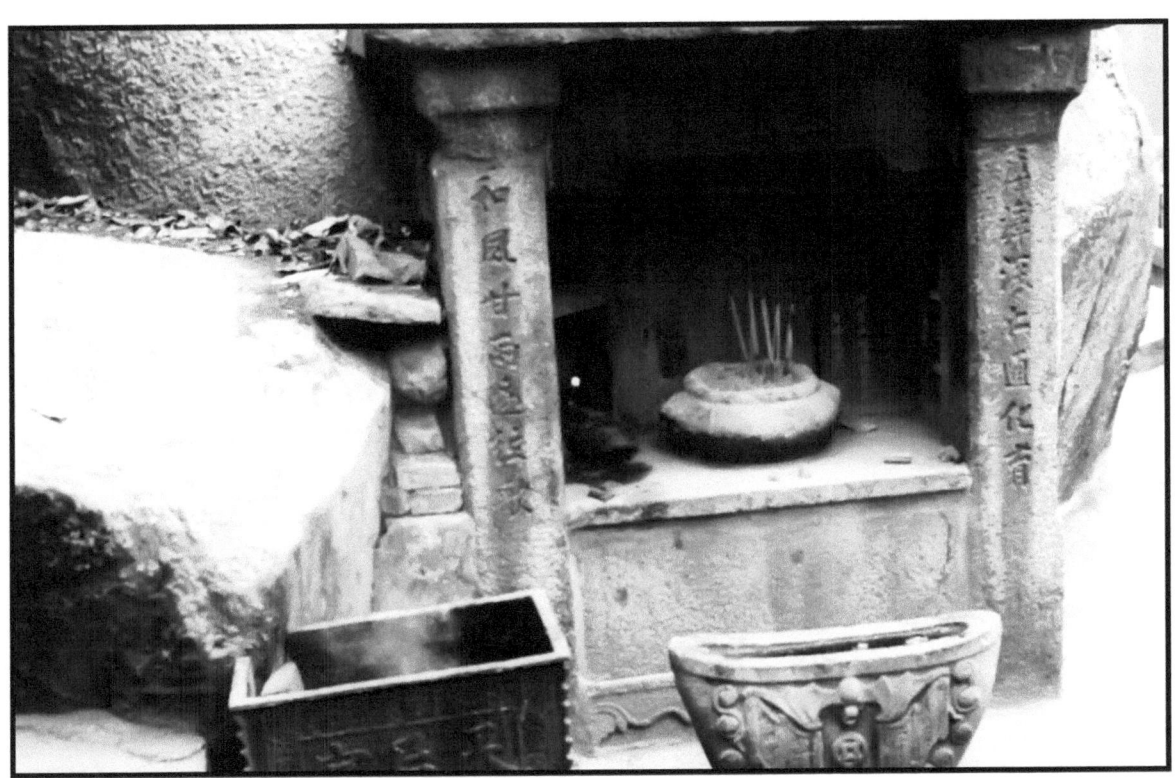

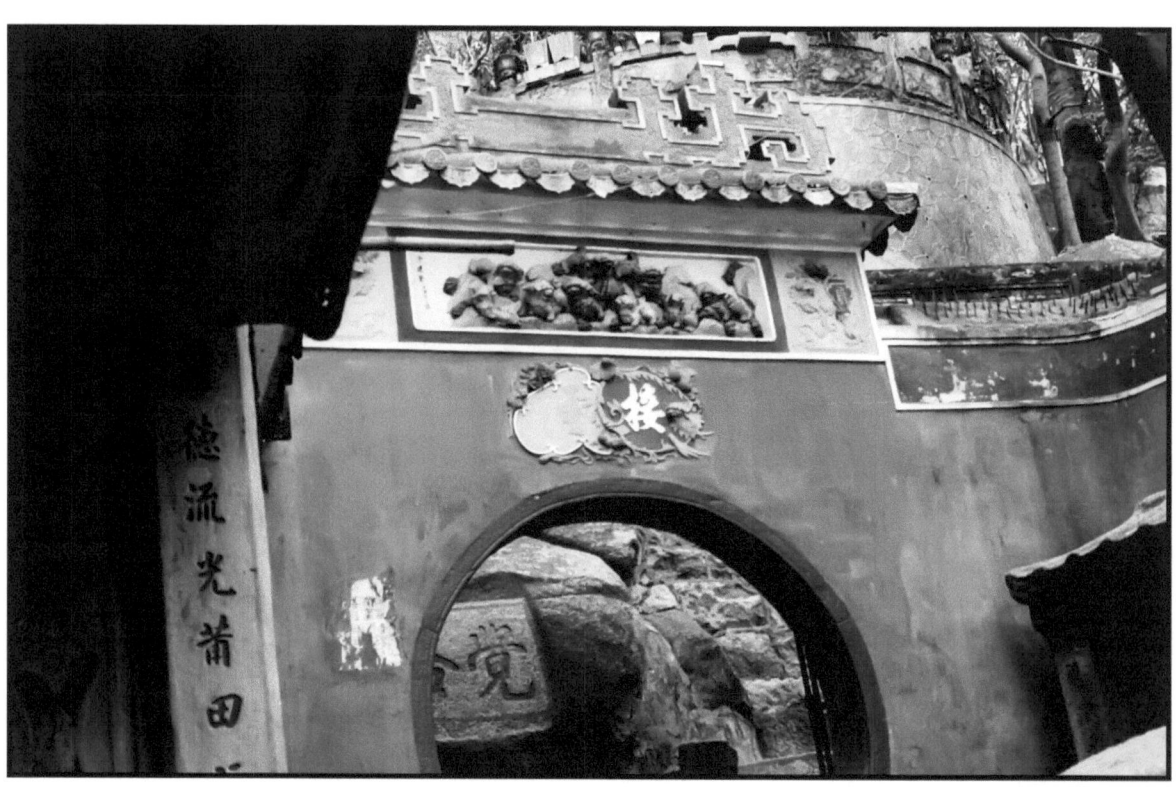

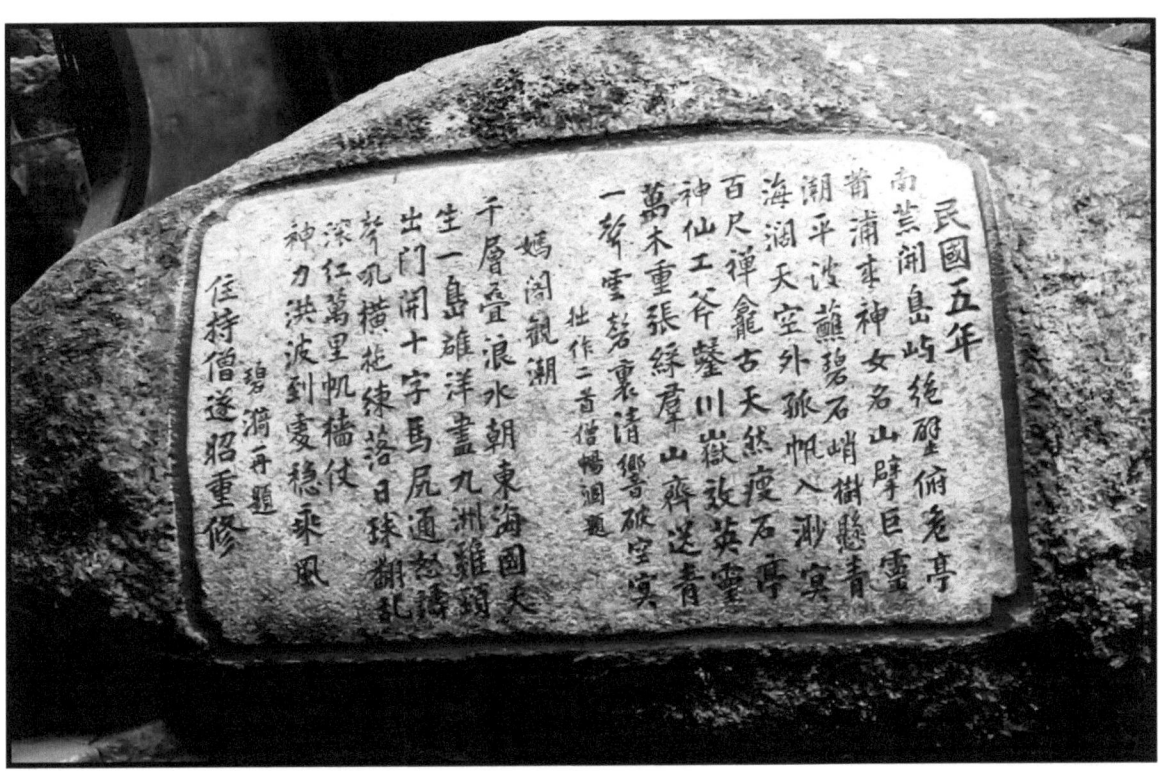

民國五年南荒閒島嶼絕壁俯兔亭
背浦來神女名山壁巨靈
暗浦波蘸碧石峭樹懸青
潮平波蘸碧帆入渺溟
海湖天空外孤帆入渺溟
百尺禪龕古天然瘦石亭
神仙工斧鑿川嶽放英靈
萬木重張綠摩山齊送青
一聲雲磬裏清響破空冥
　　　　拙作二首借暢週題

媽閣觀潮
千層疊浪水朝東海國天
生一島雄洋盡九洲雞頭
出門開十字馬尻通松海
琴瓶橫托練落日珠潮孔
滾紅萬里帆檣伏
神力洪波到麥穩乘風
　　碧漪戶題

住持僧遂昭重修

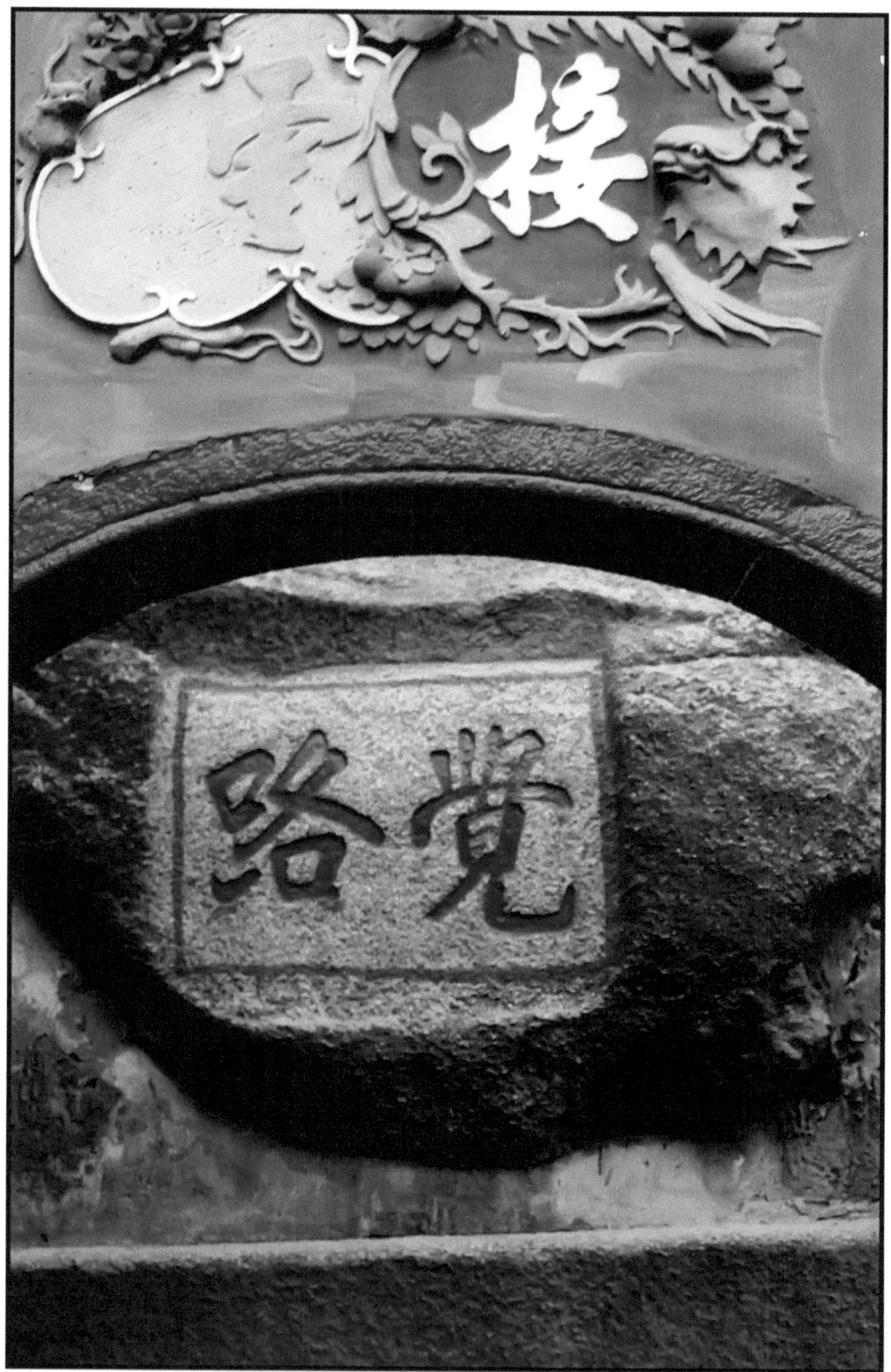

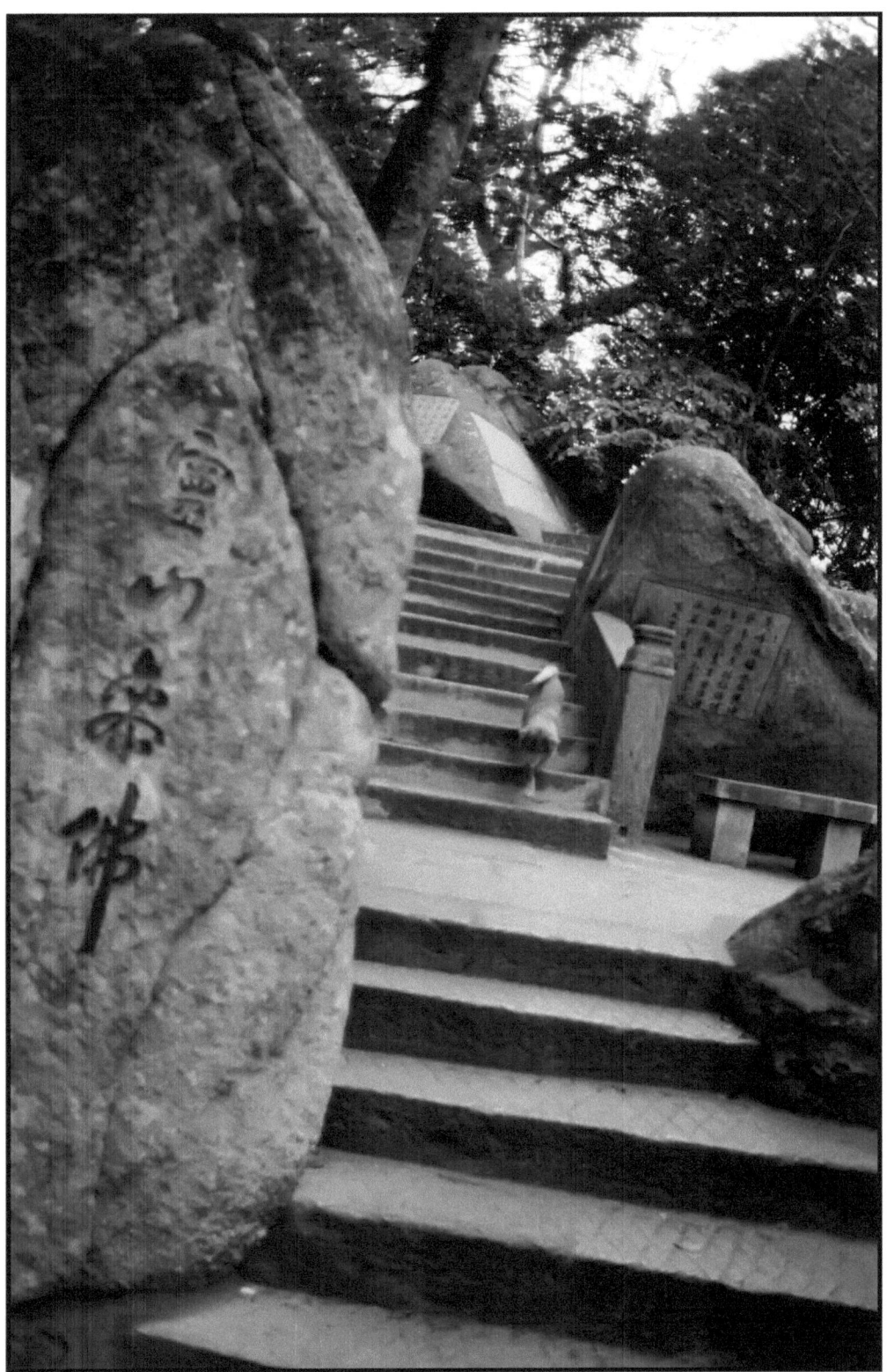

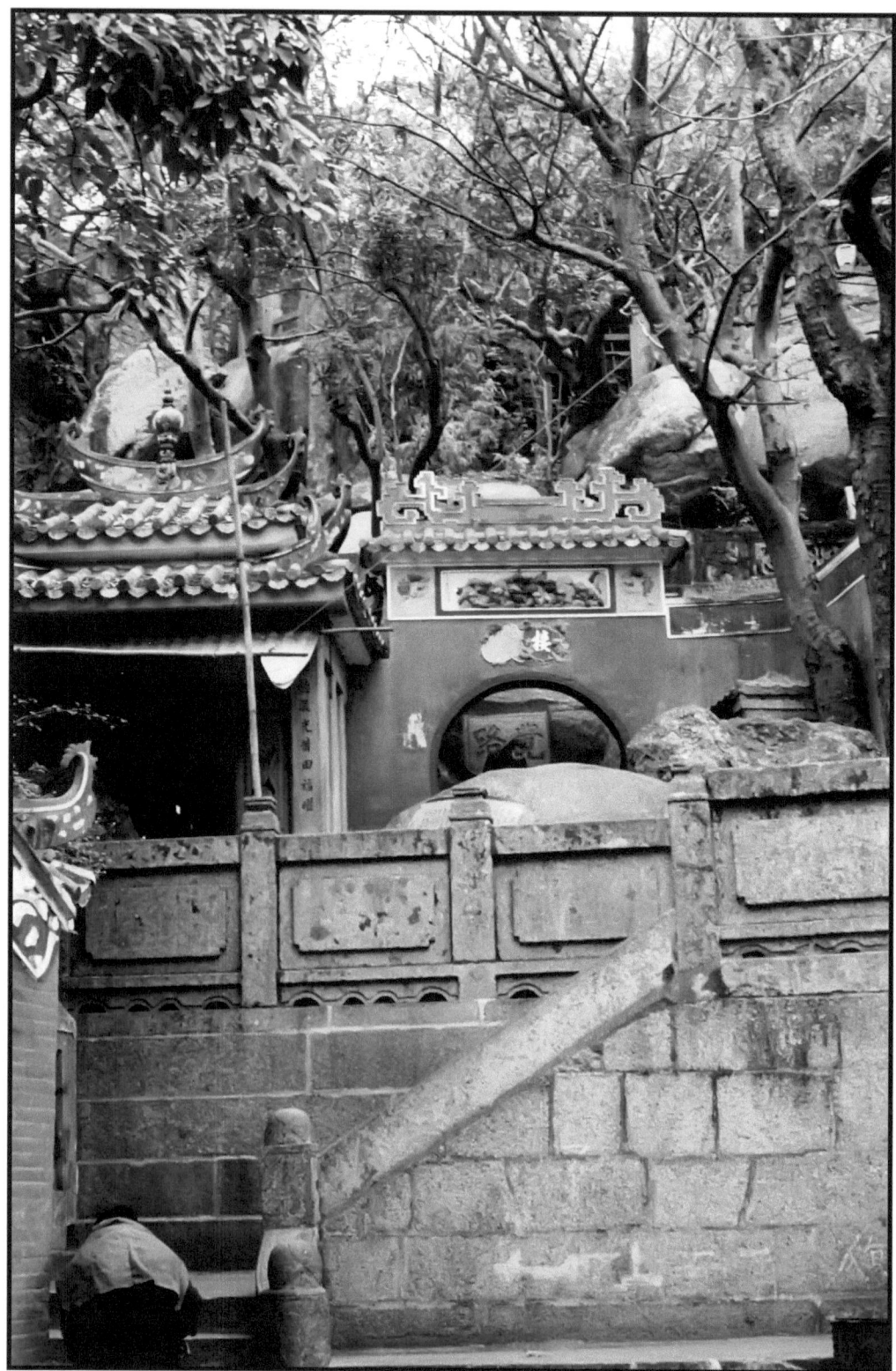

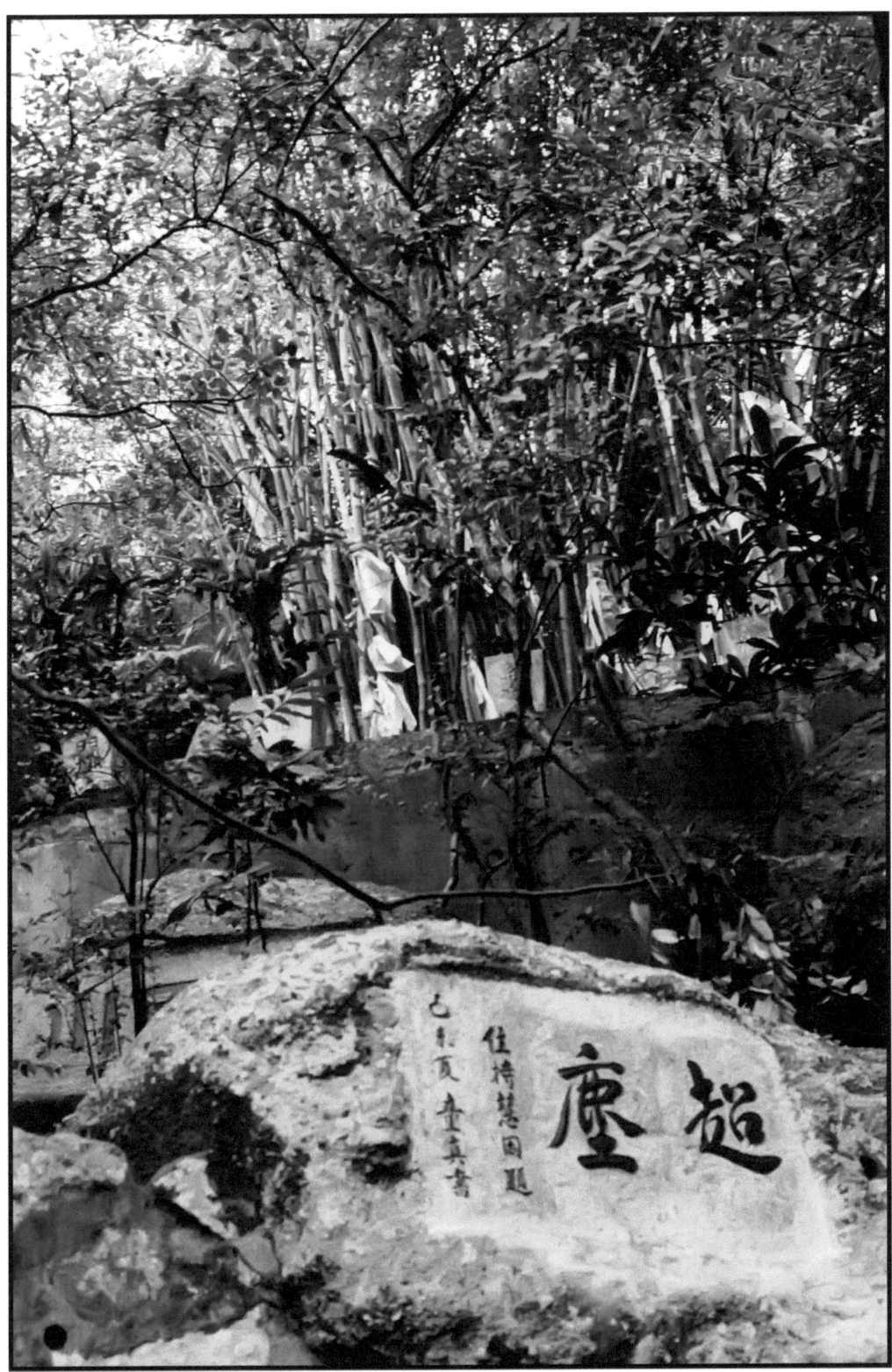

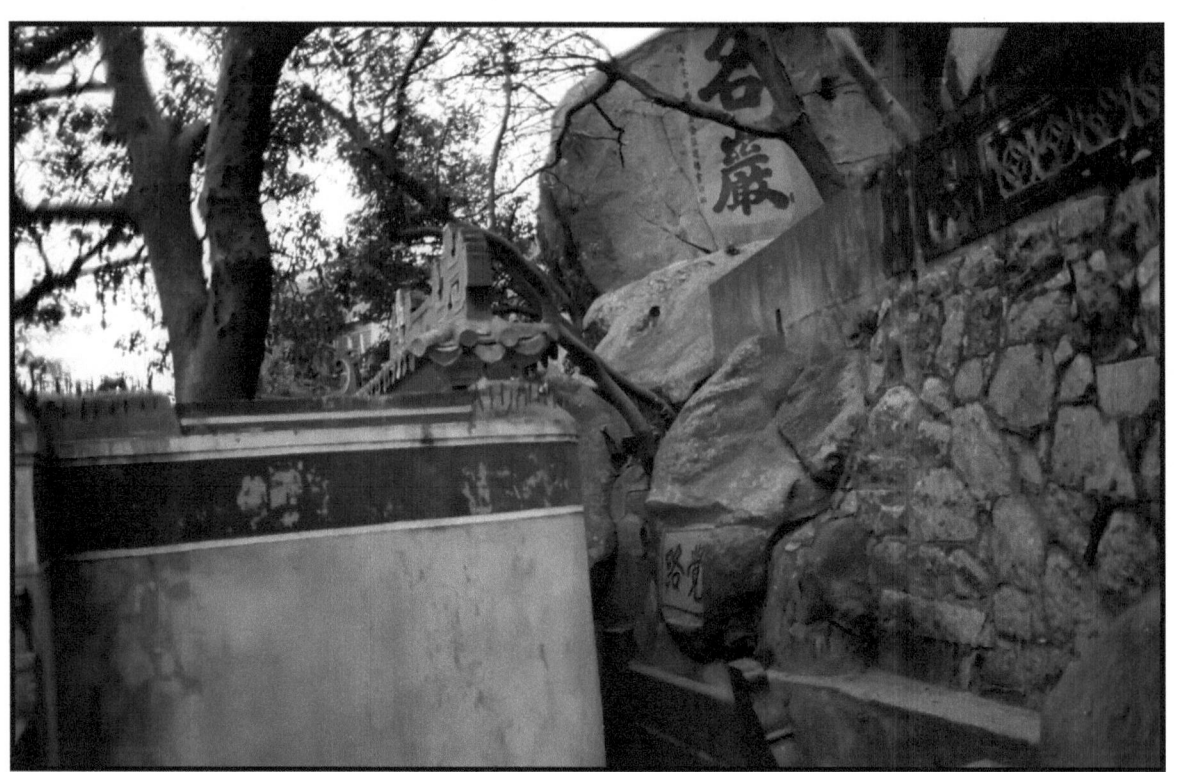

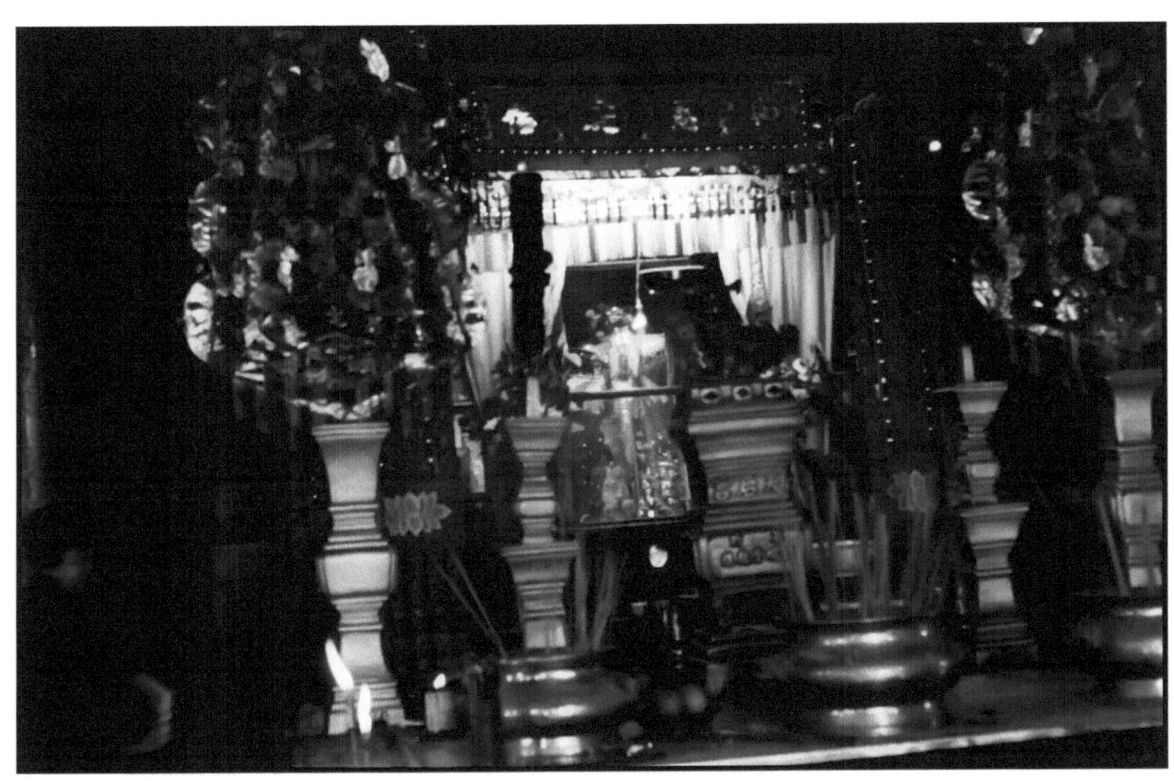

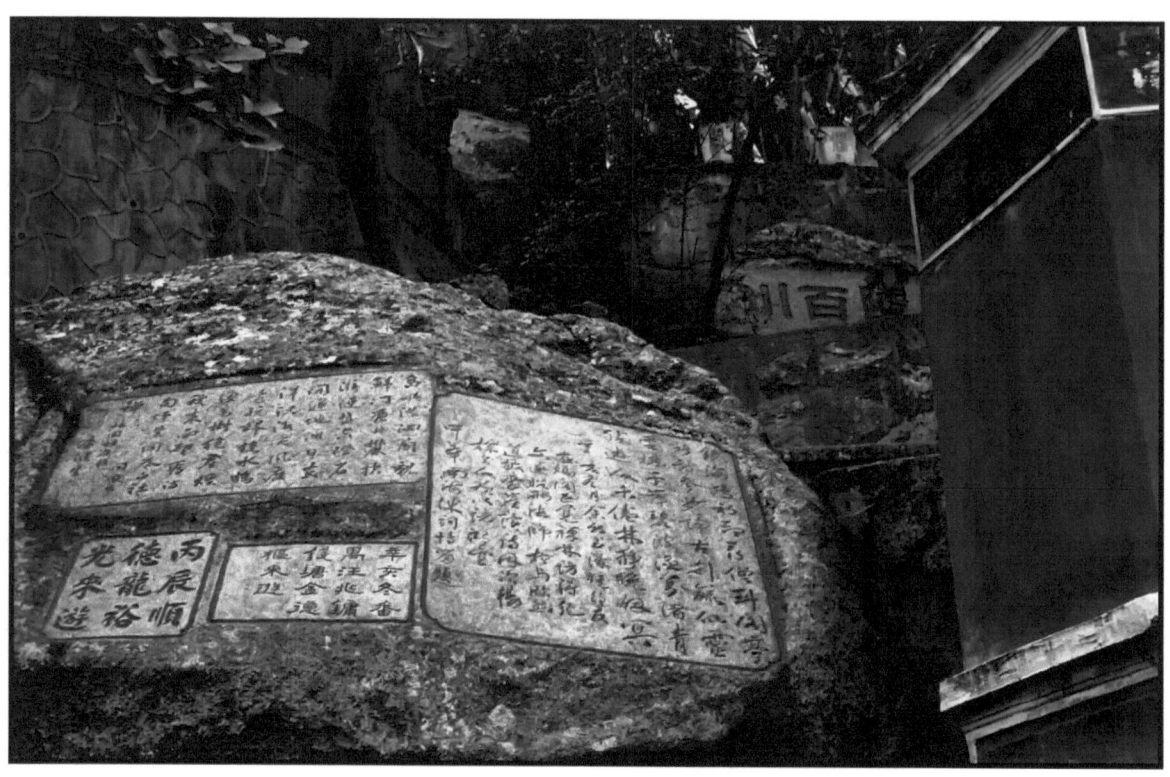

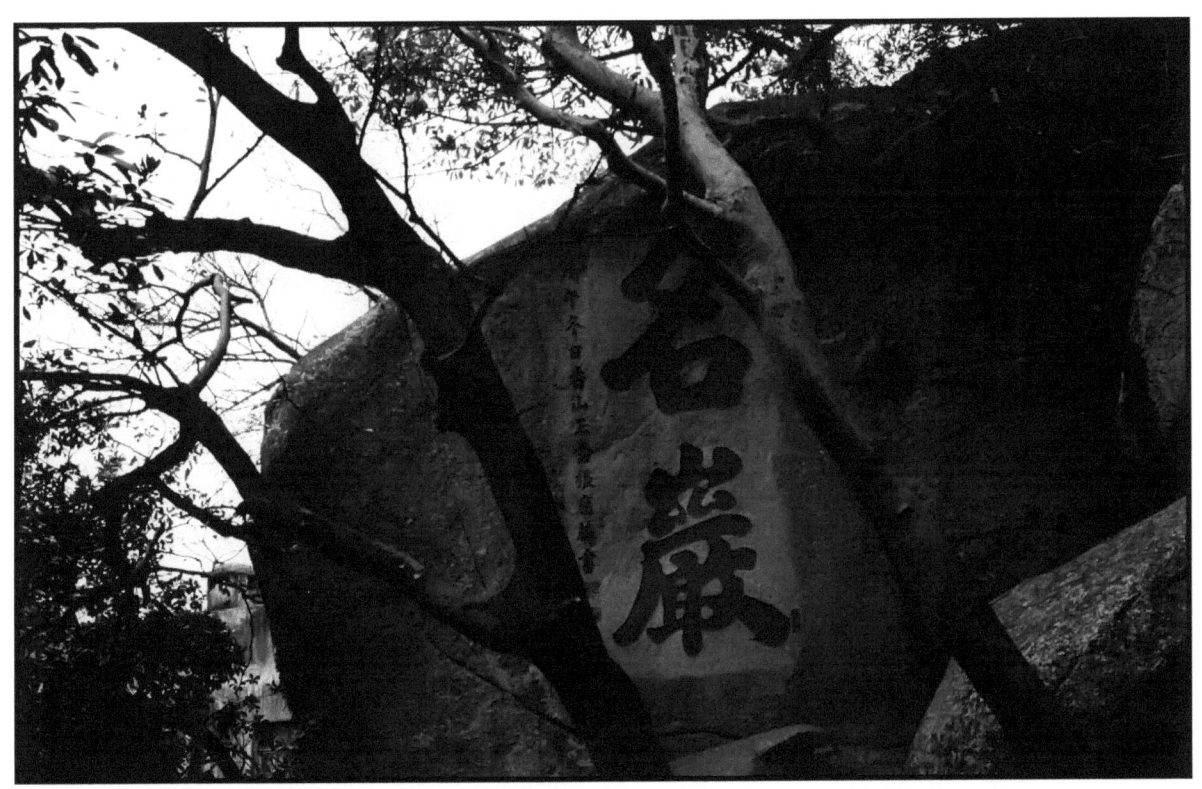

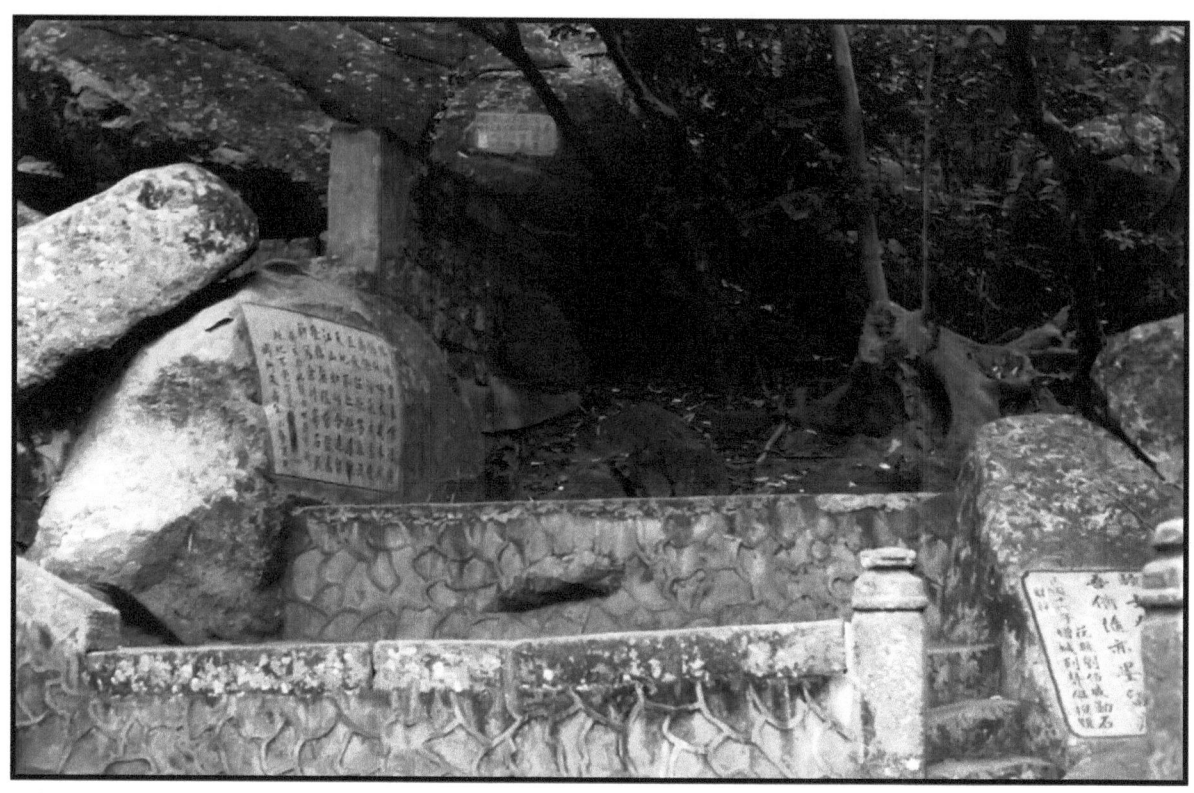

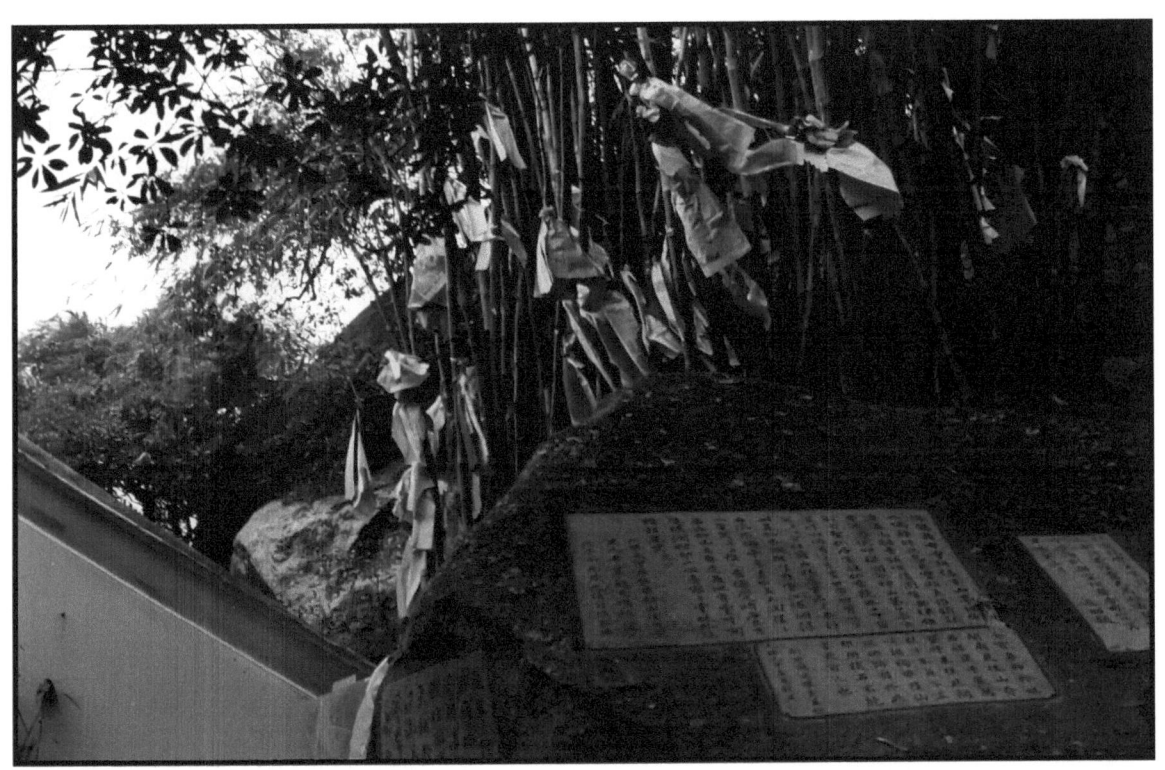

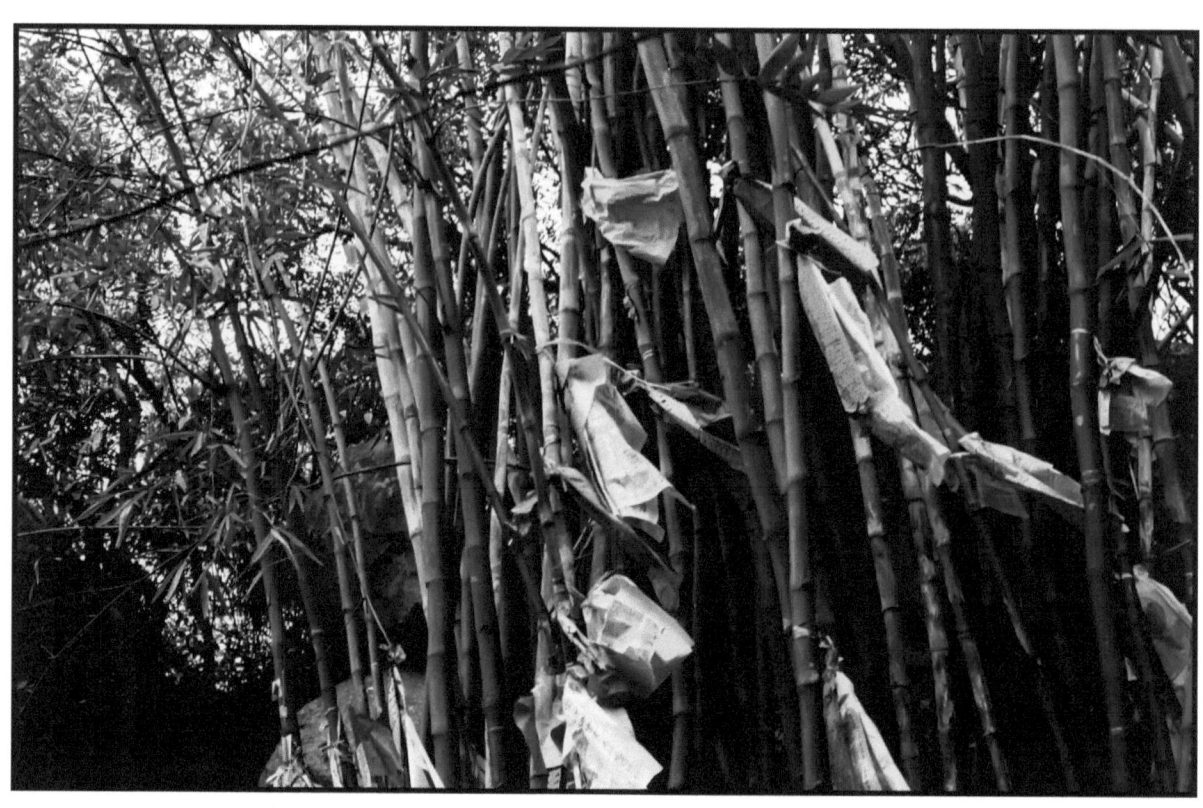

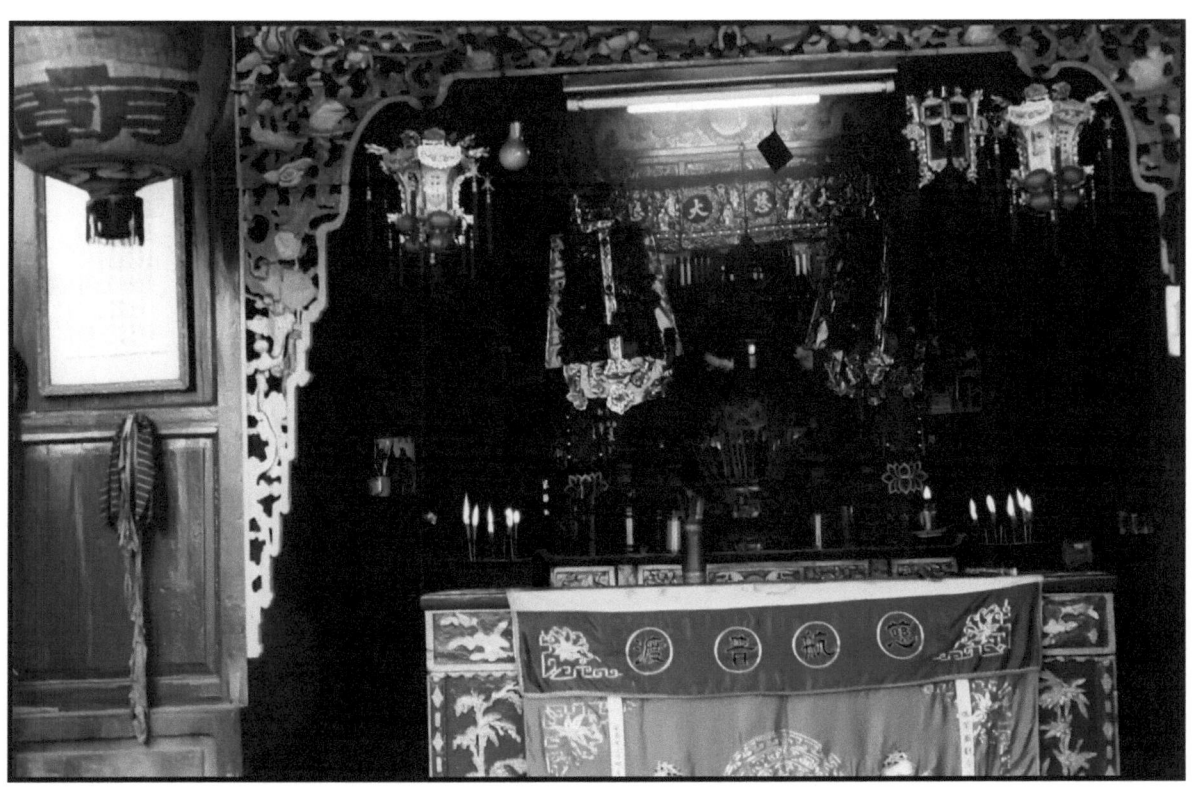

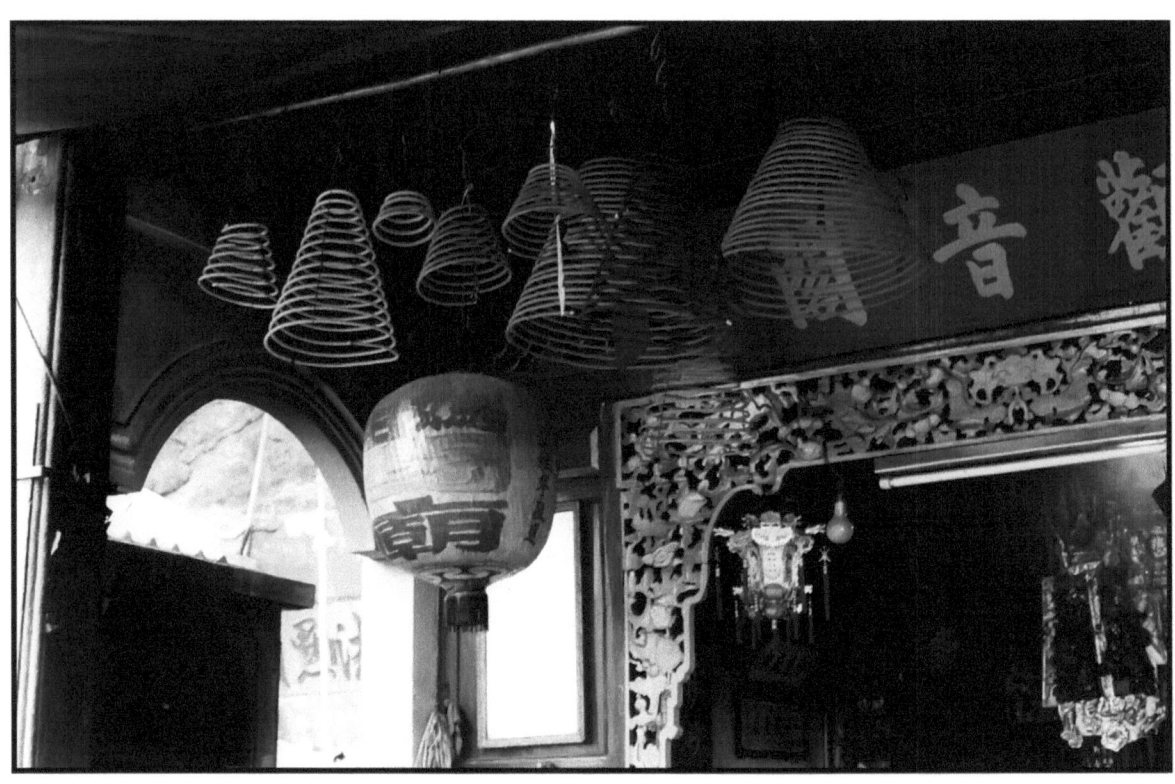

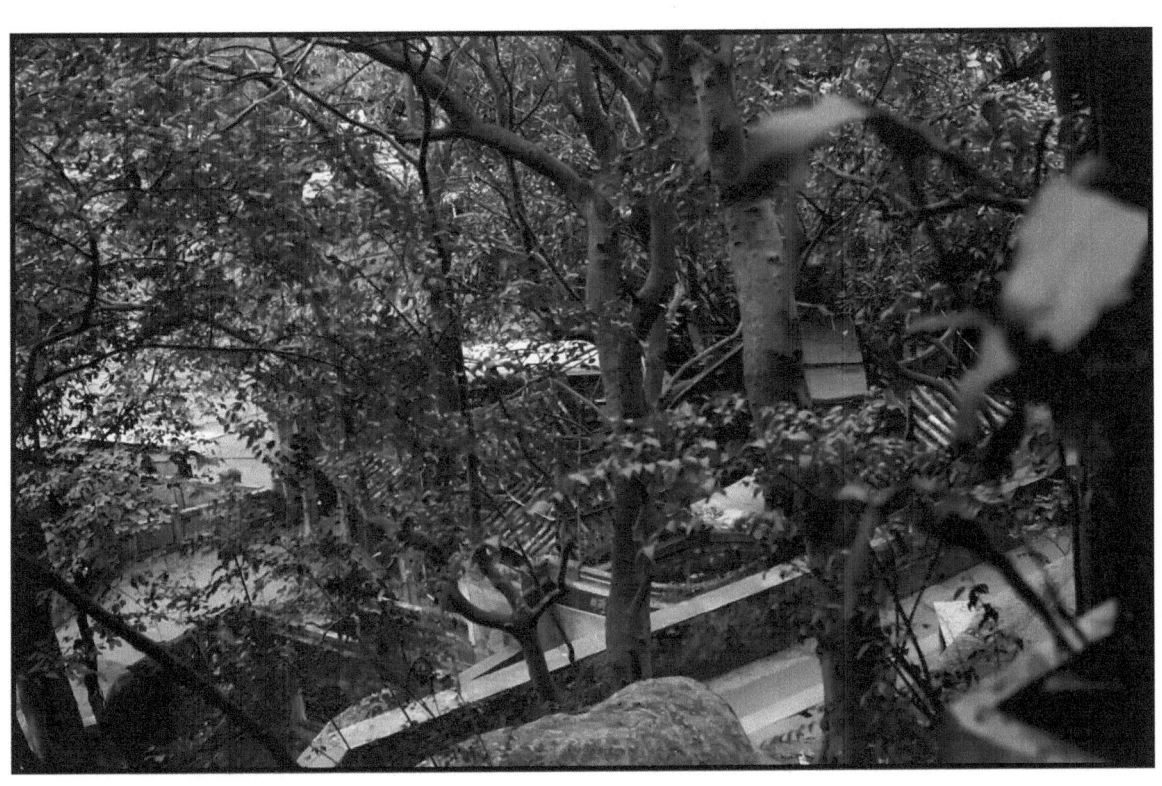

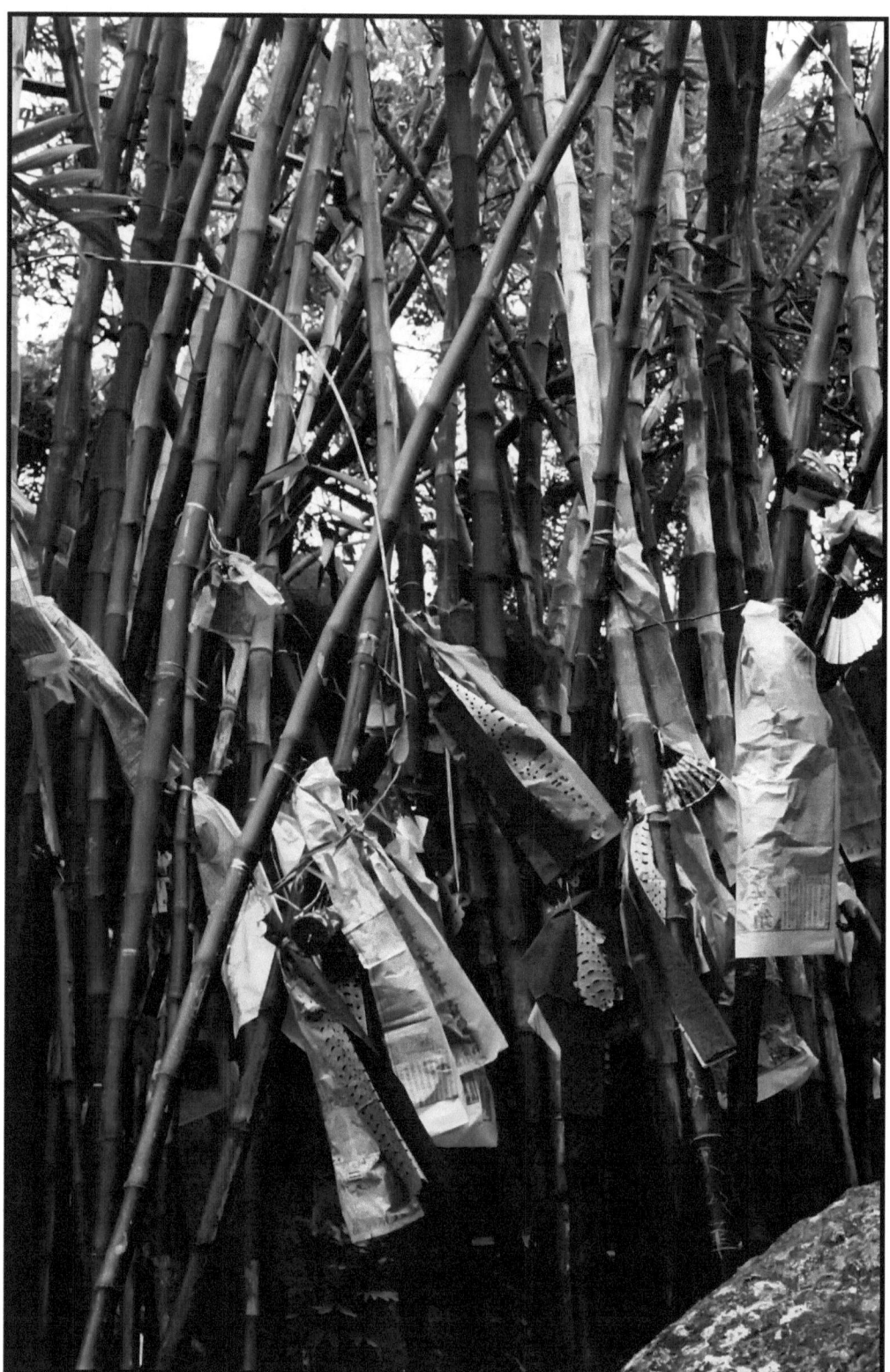

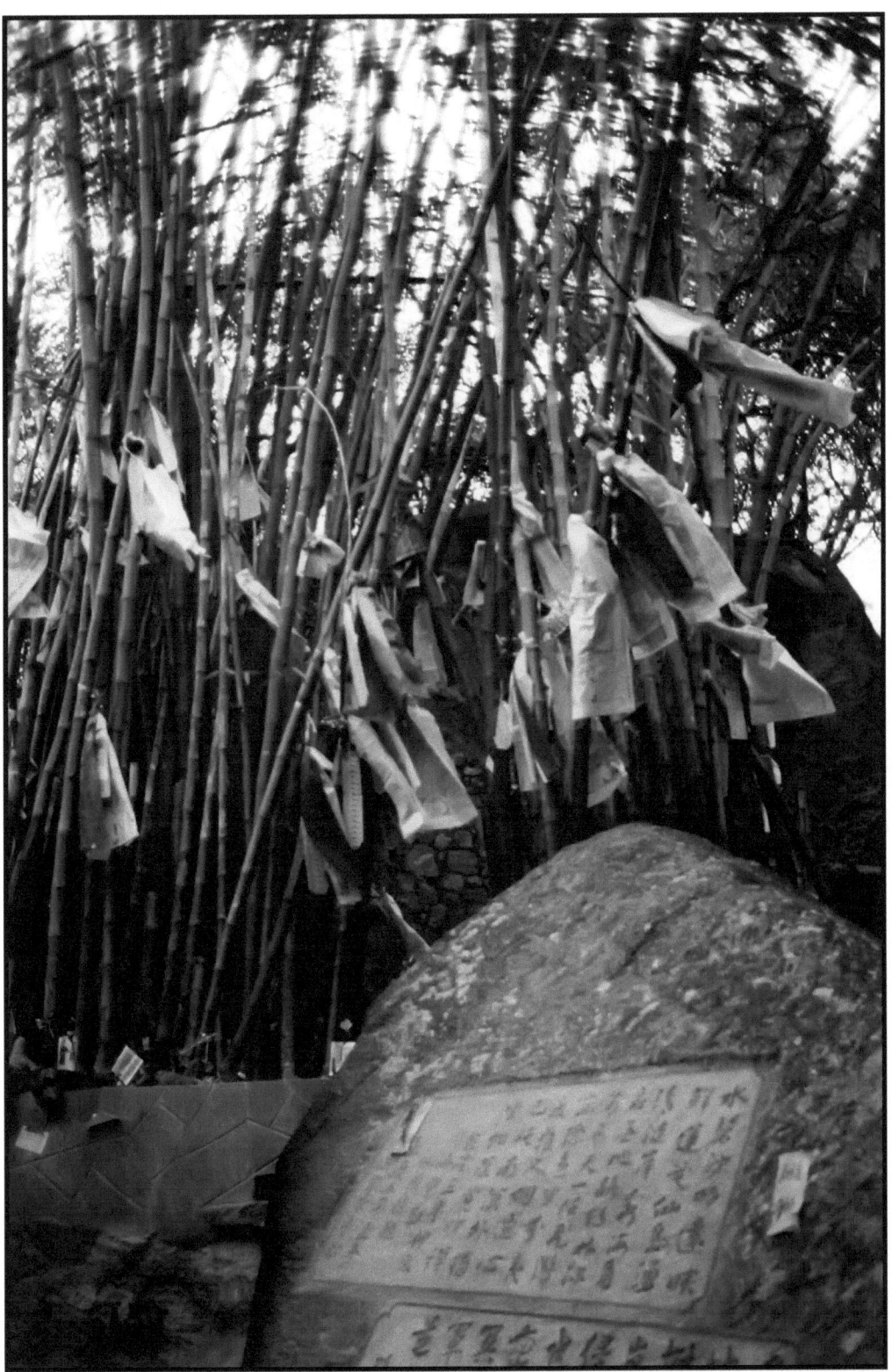

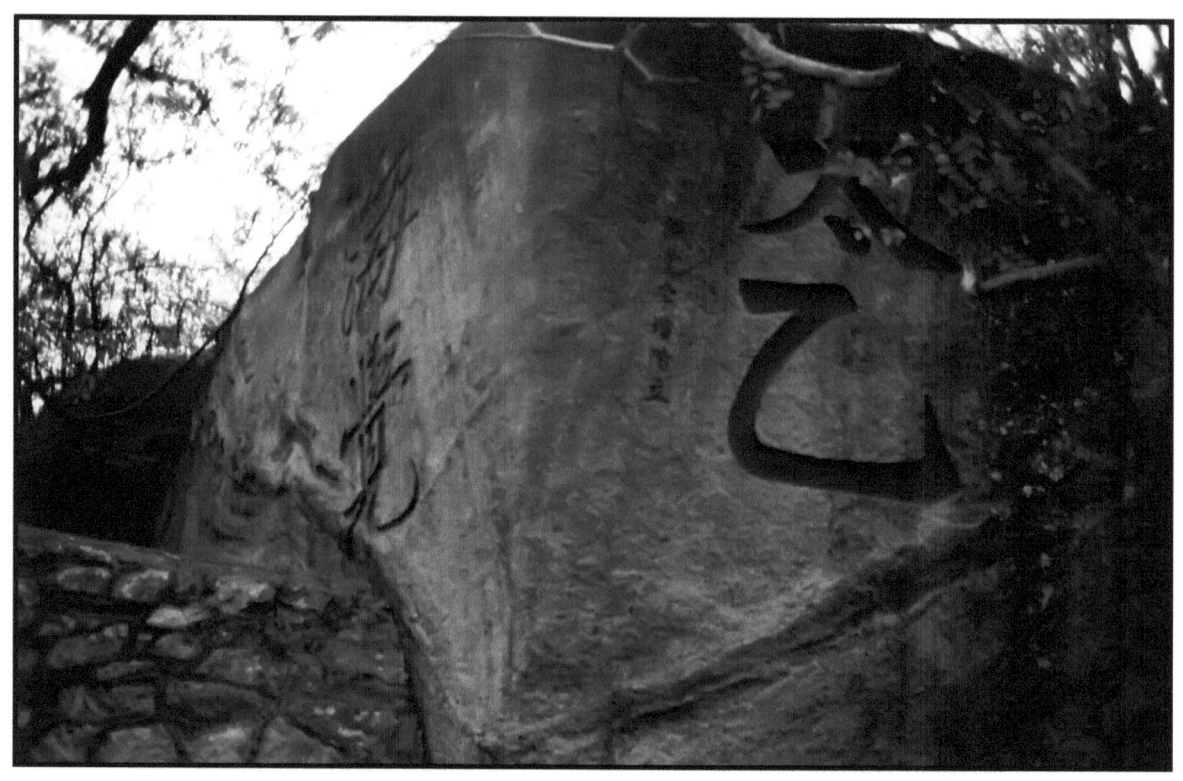

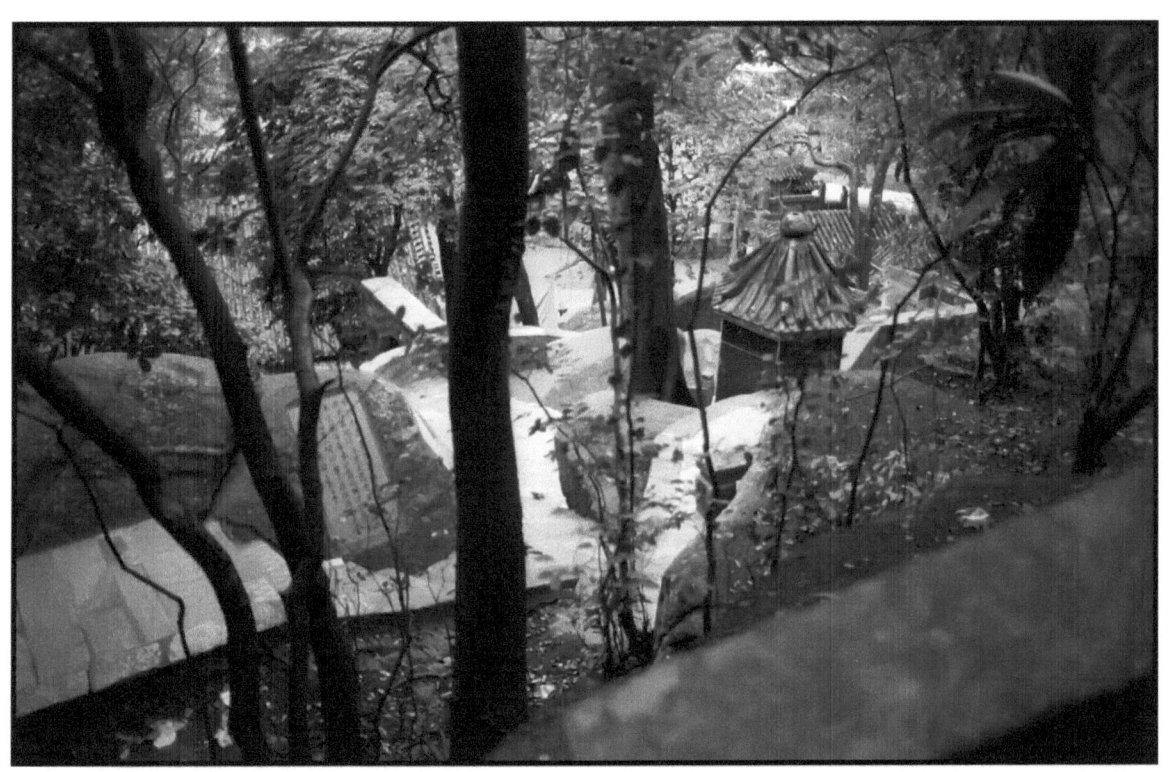

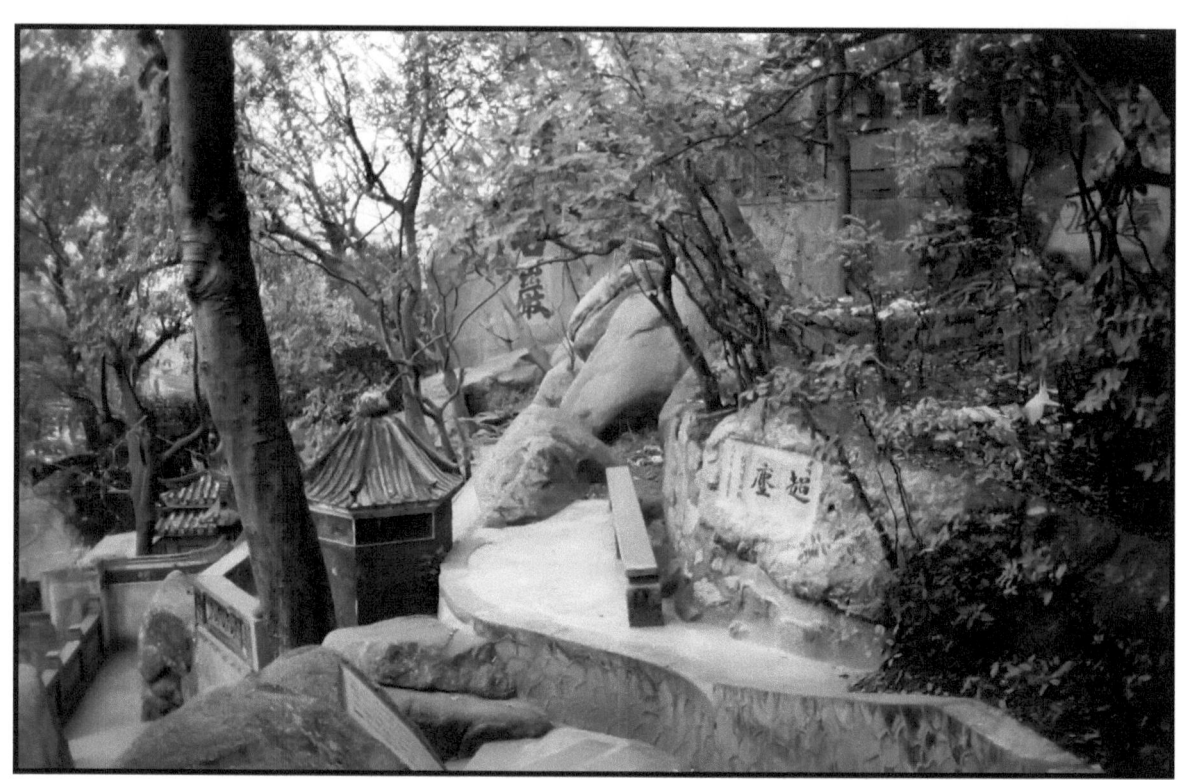

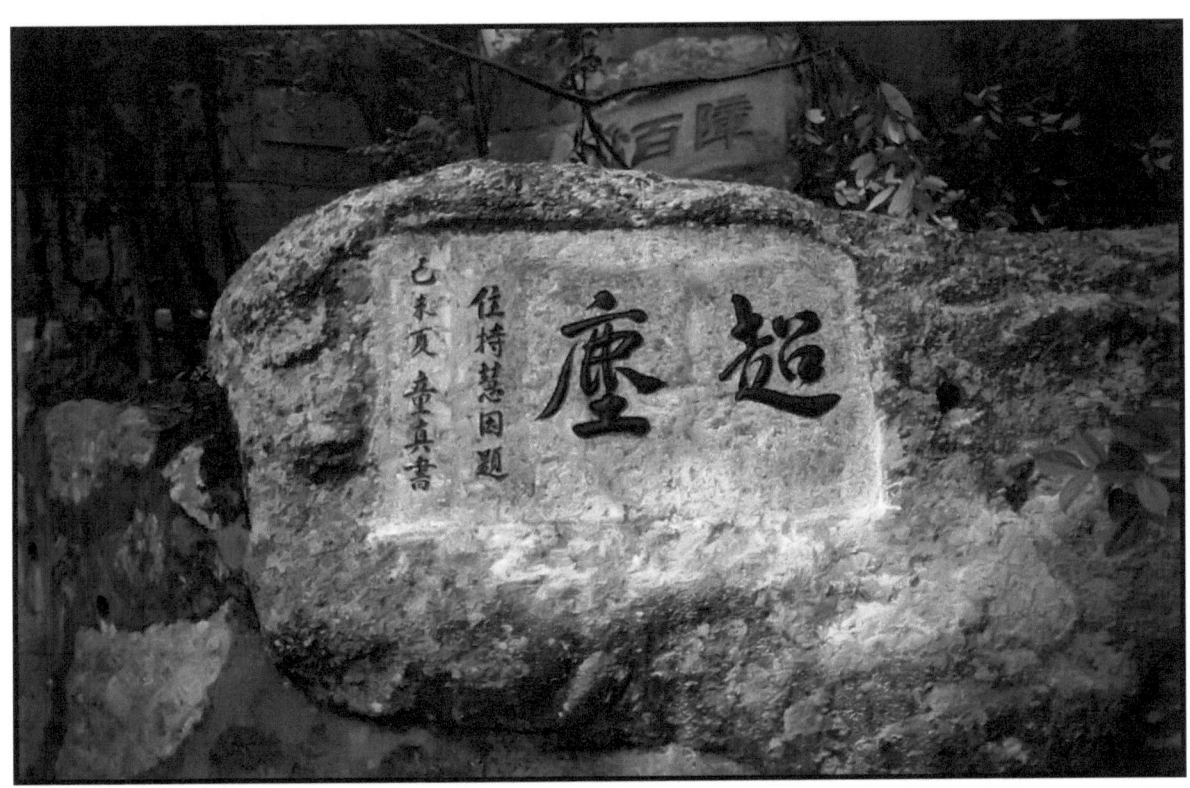

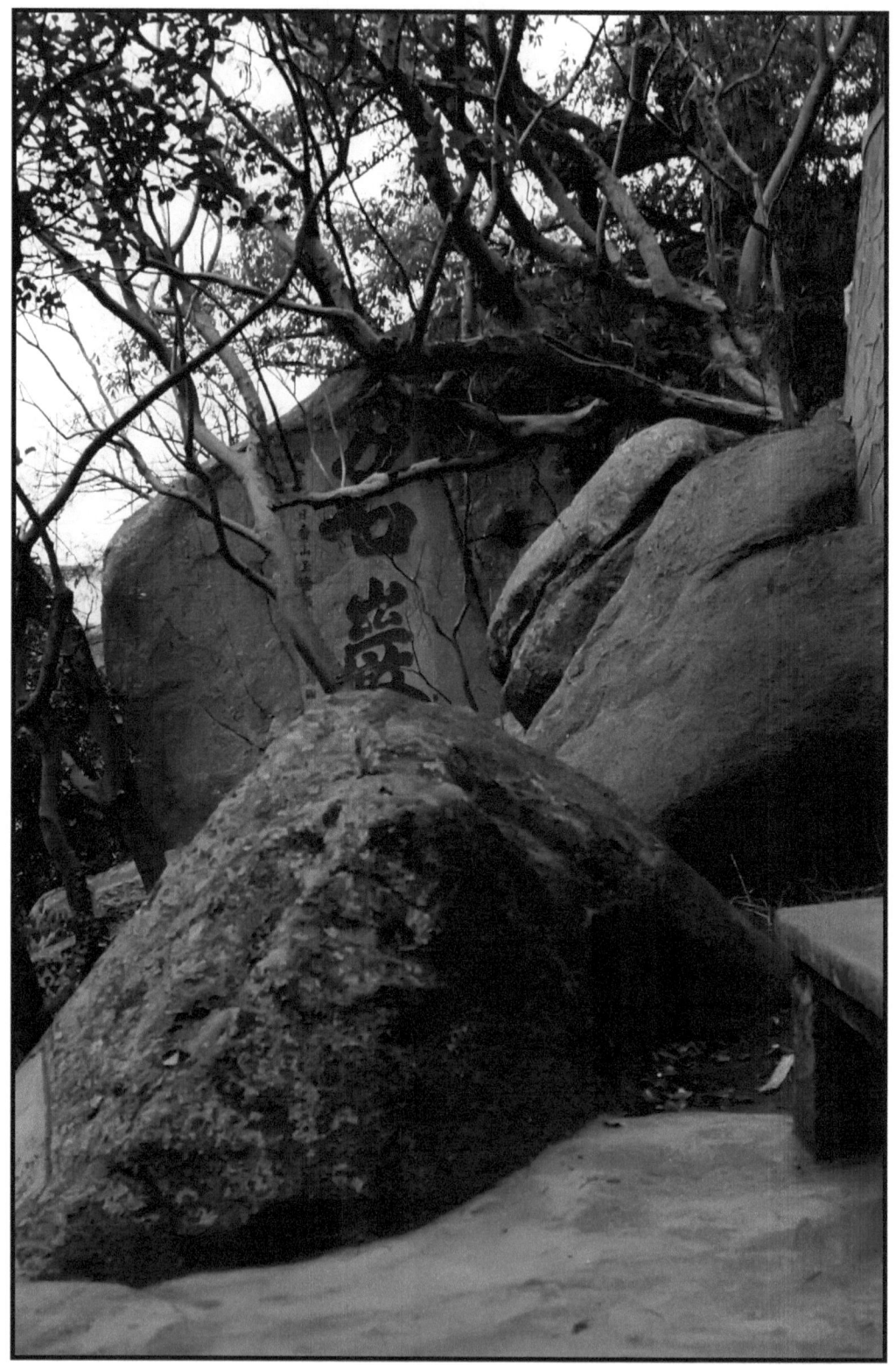

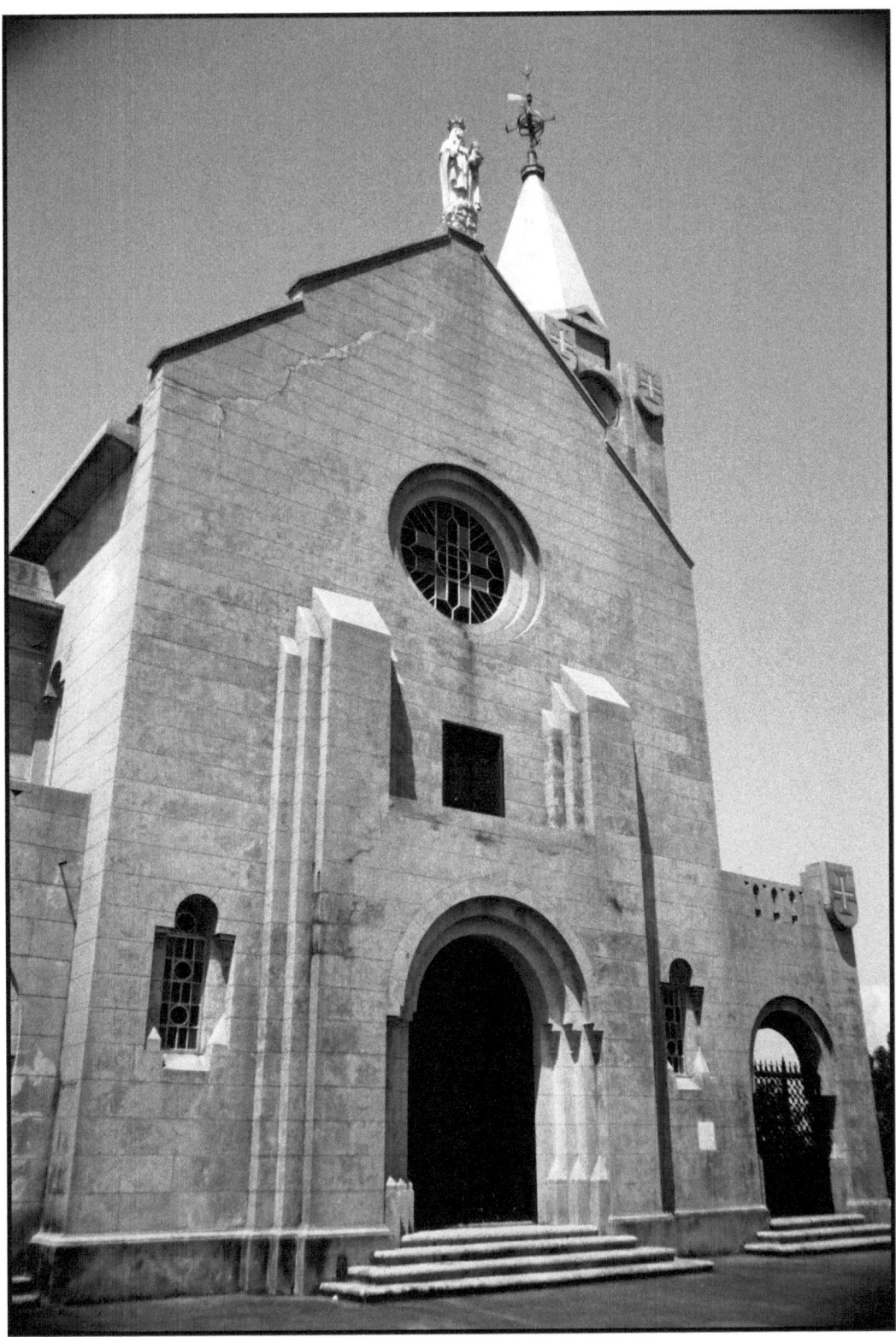

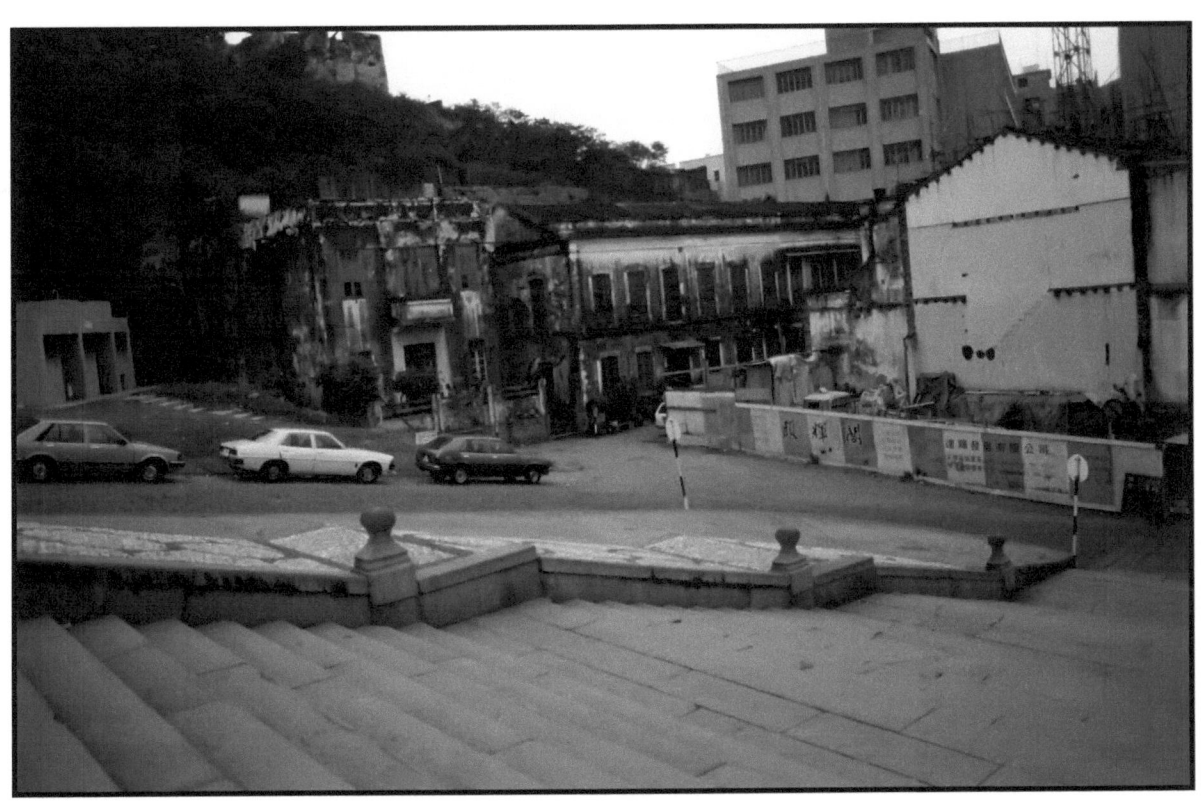

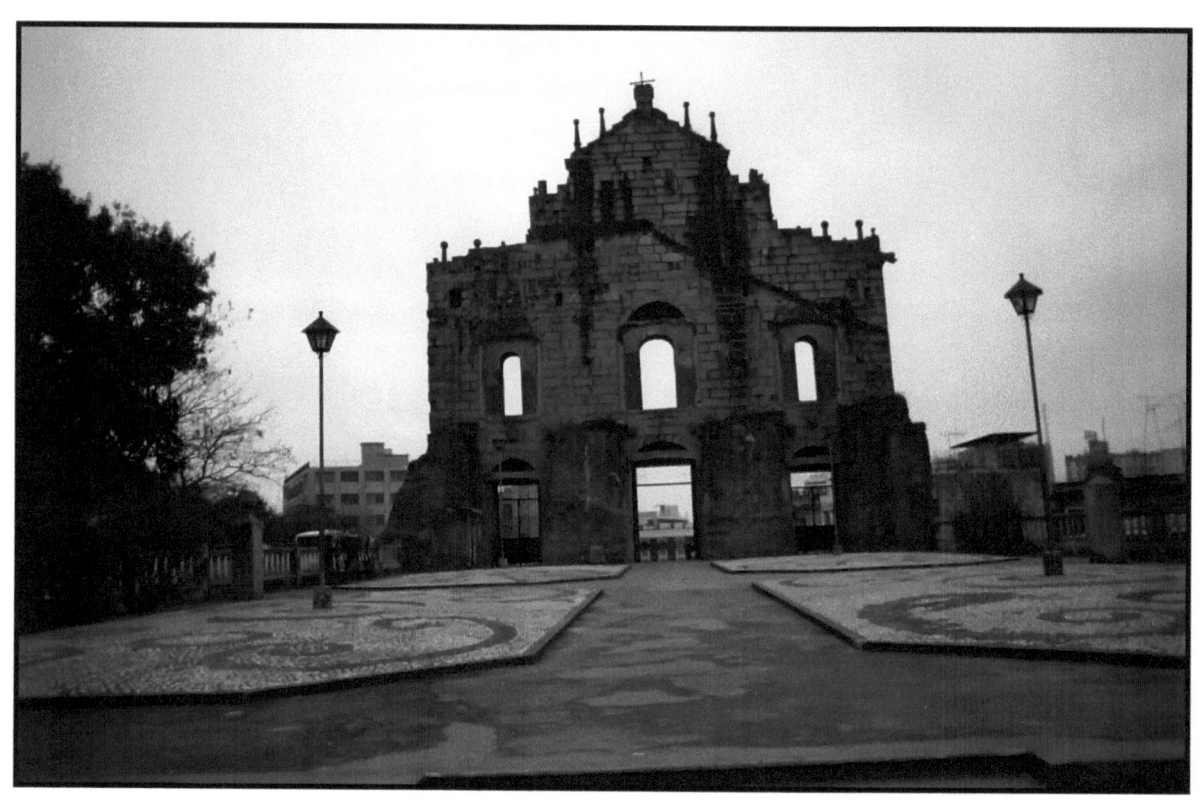

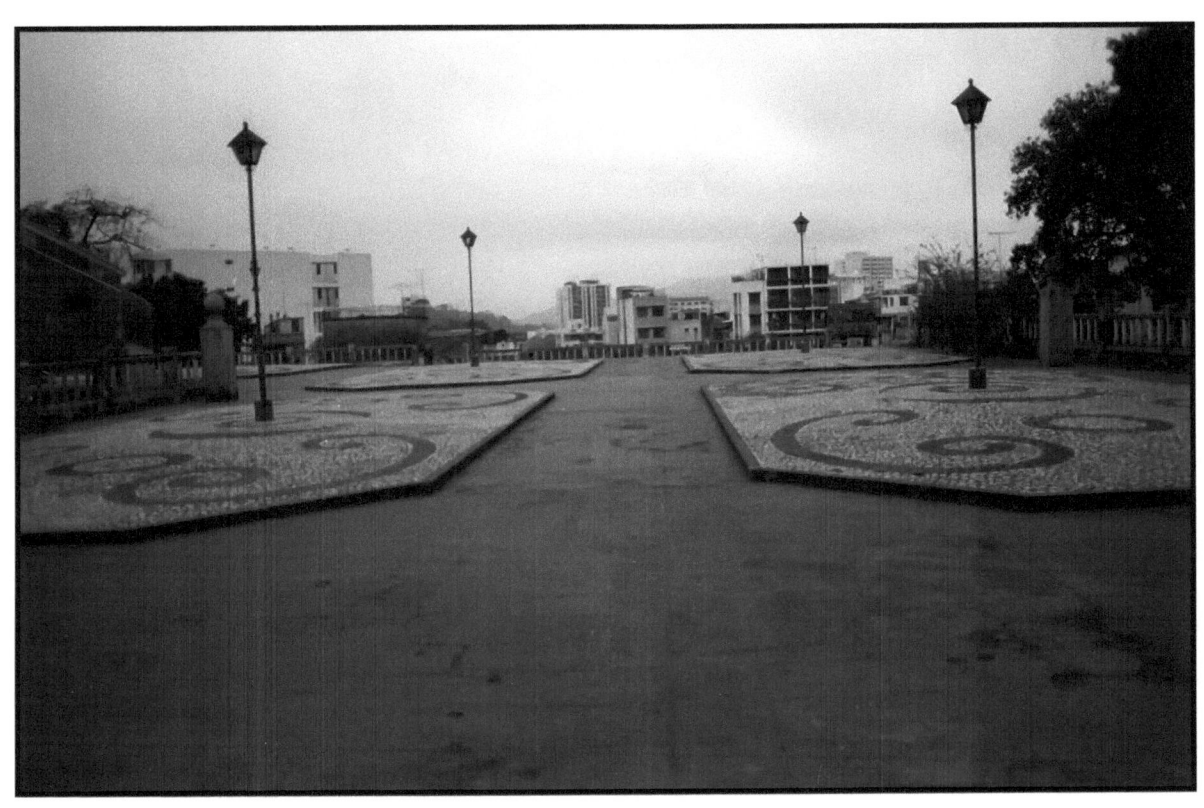

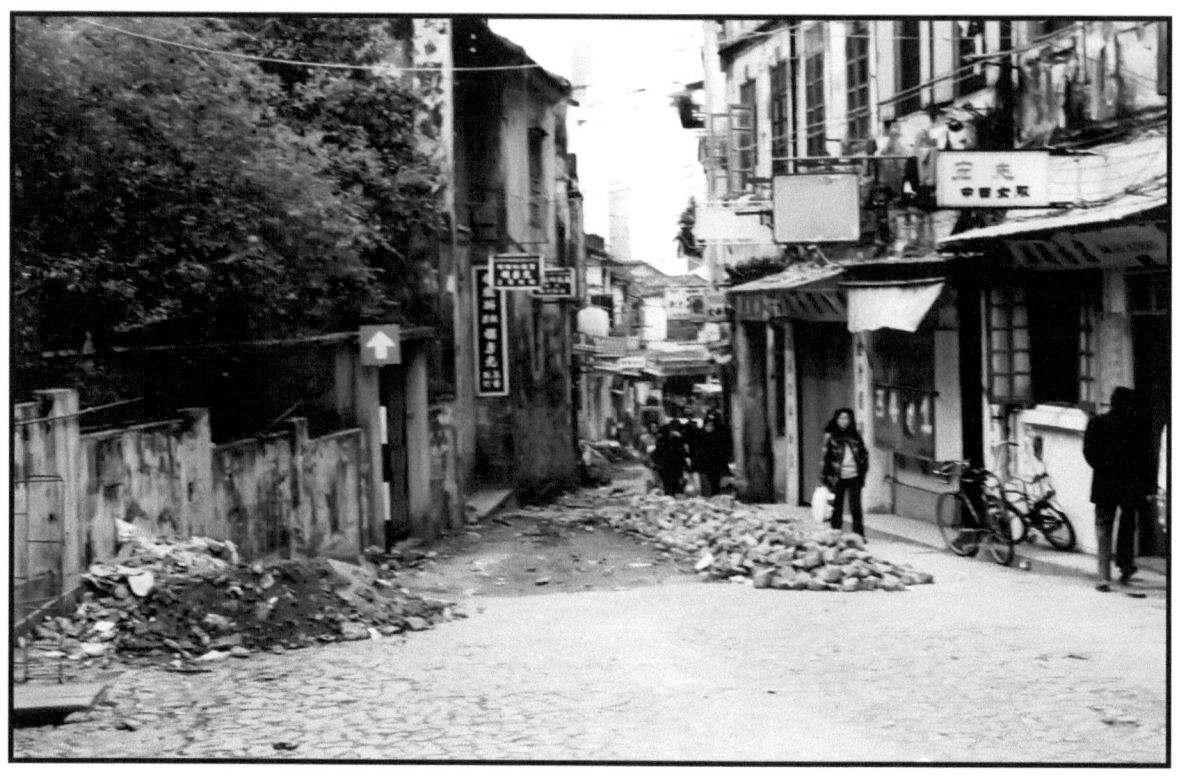

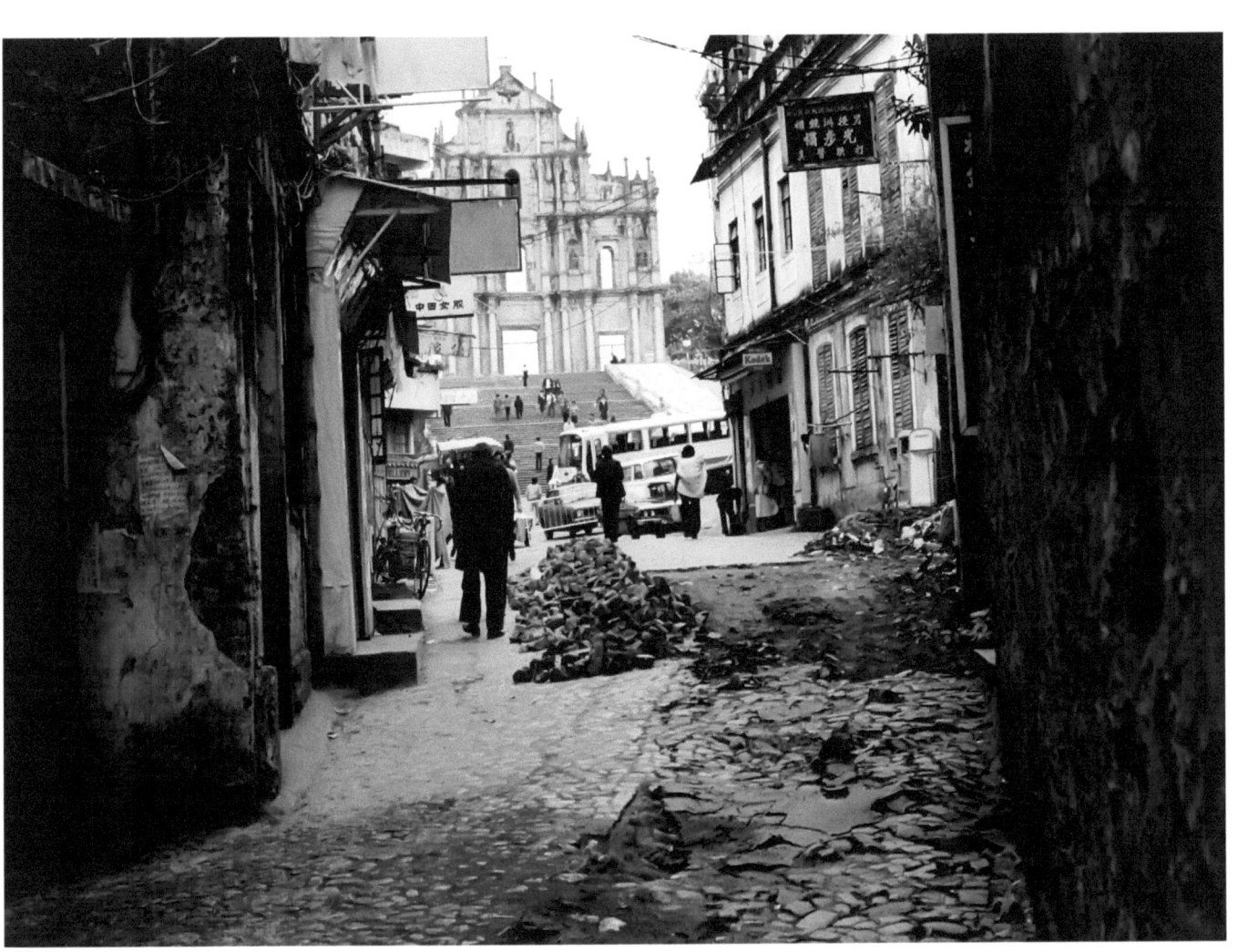

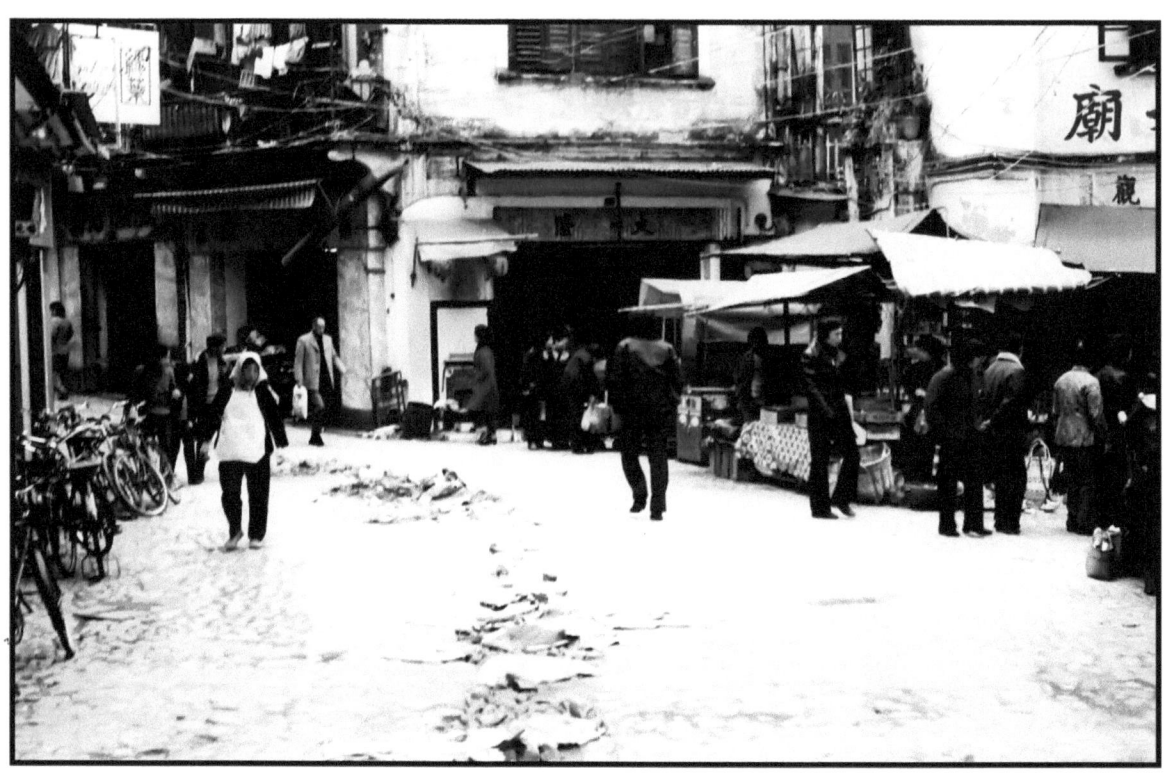

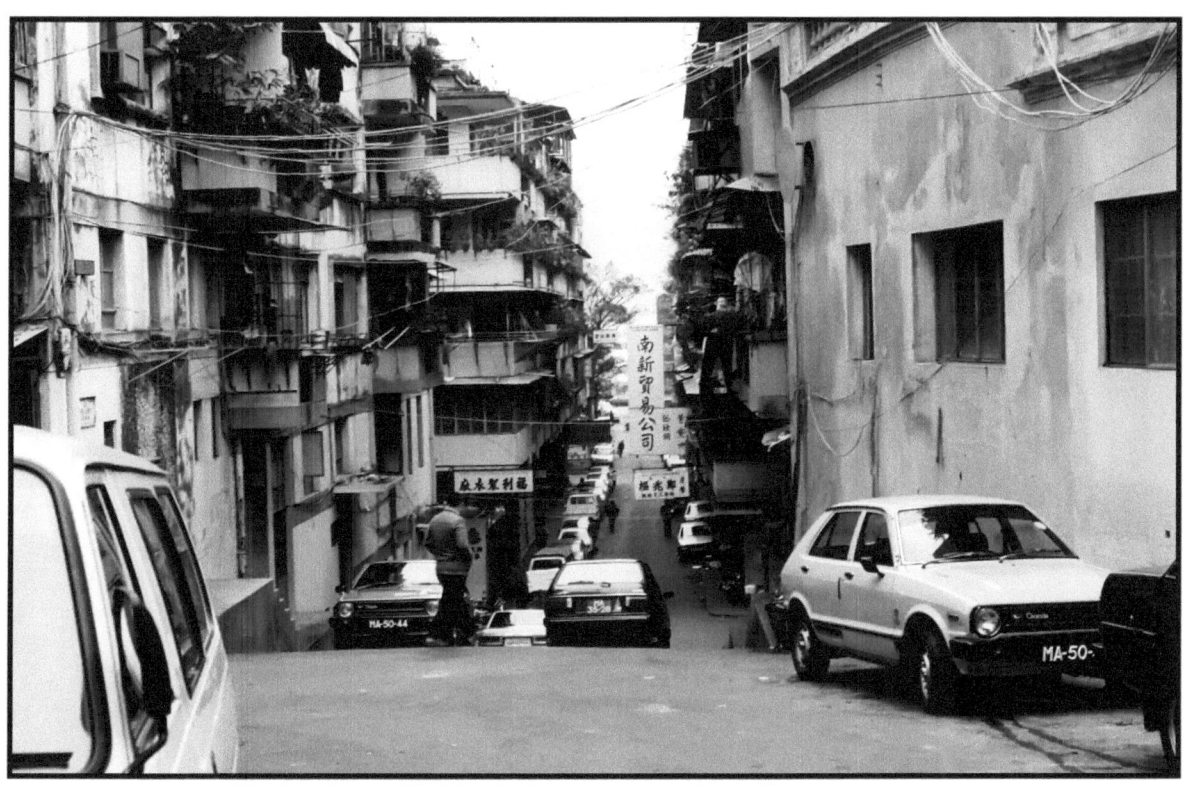

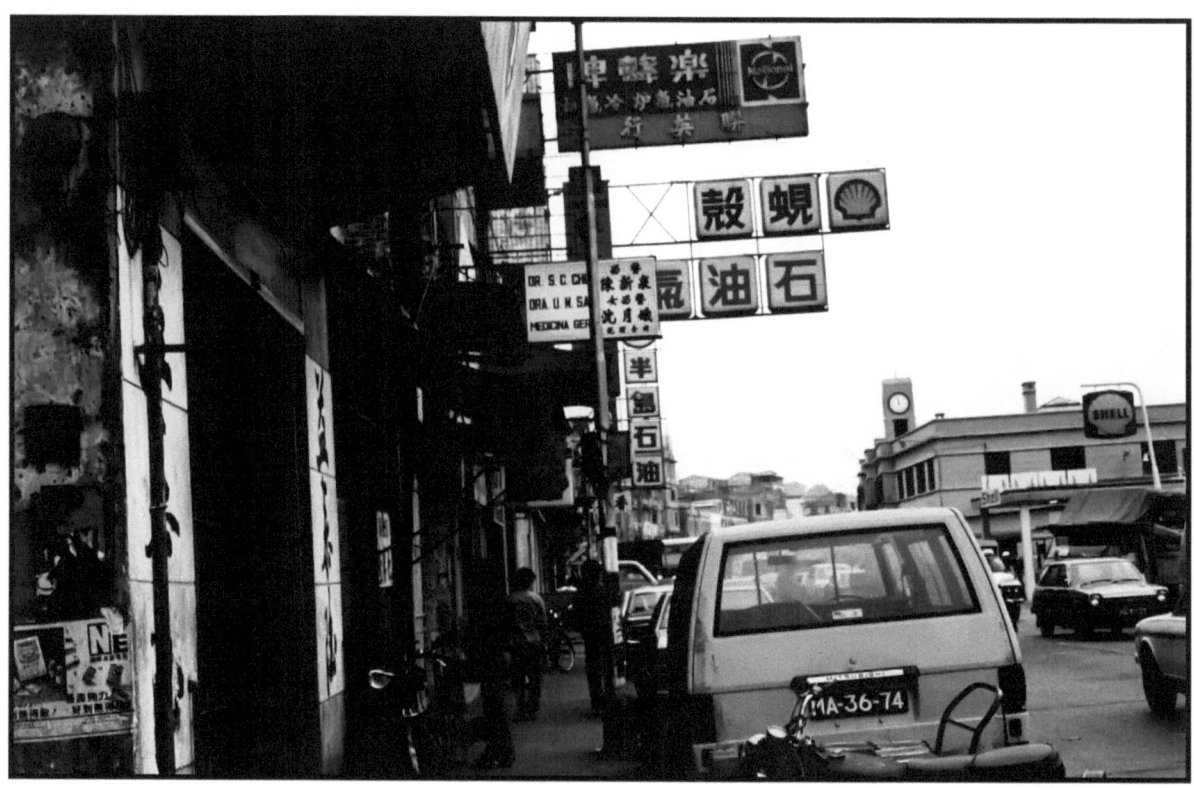

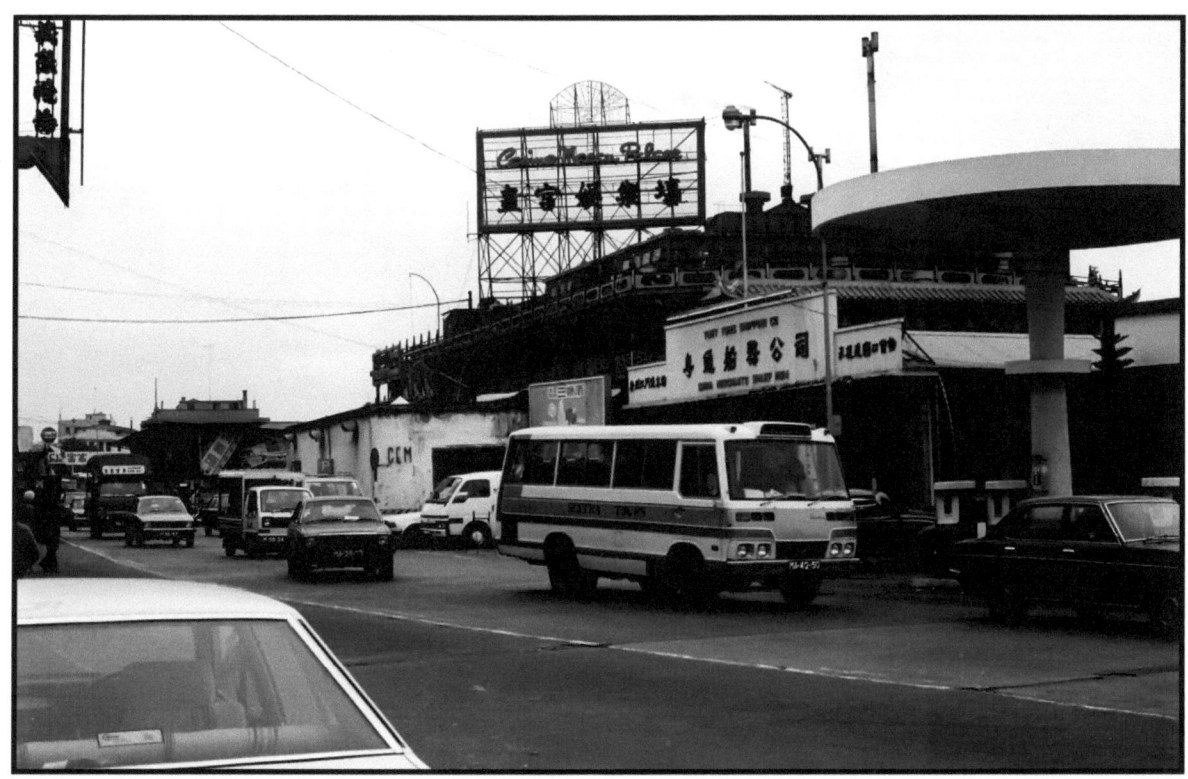

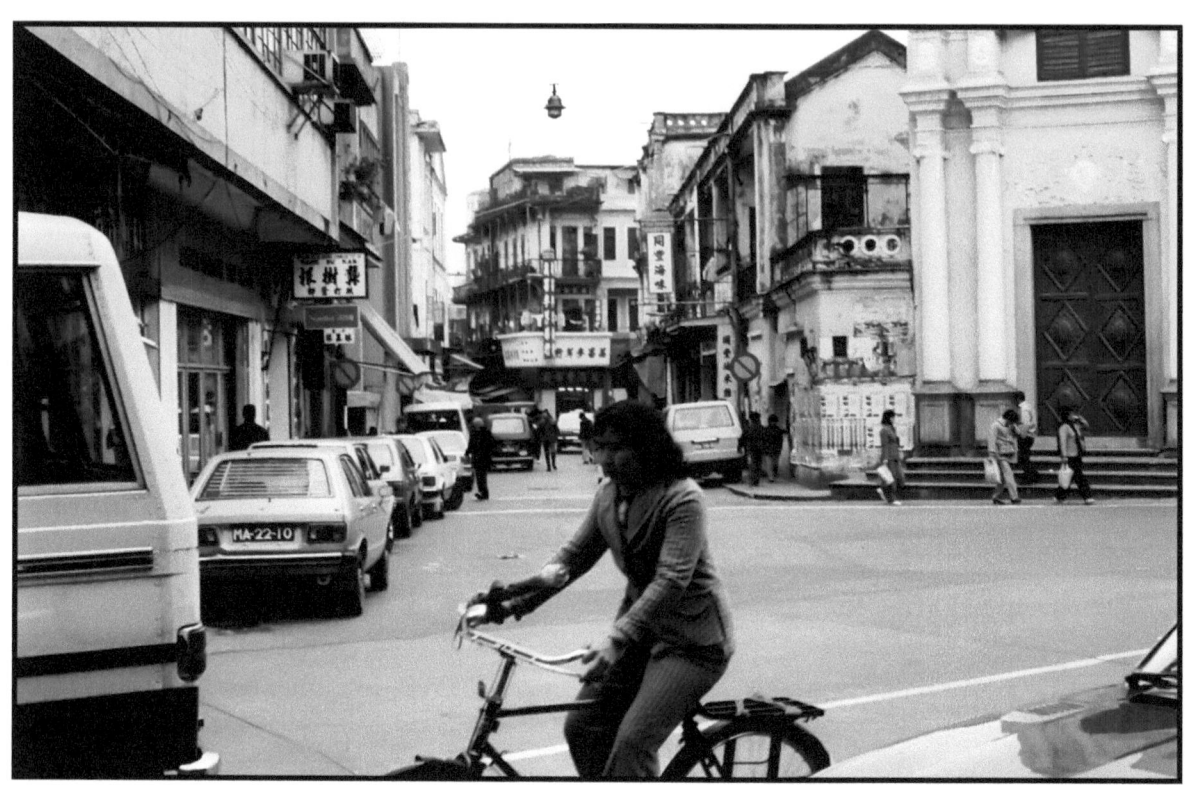

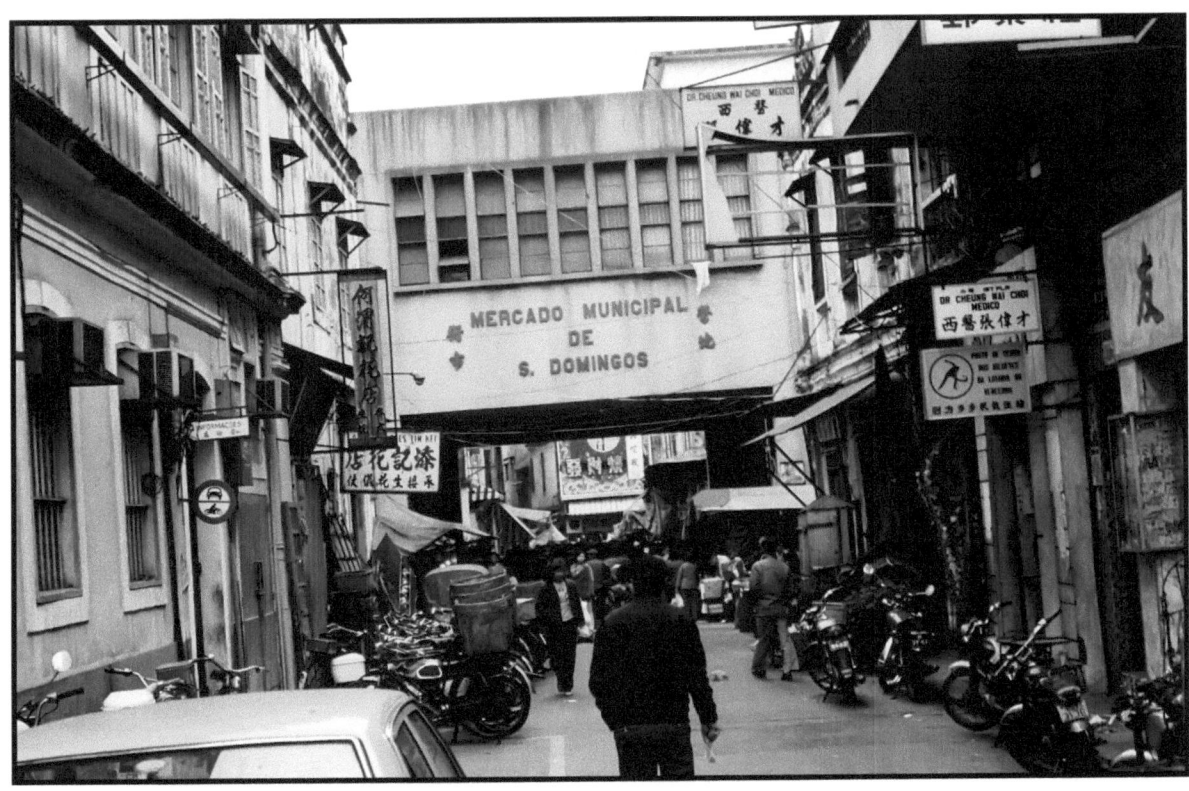

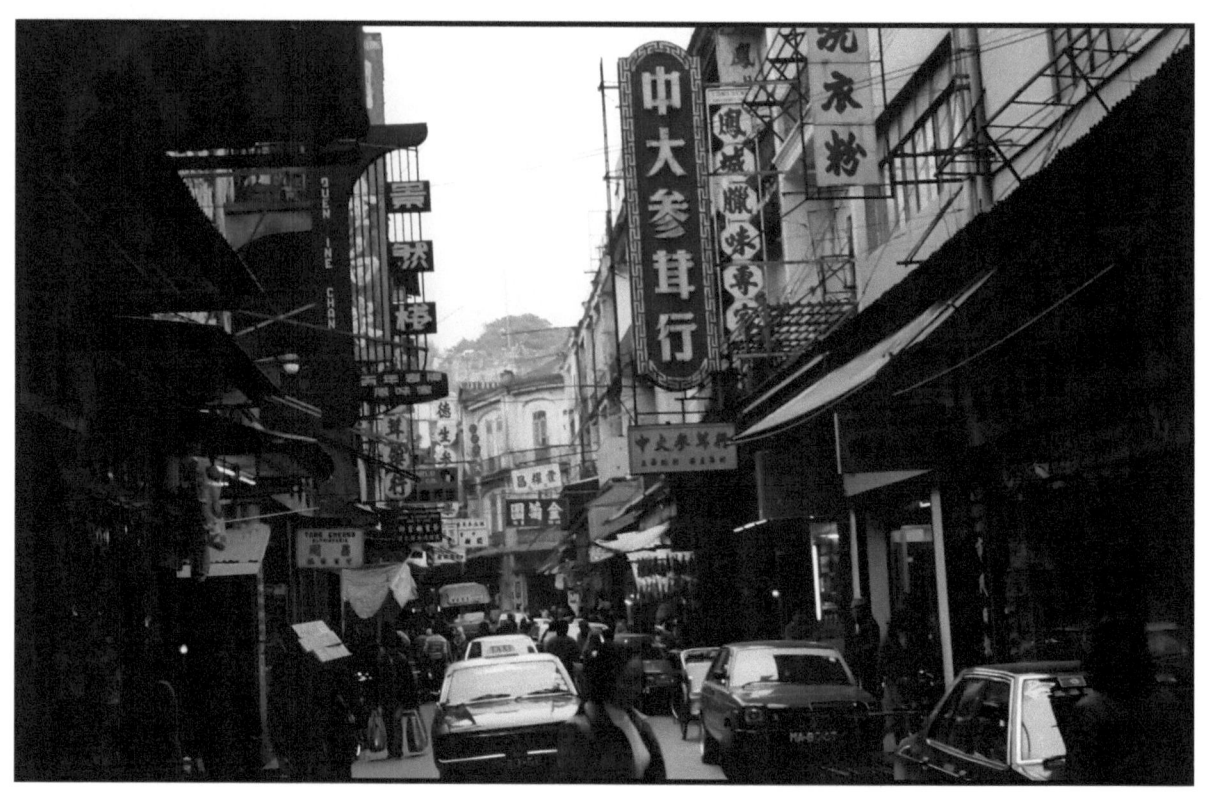

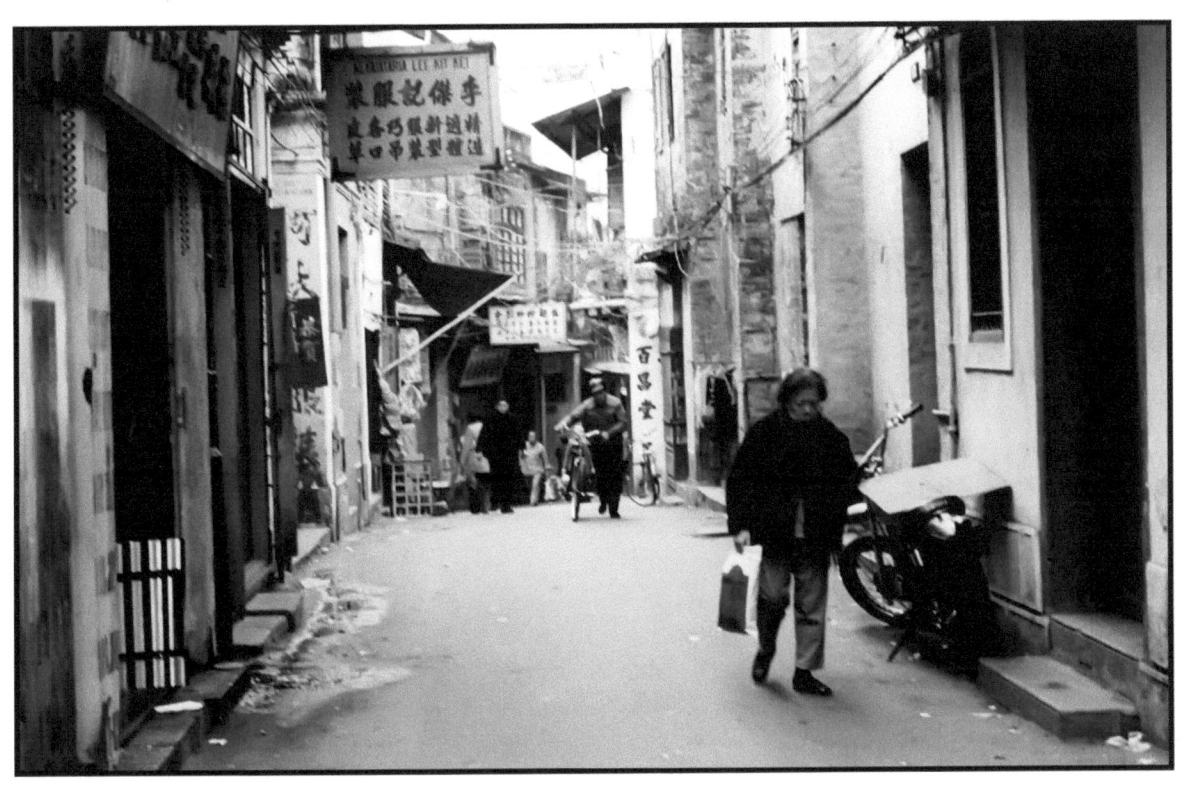

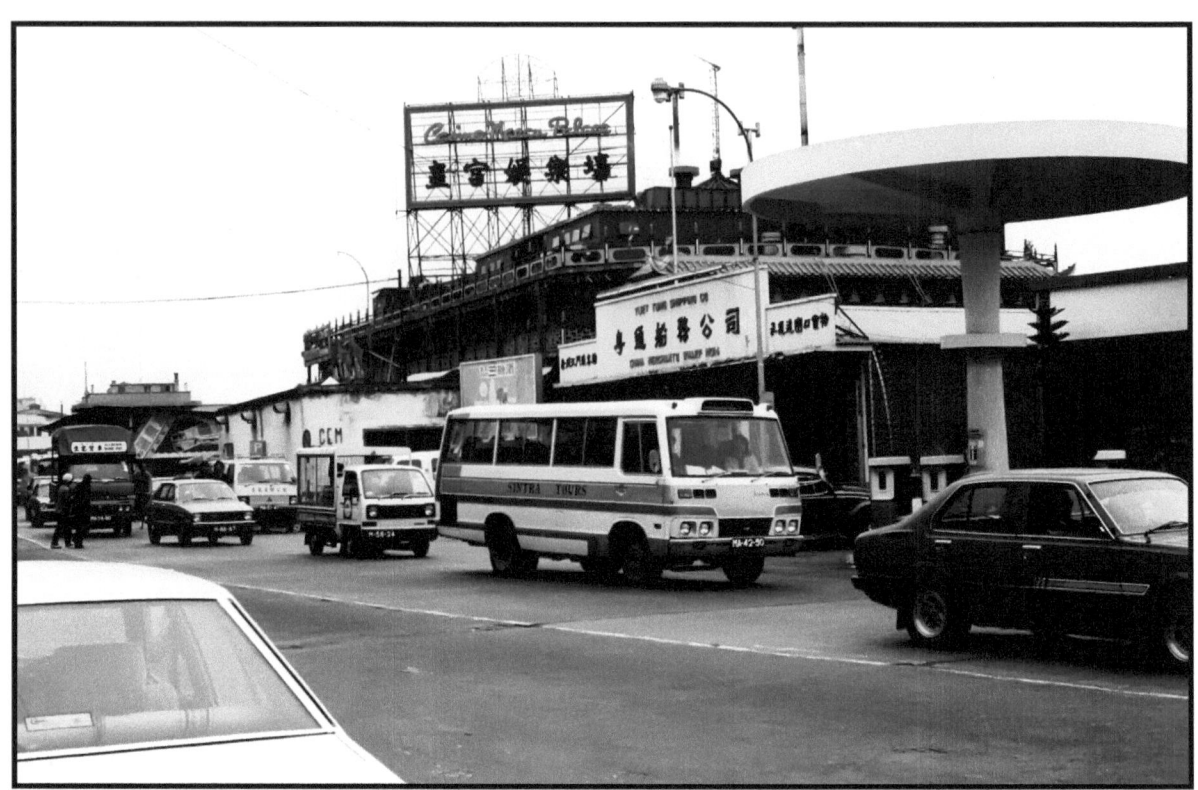

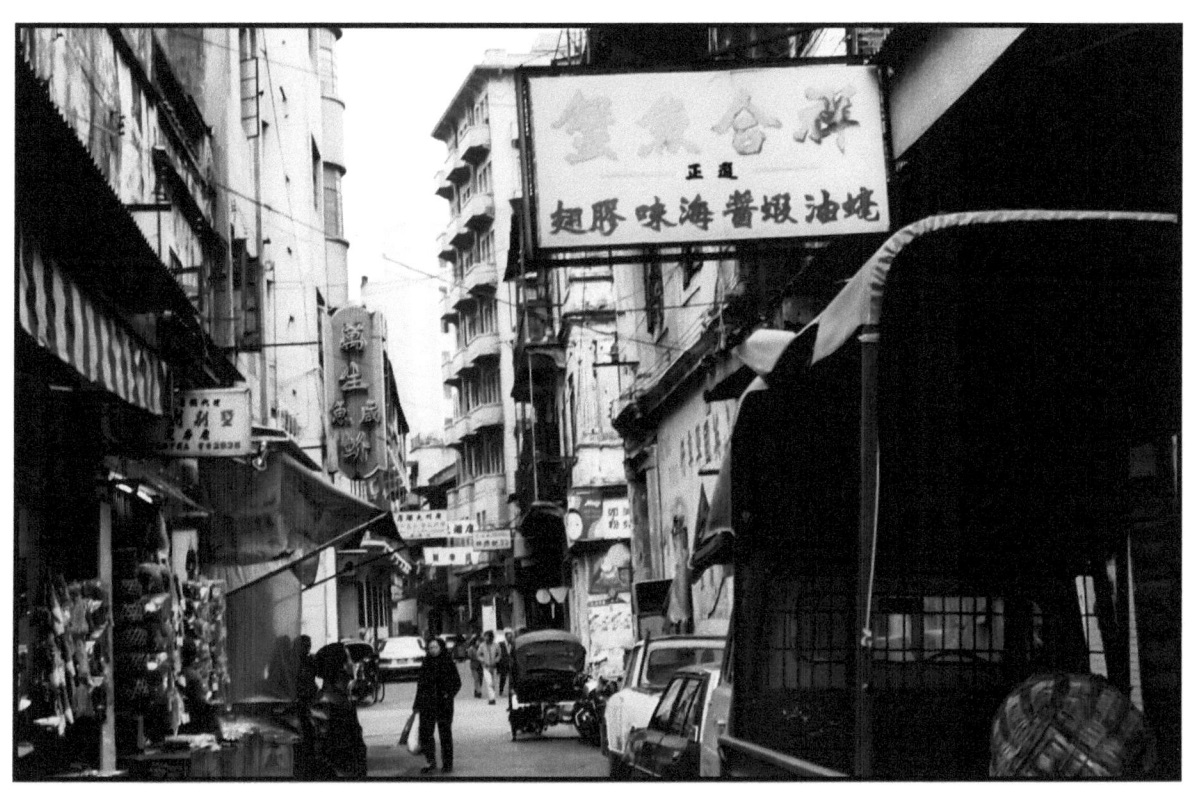

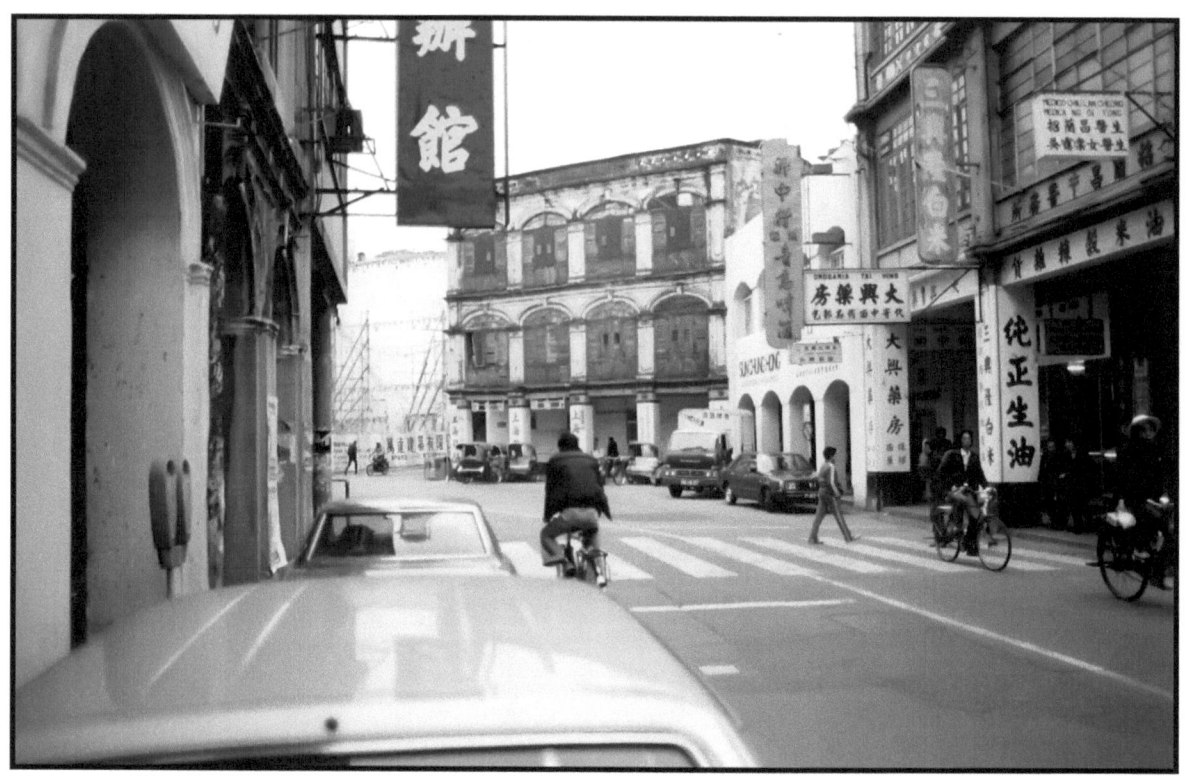

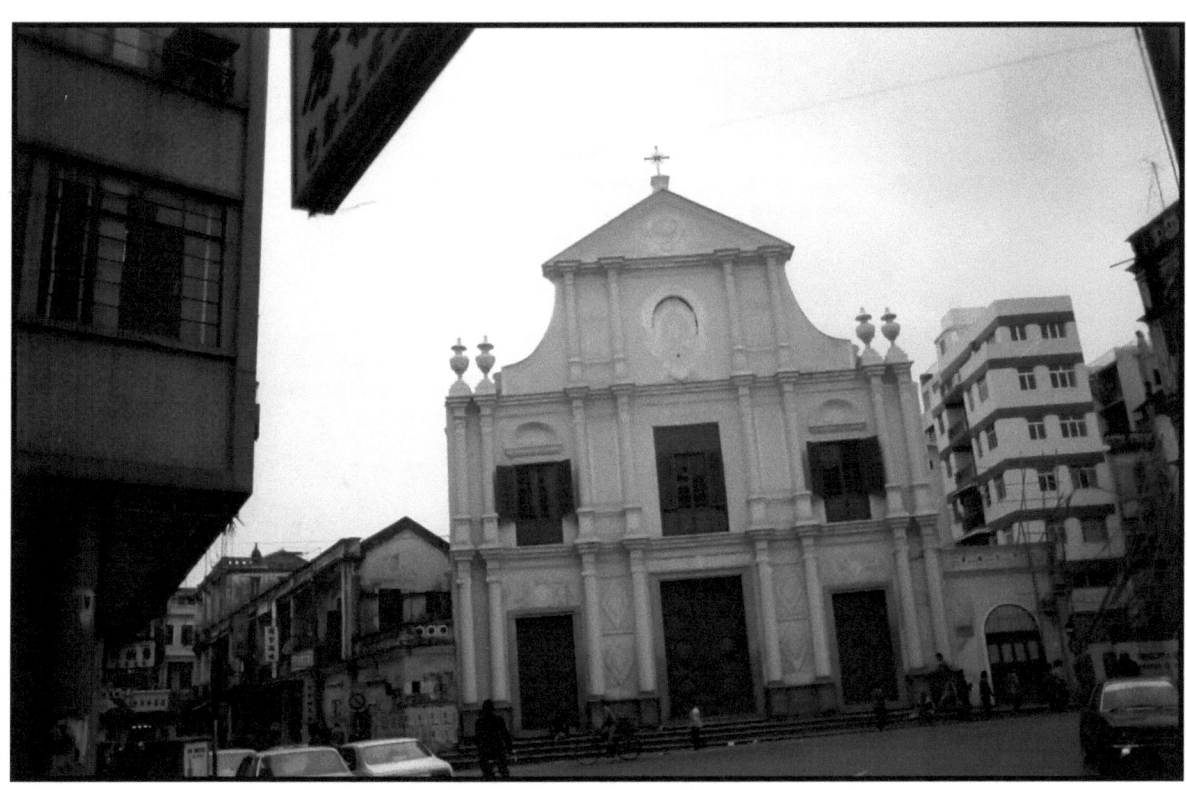

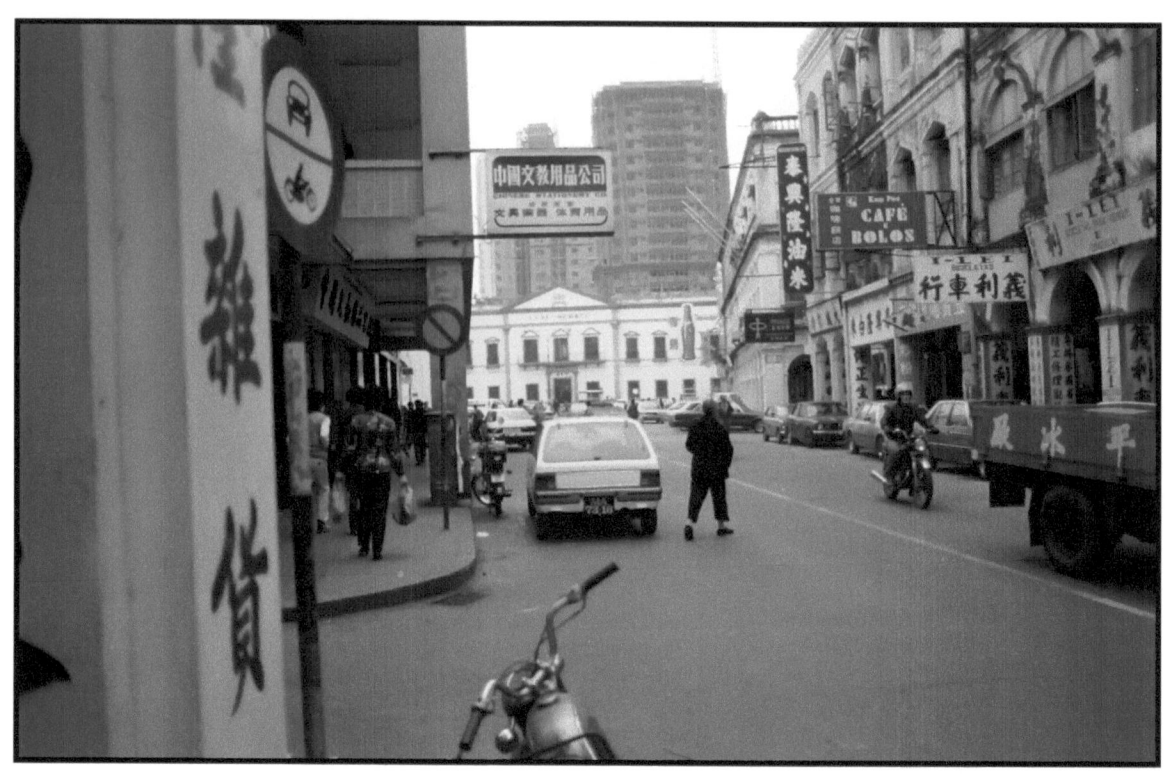

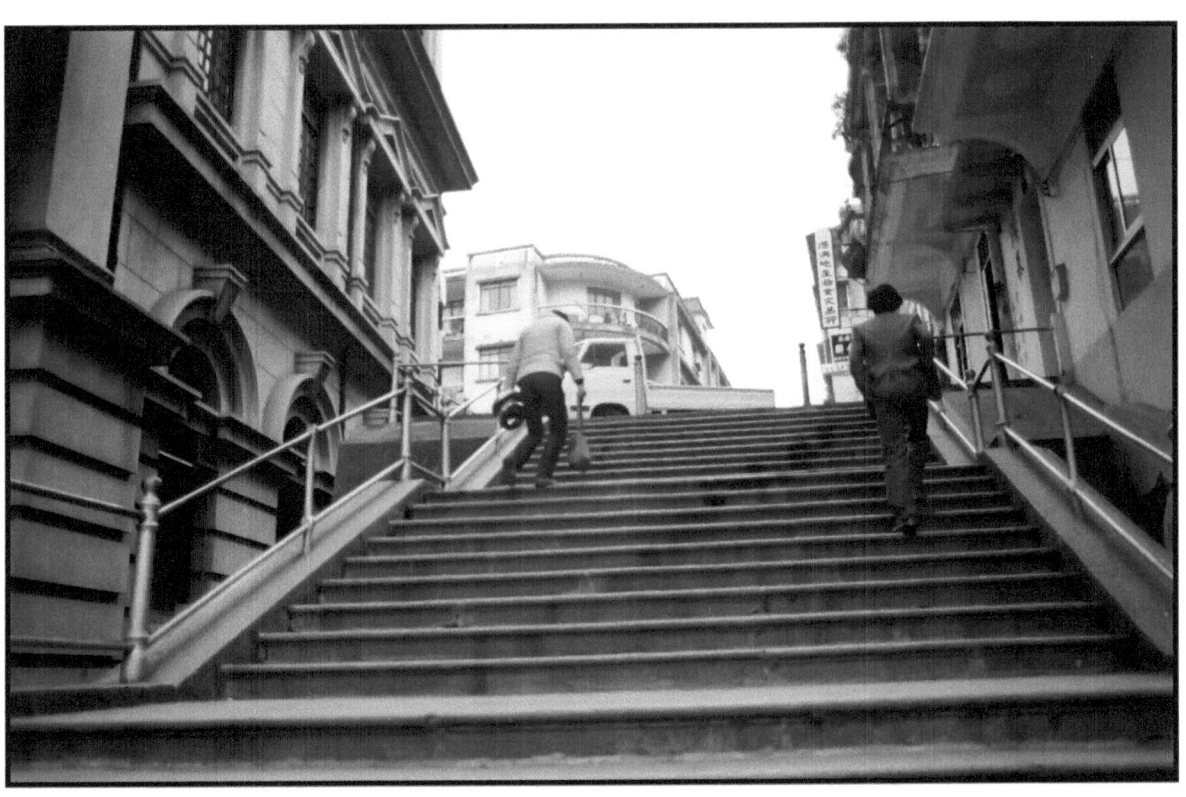

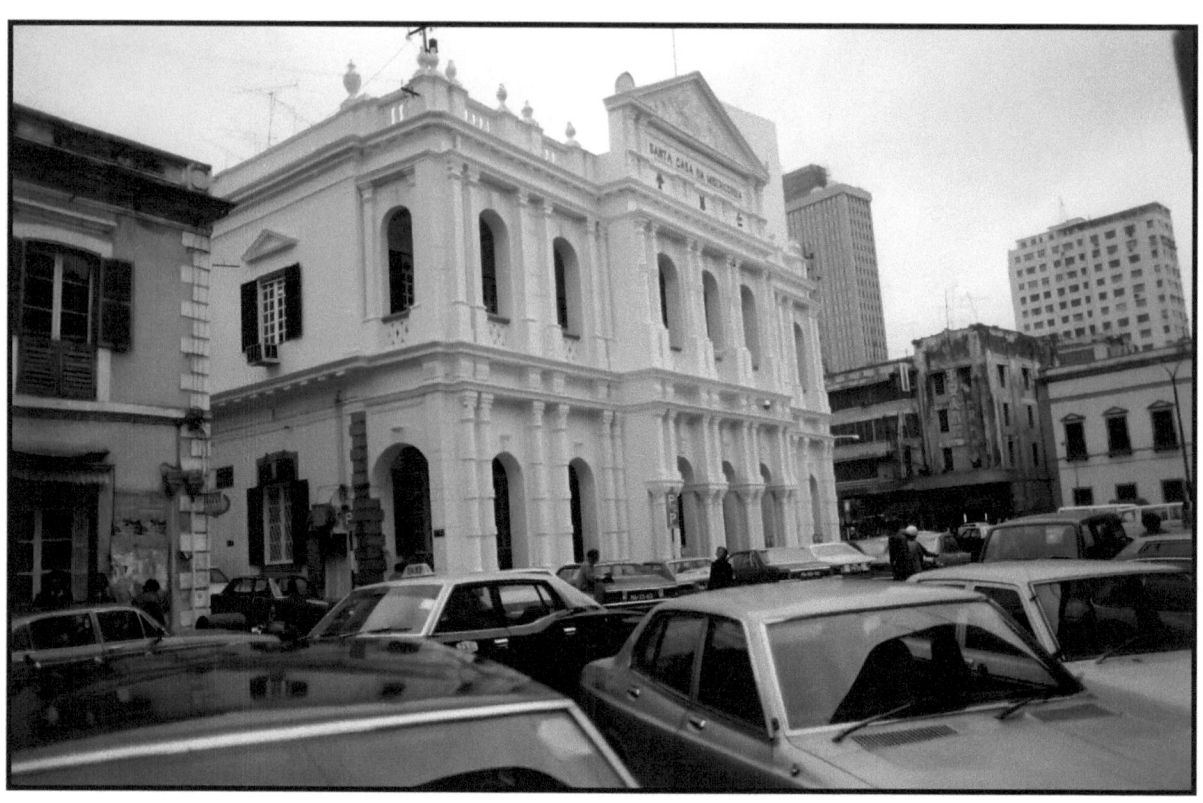

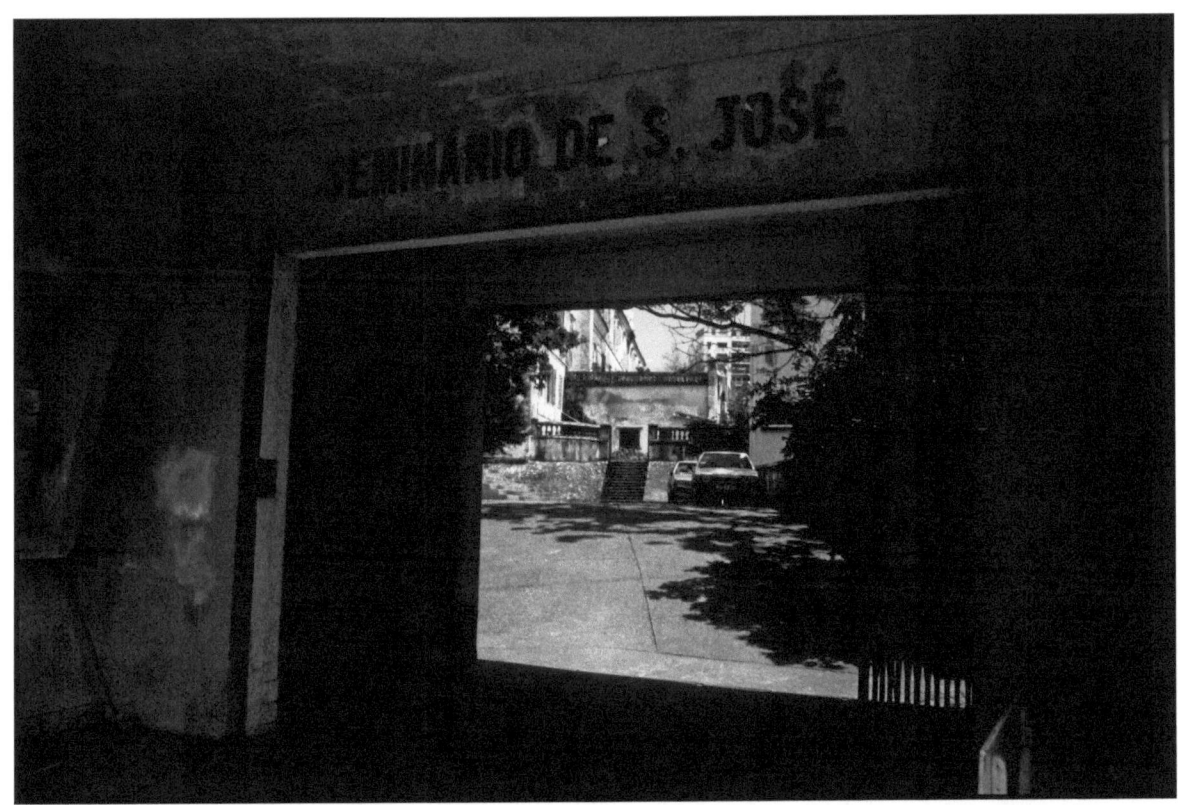

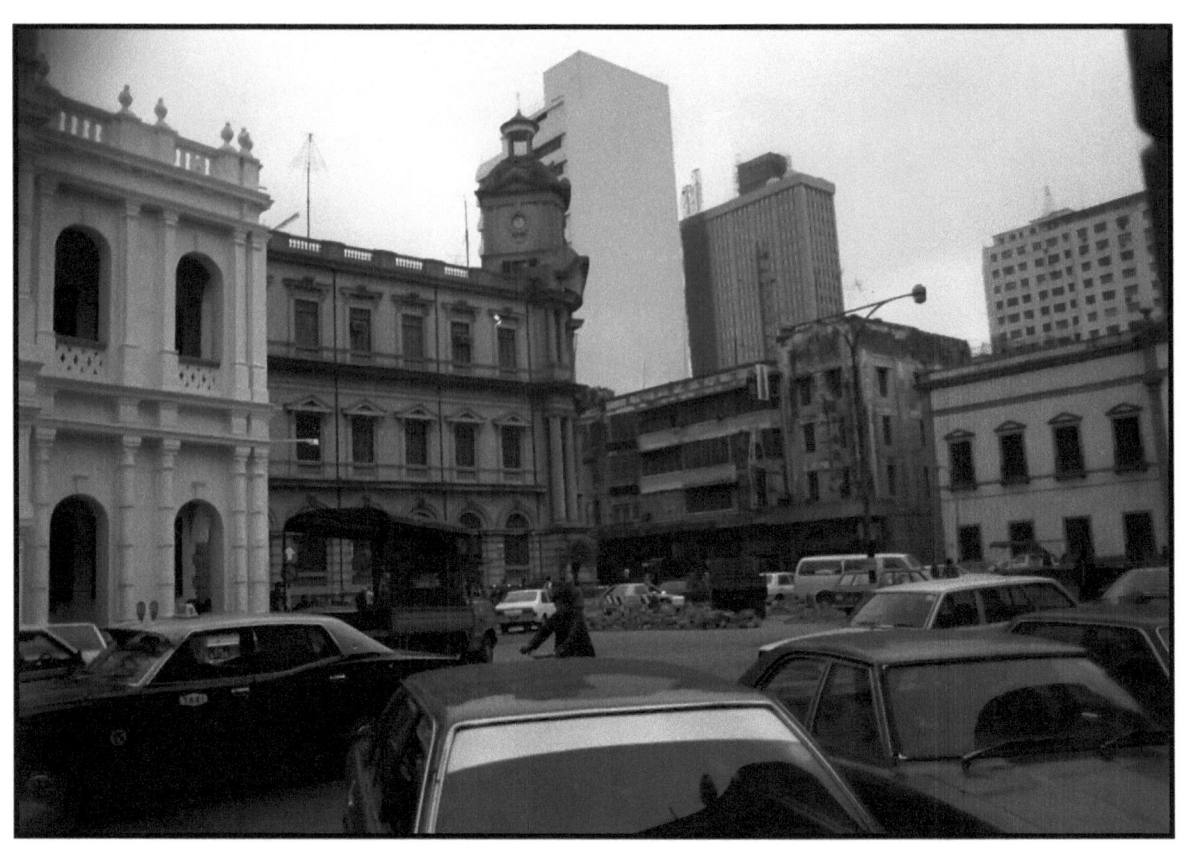

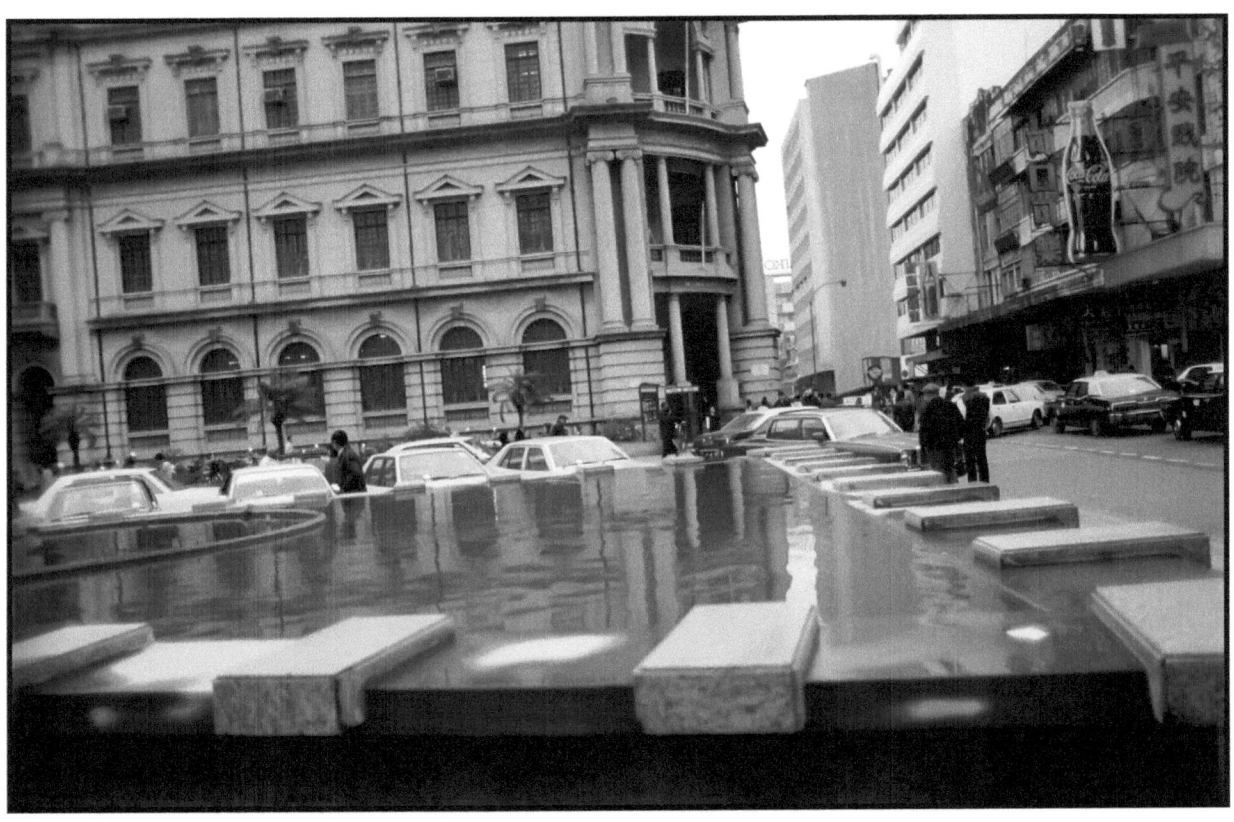

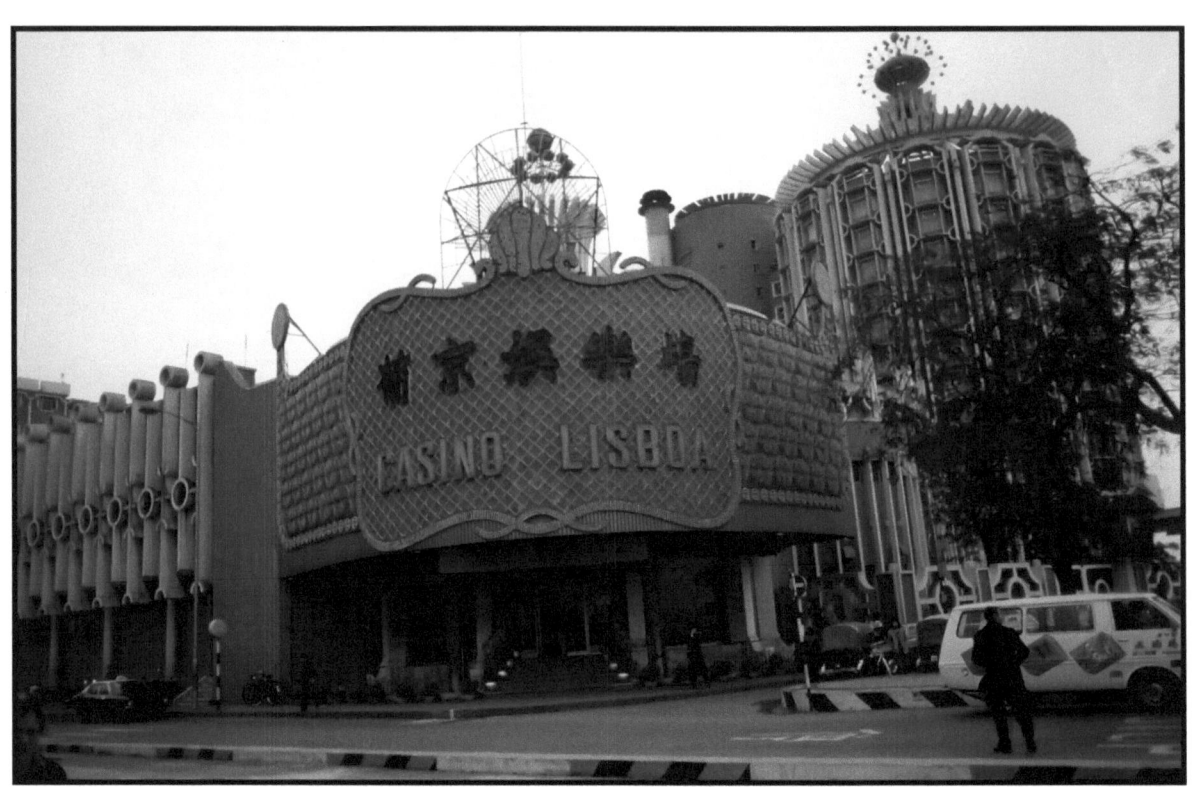

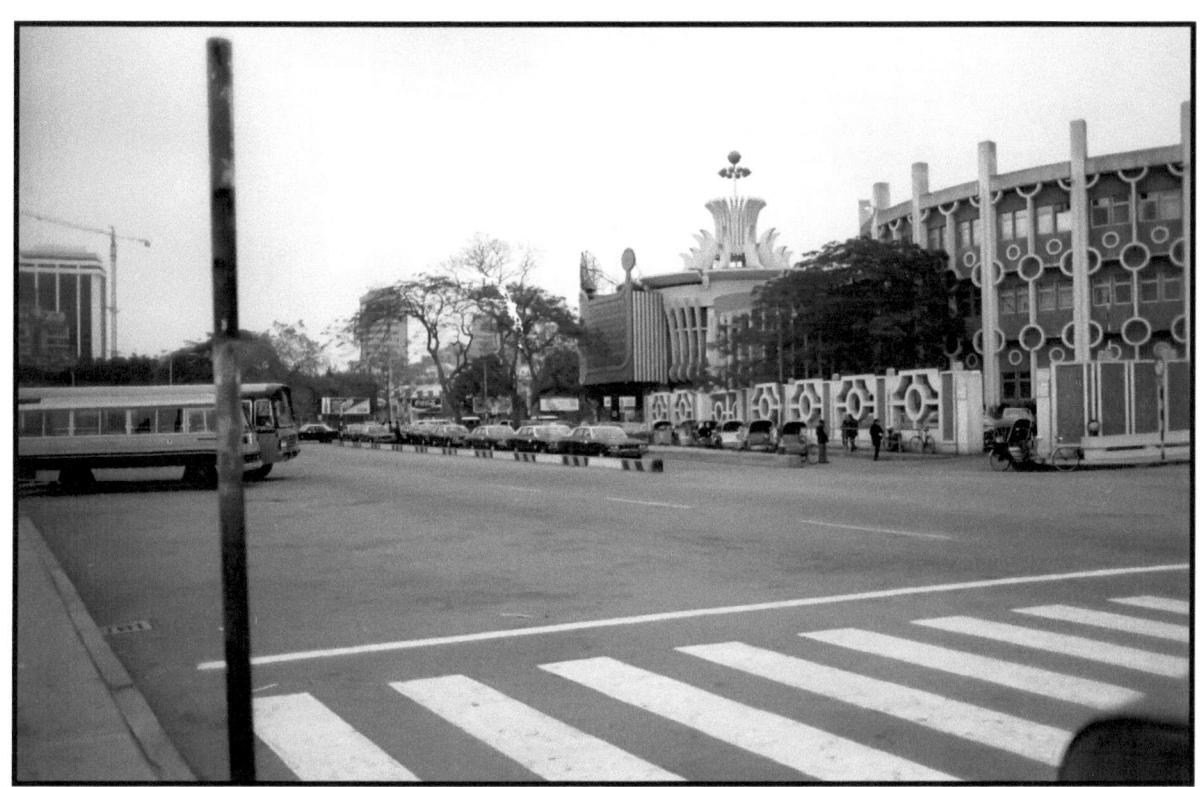

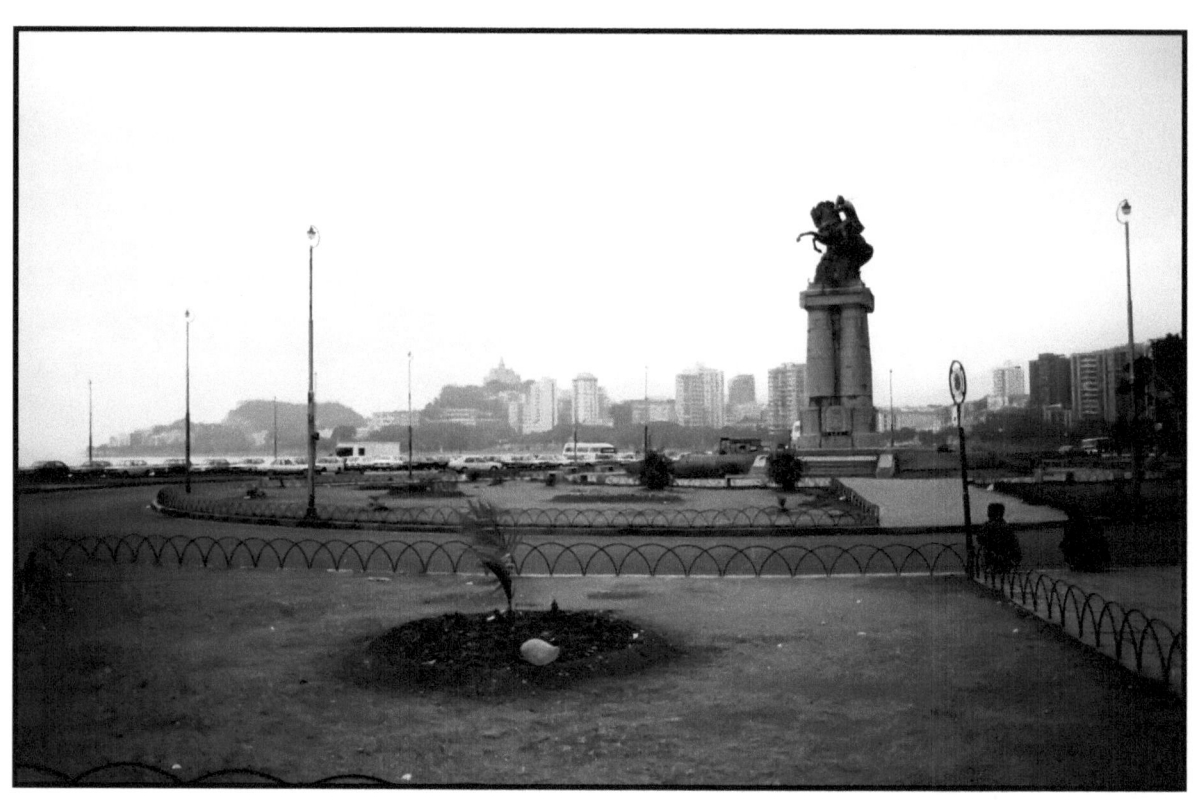

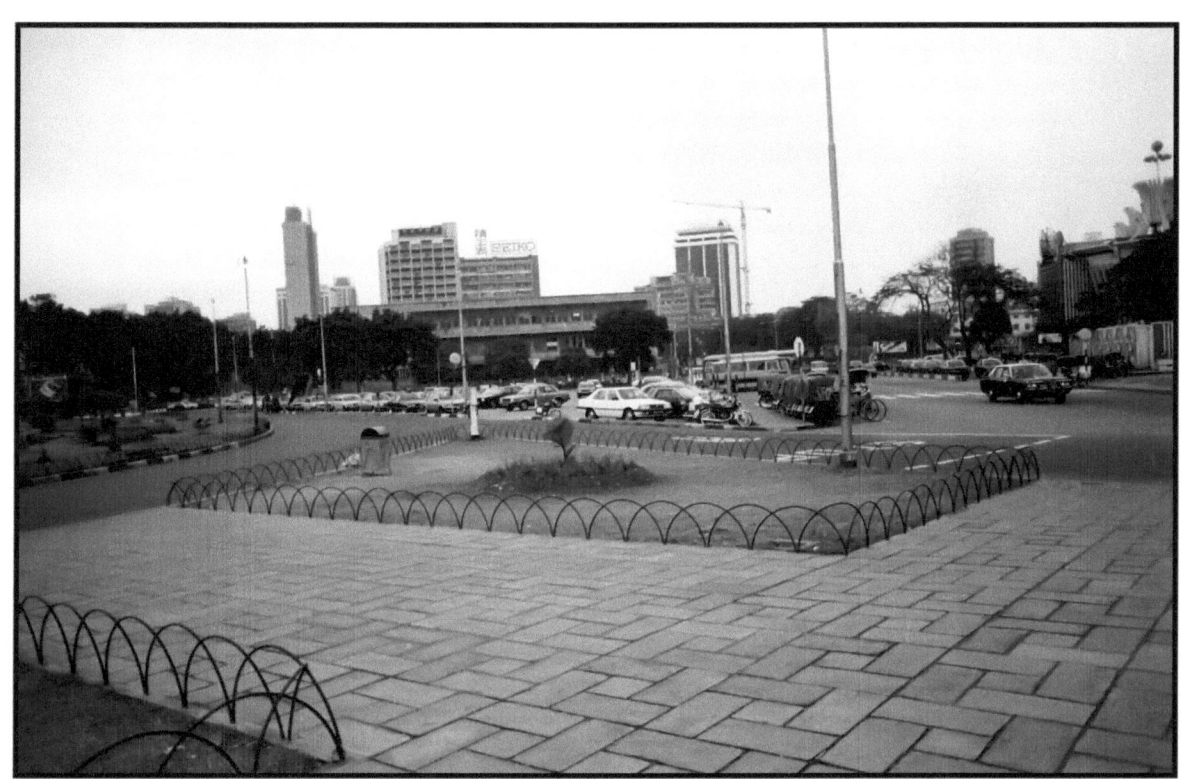

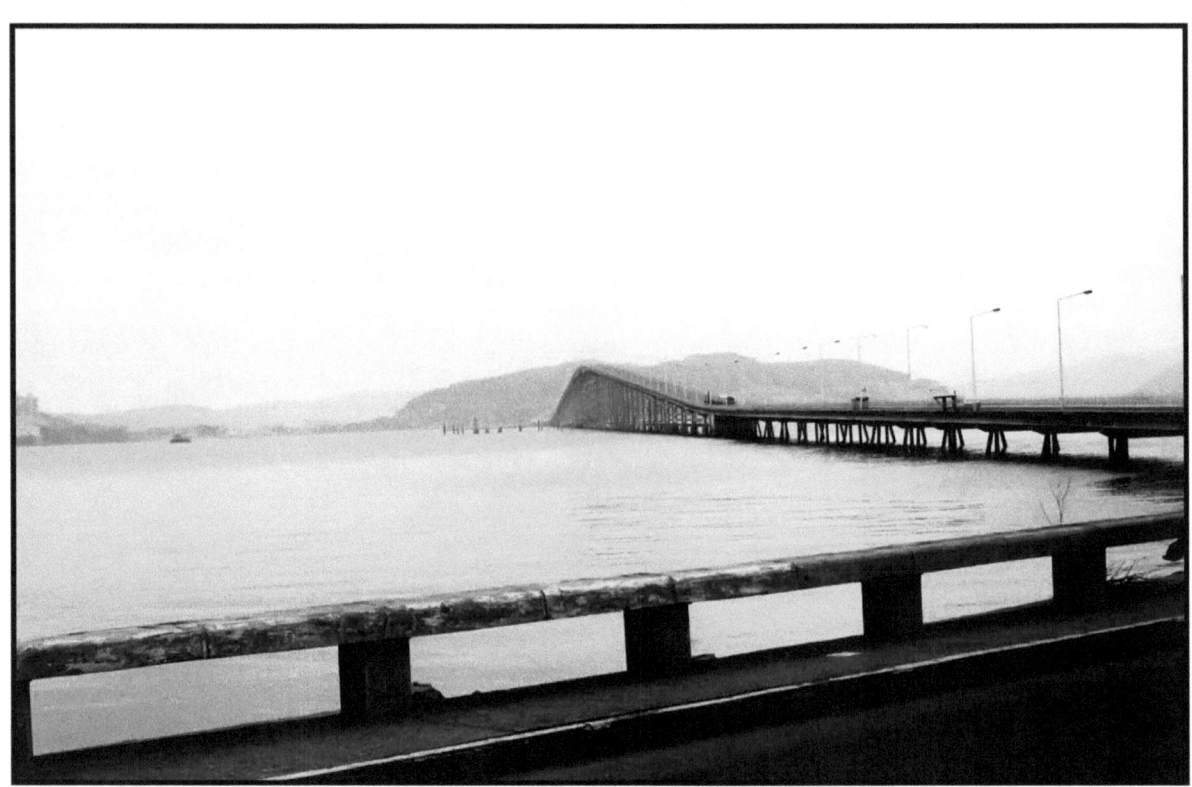

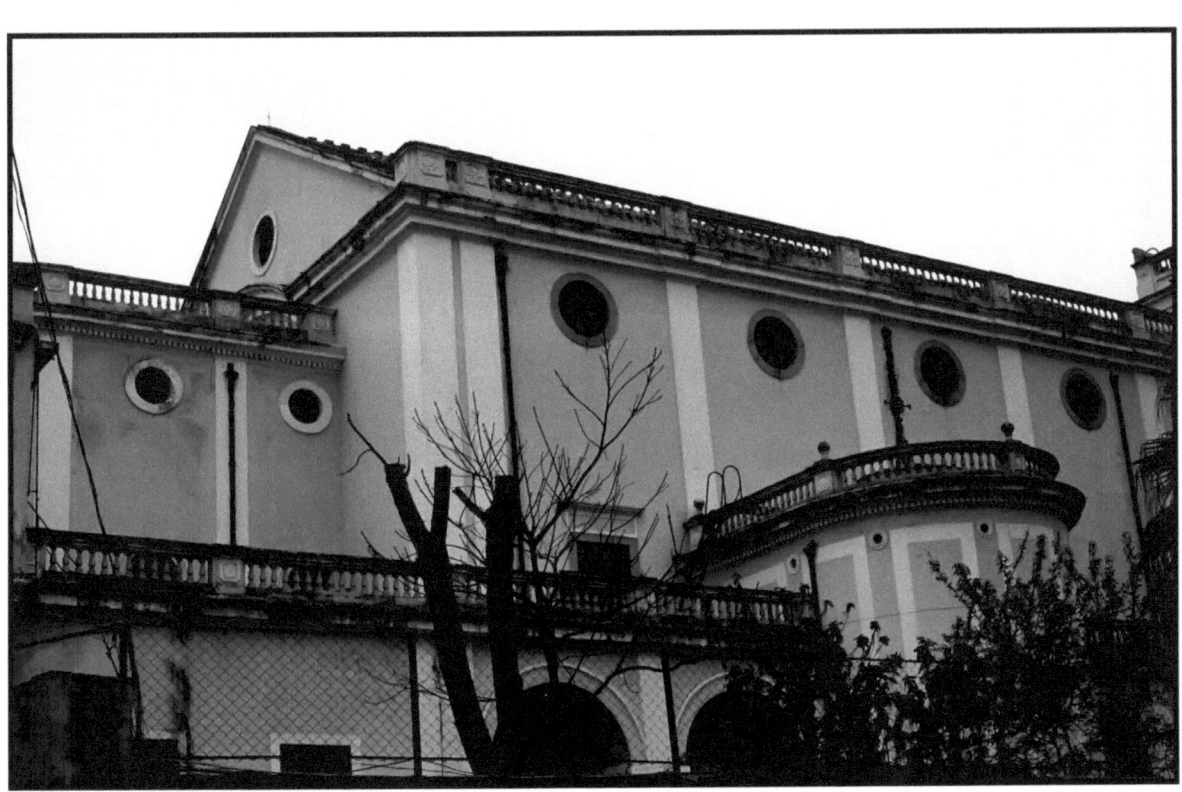

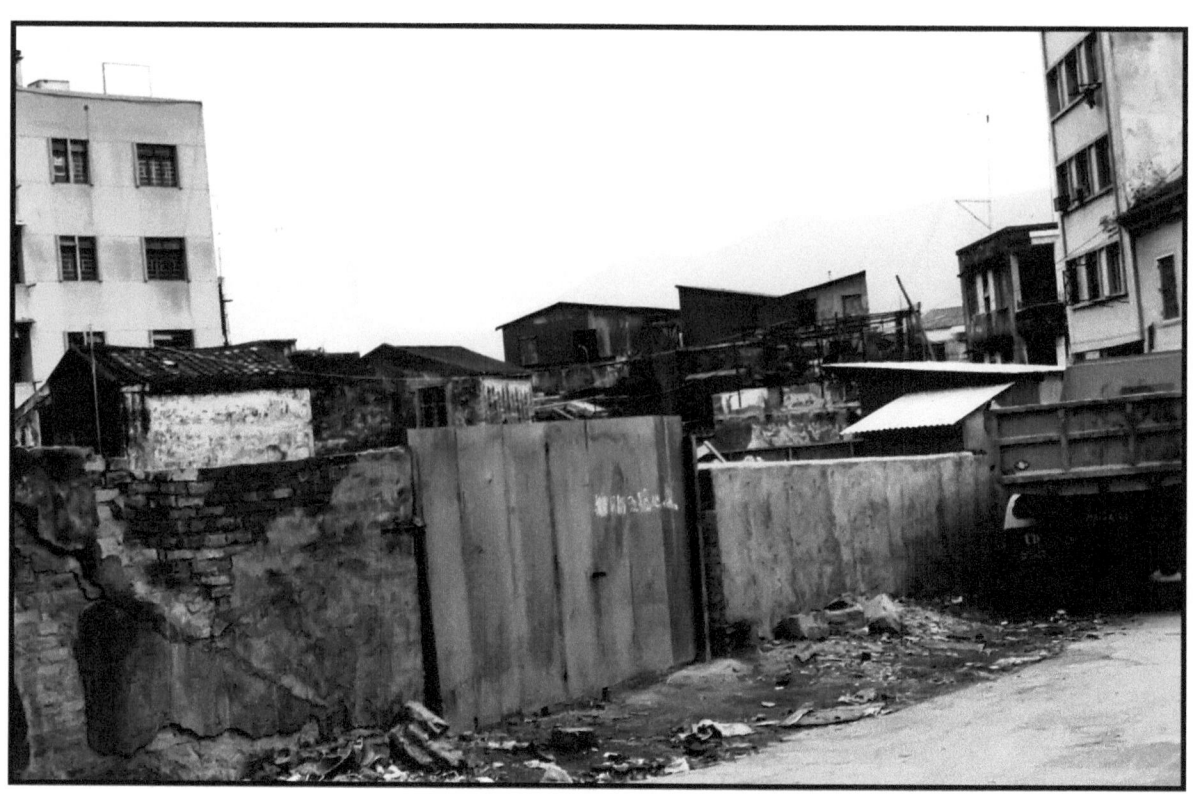

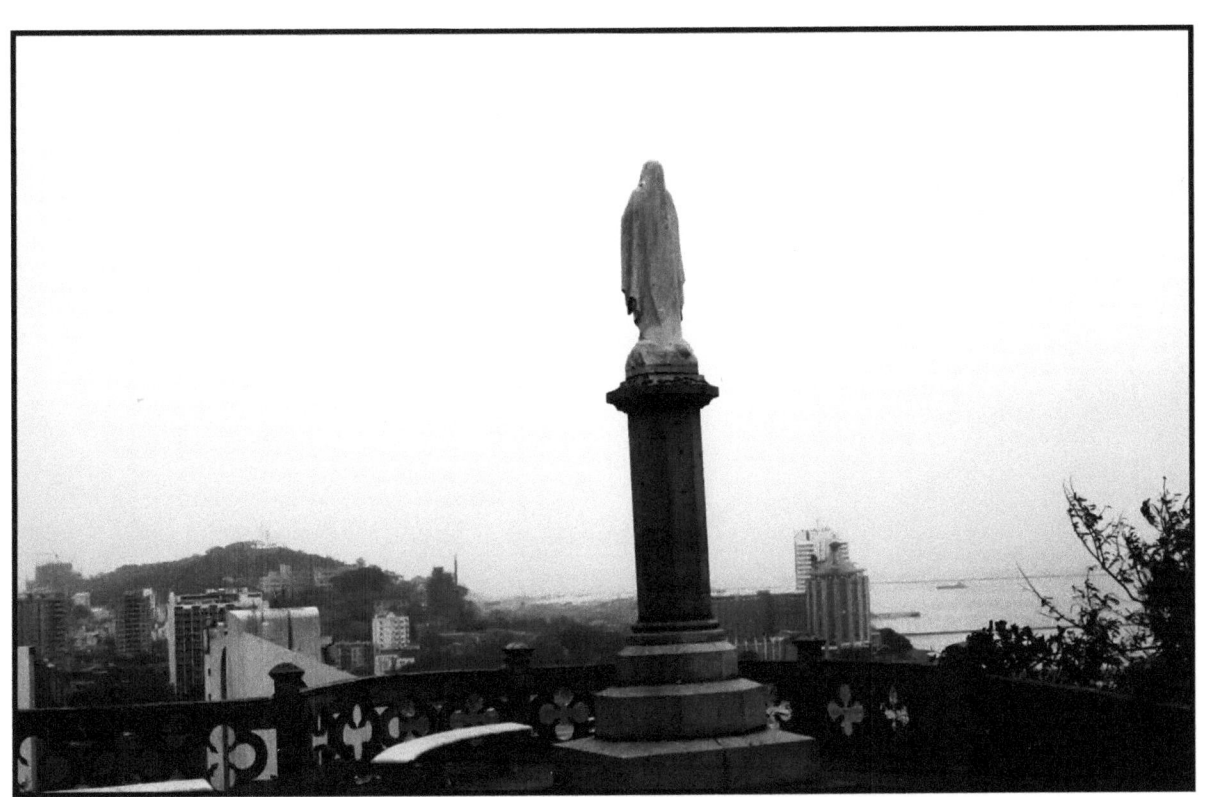

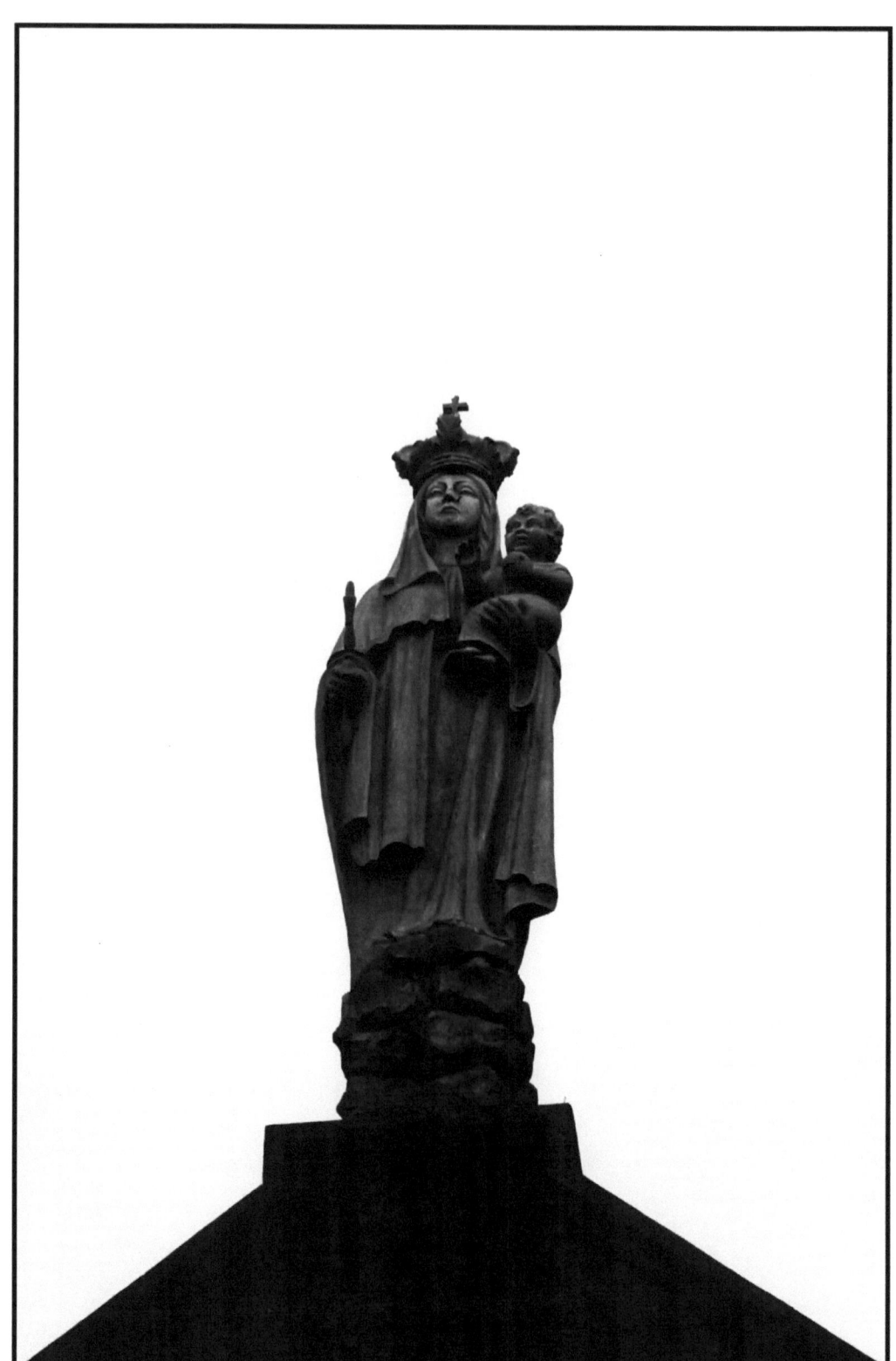

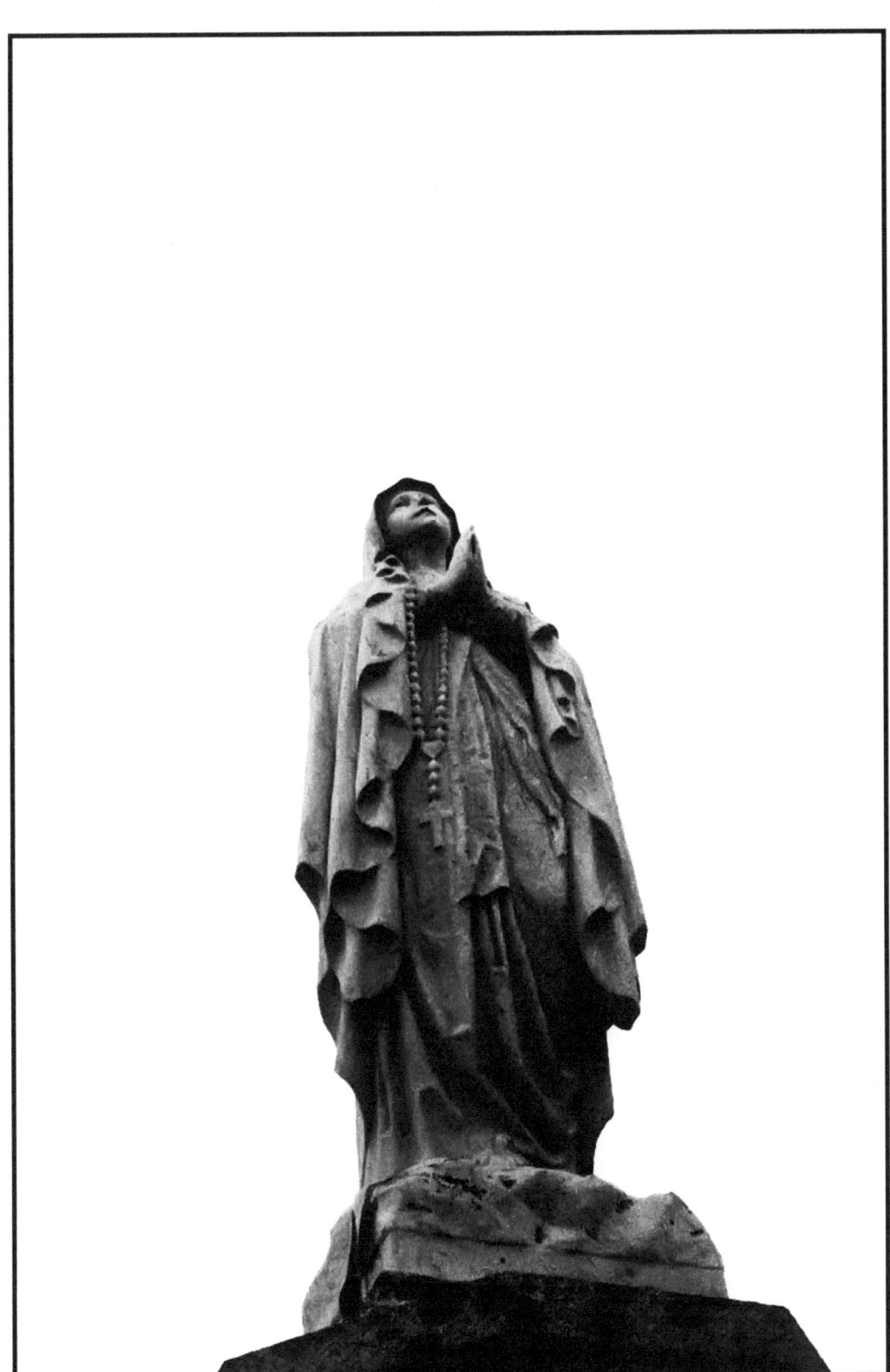

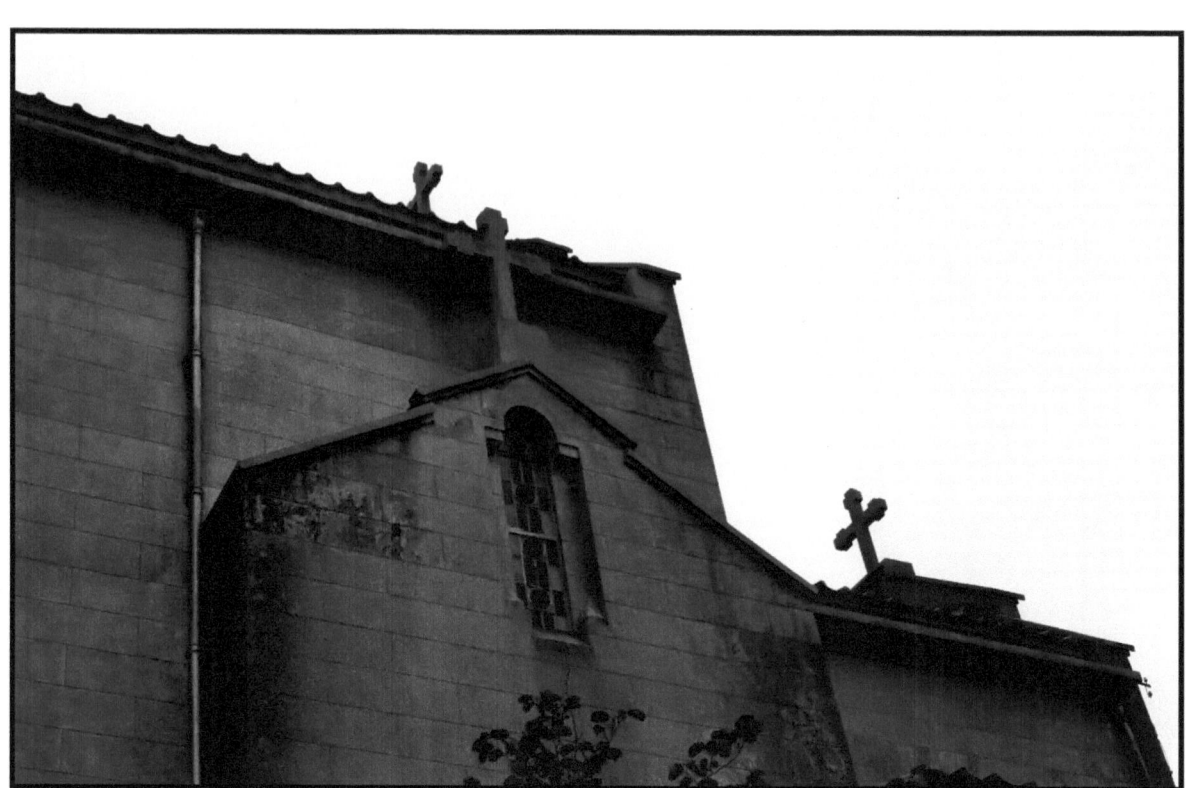

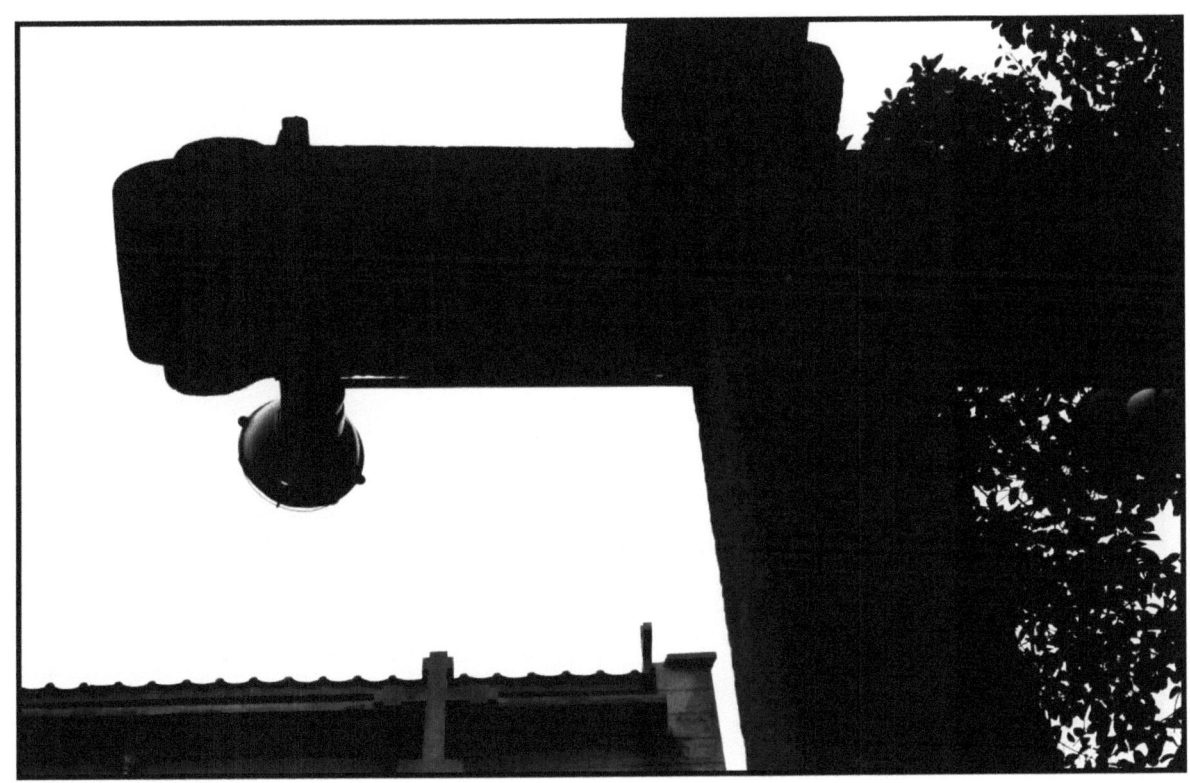

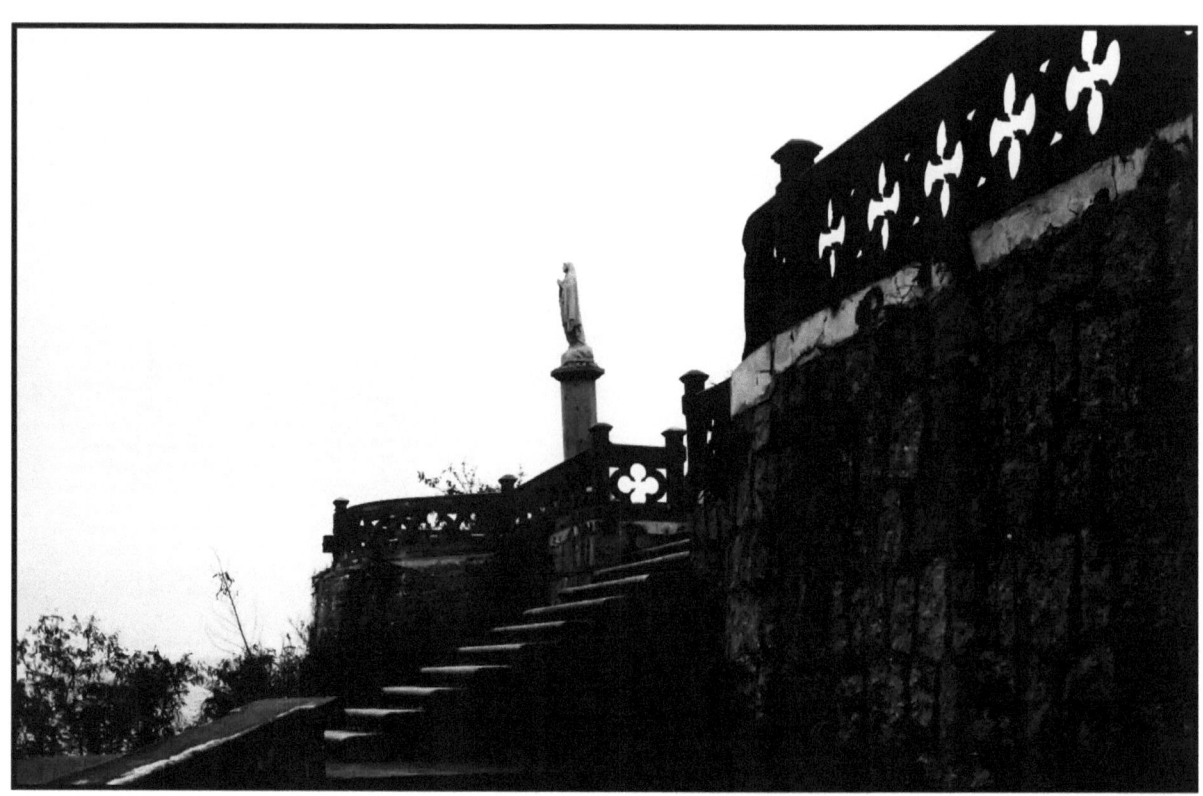

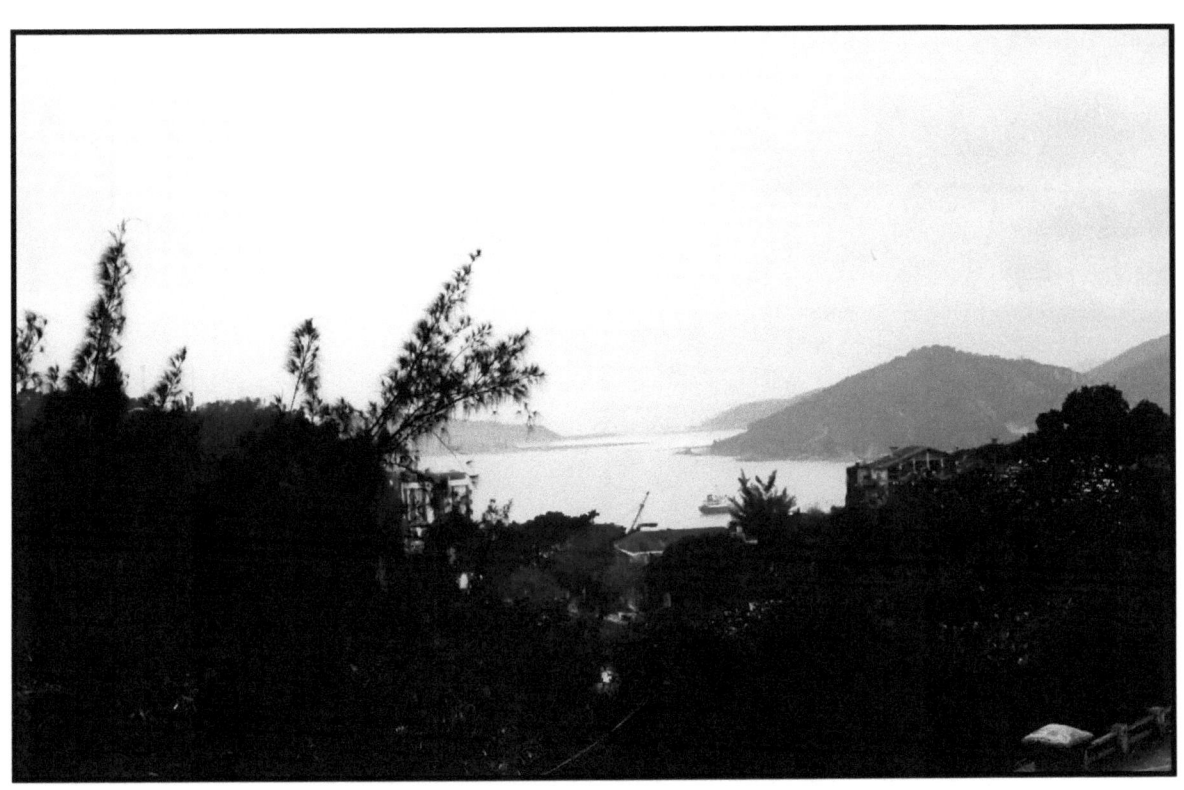

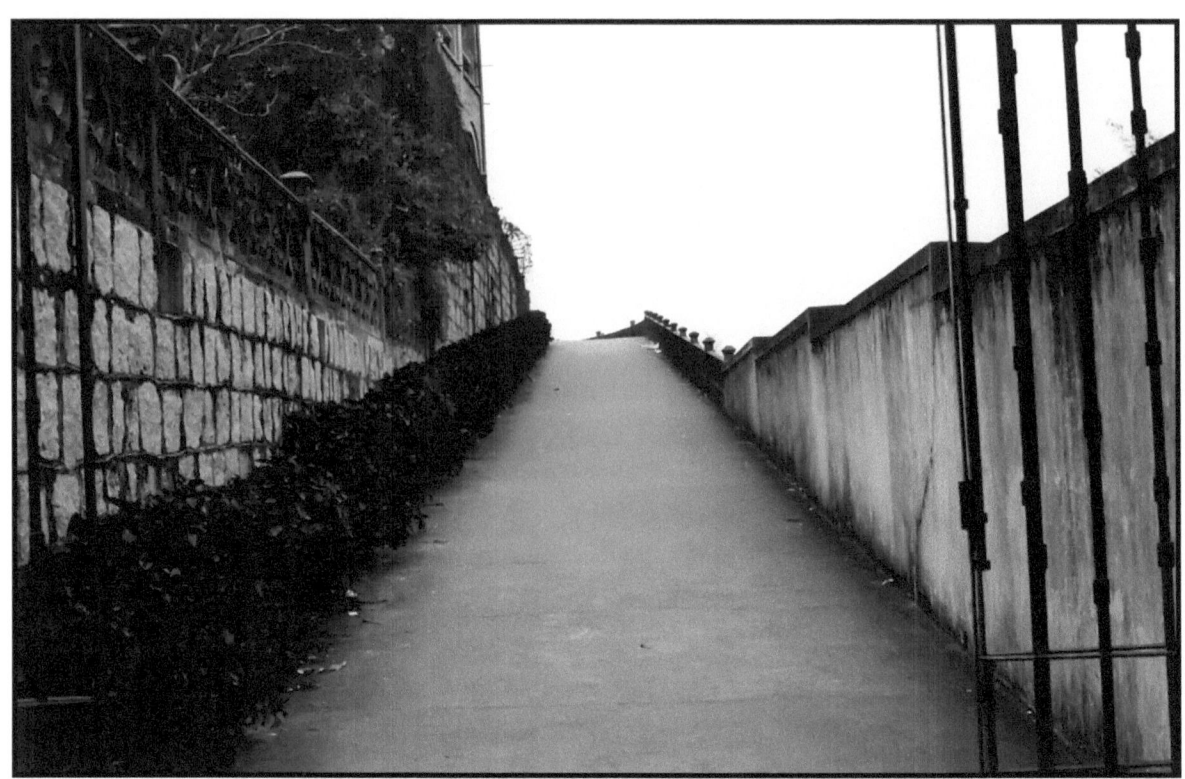

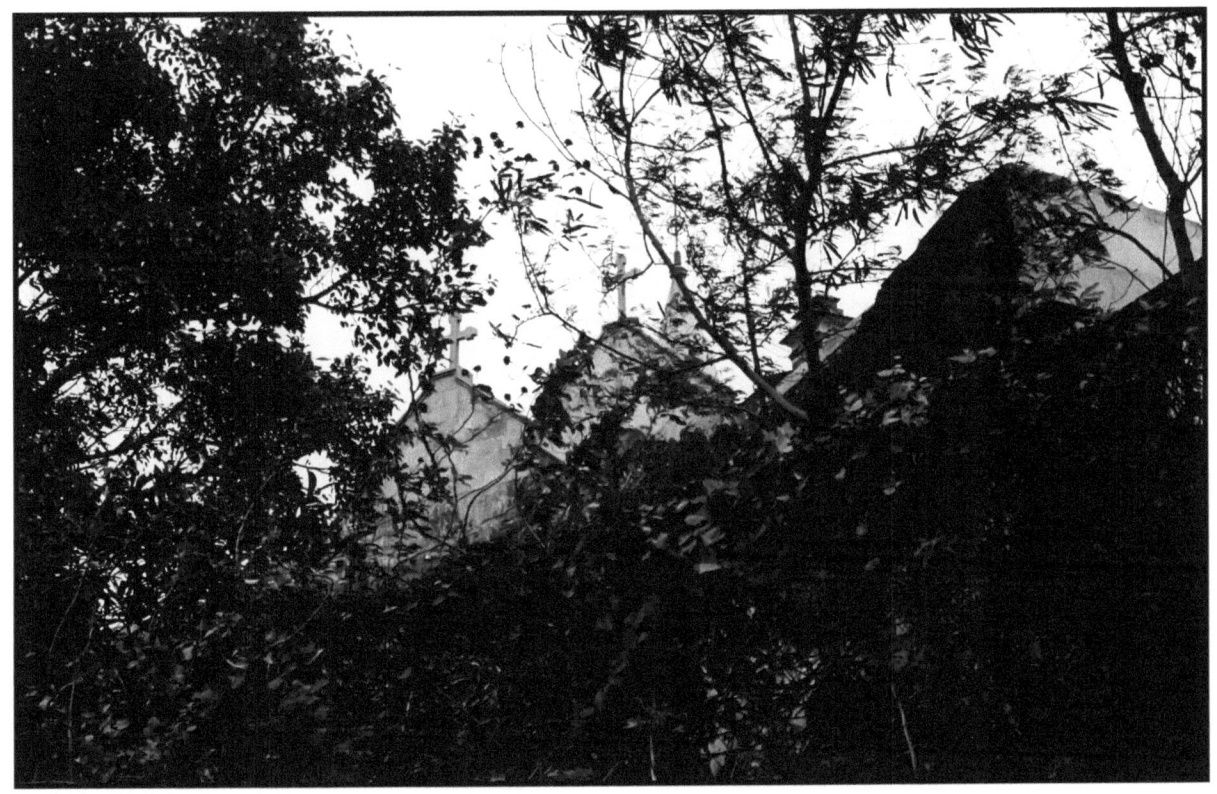

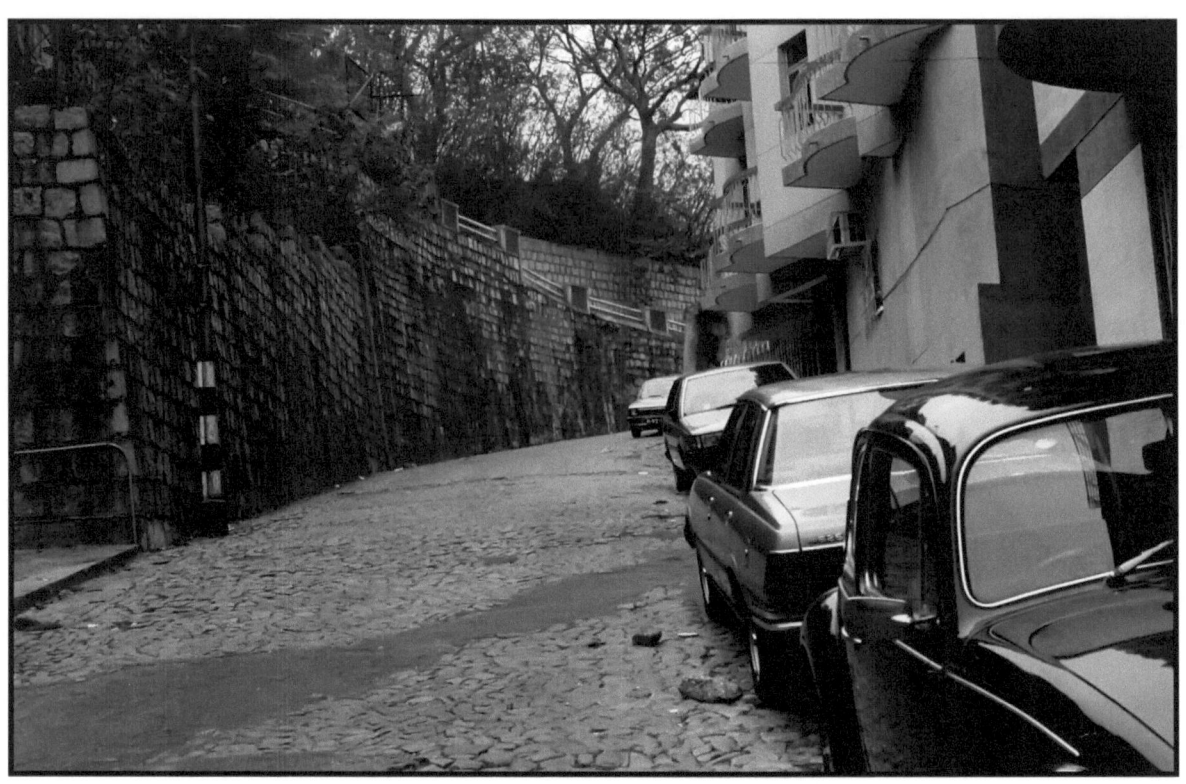

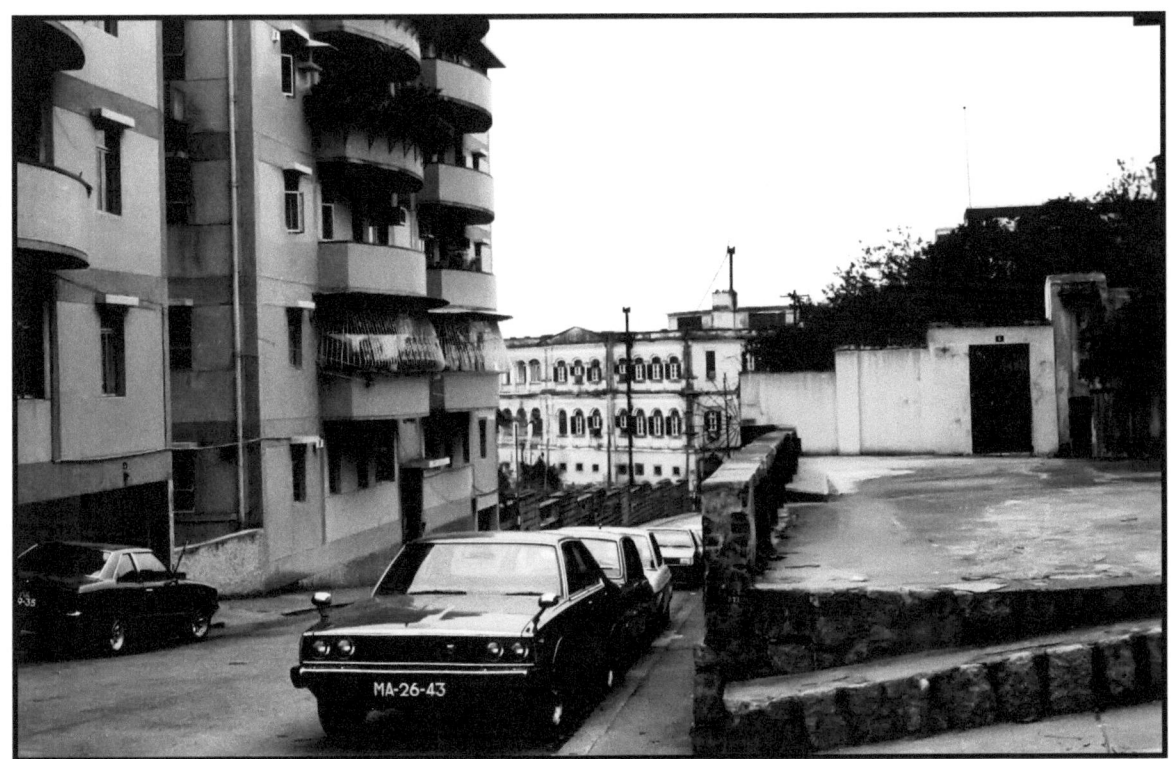

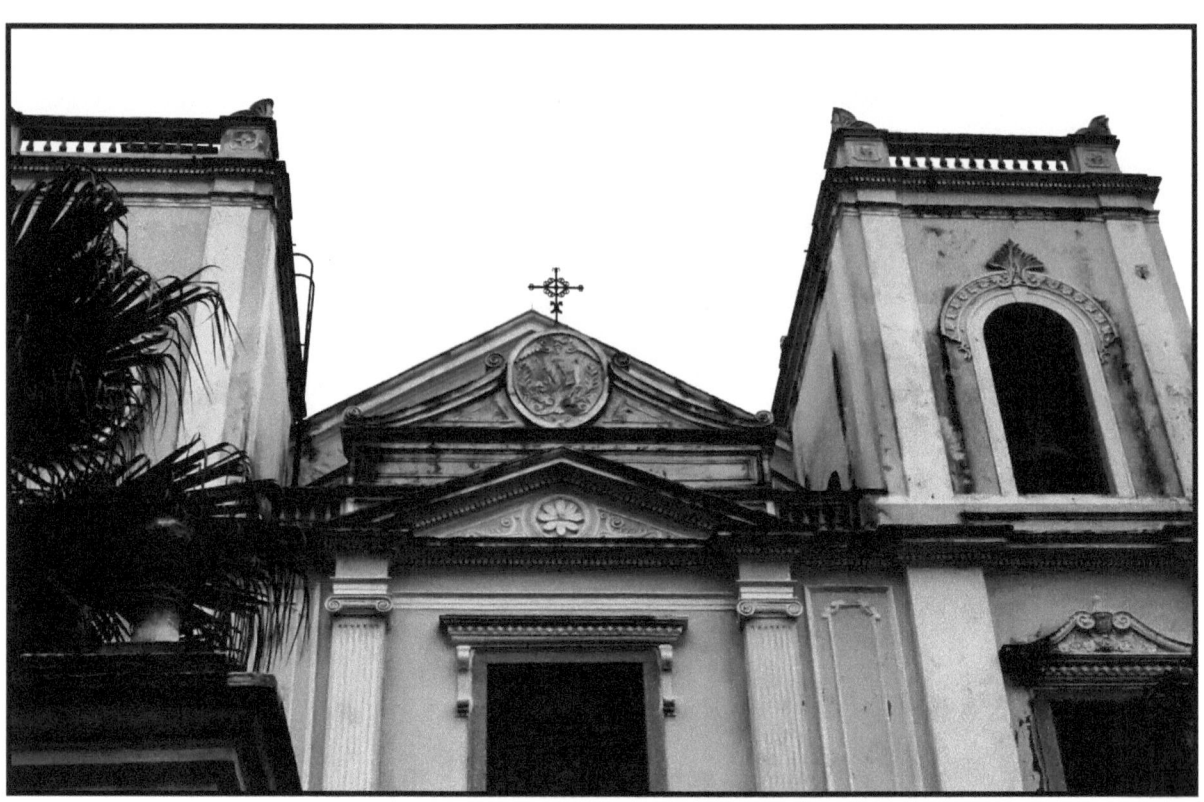

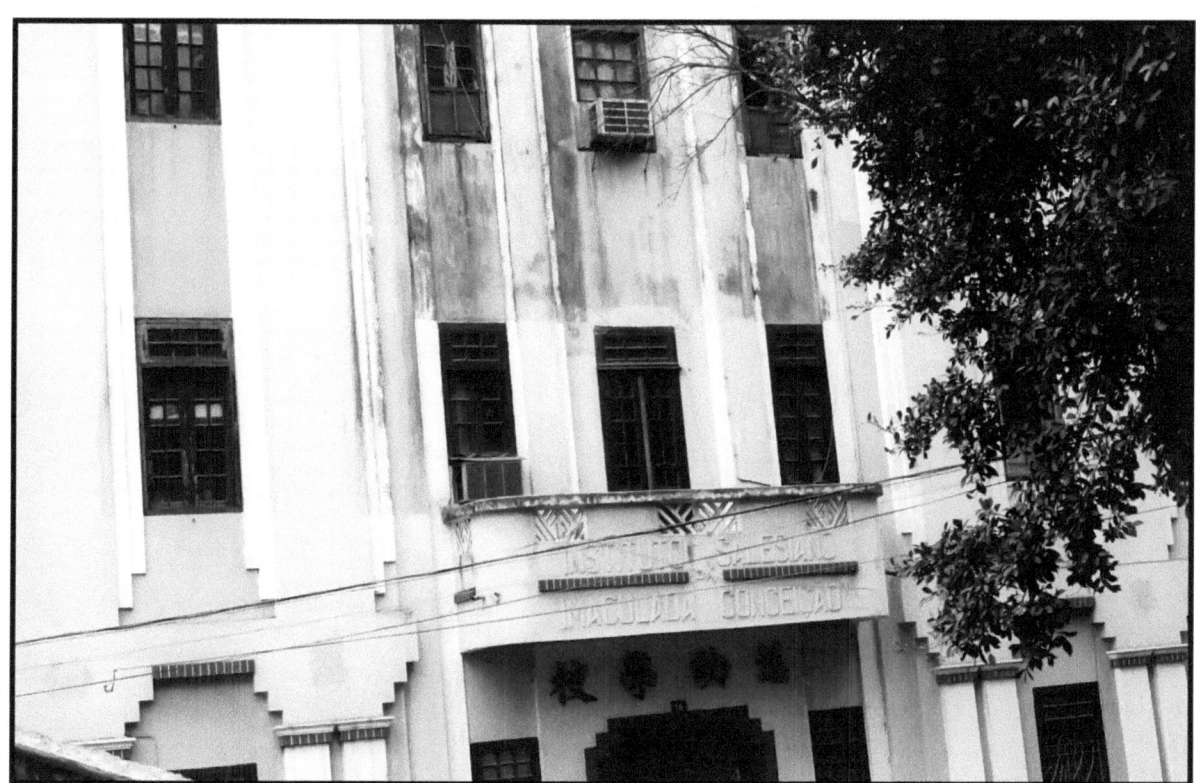

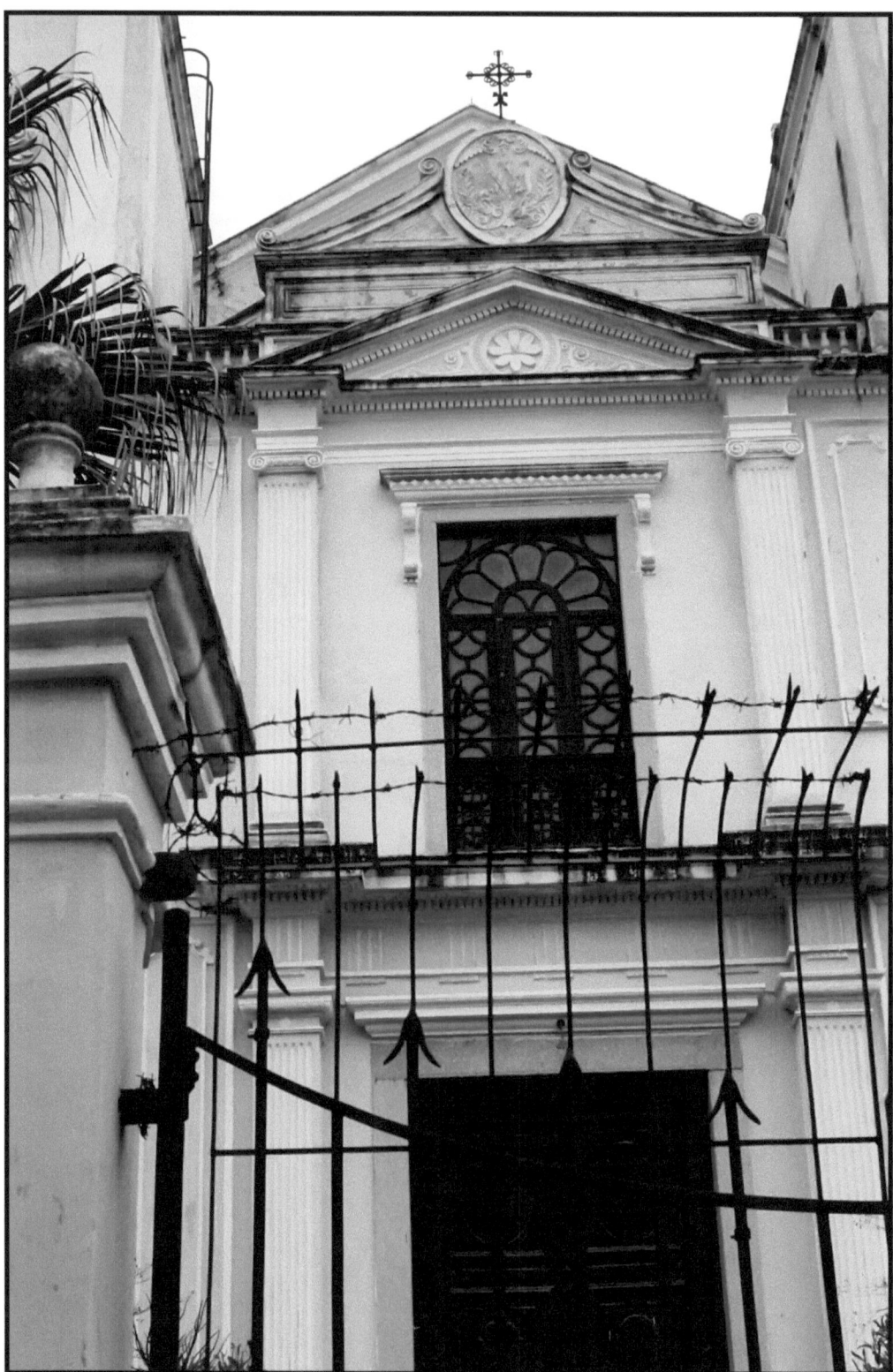

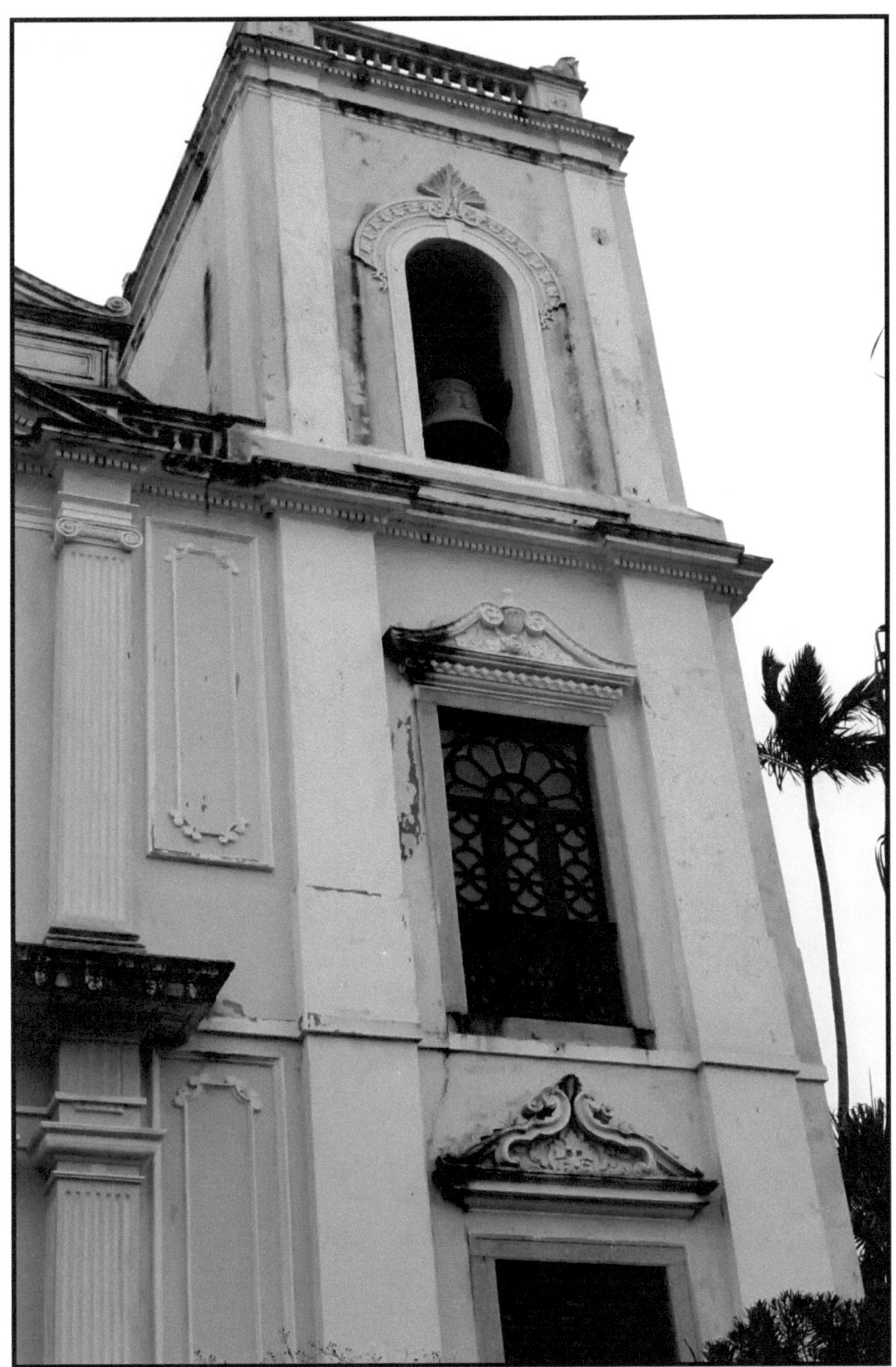

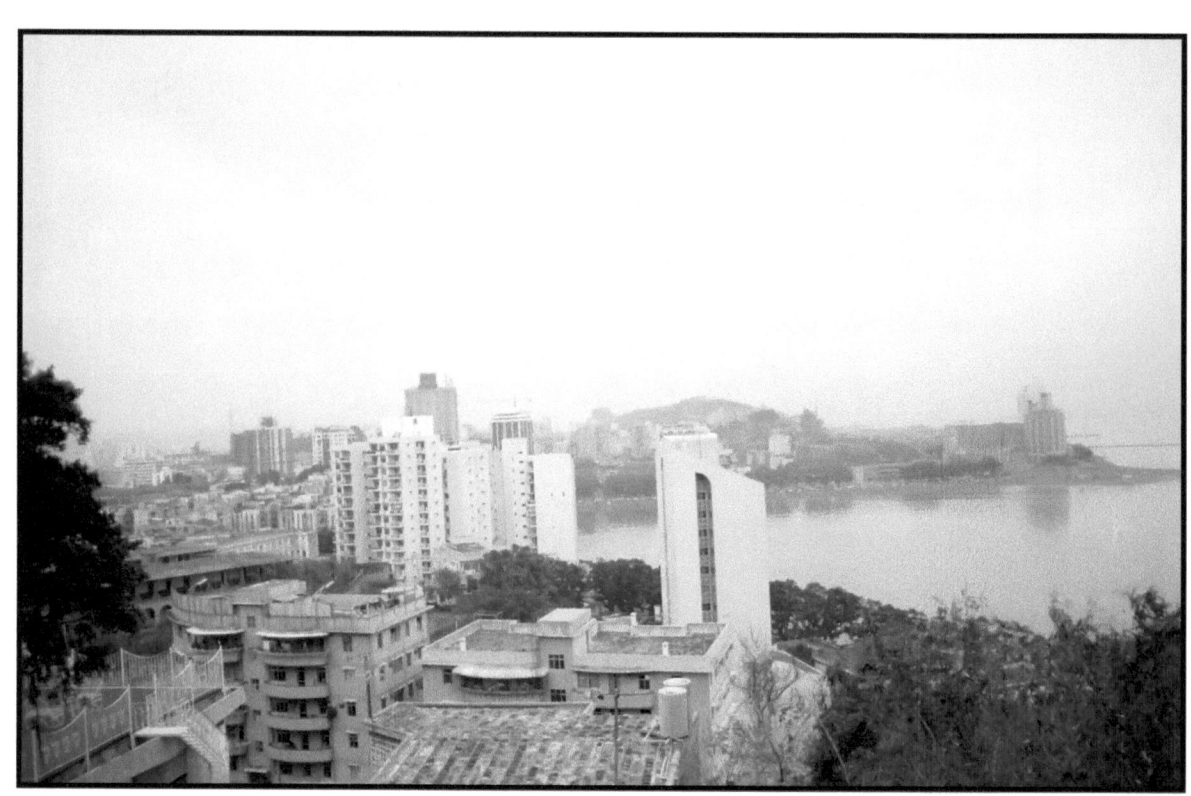

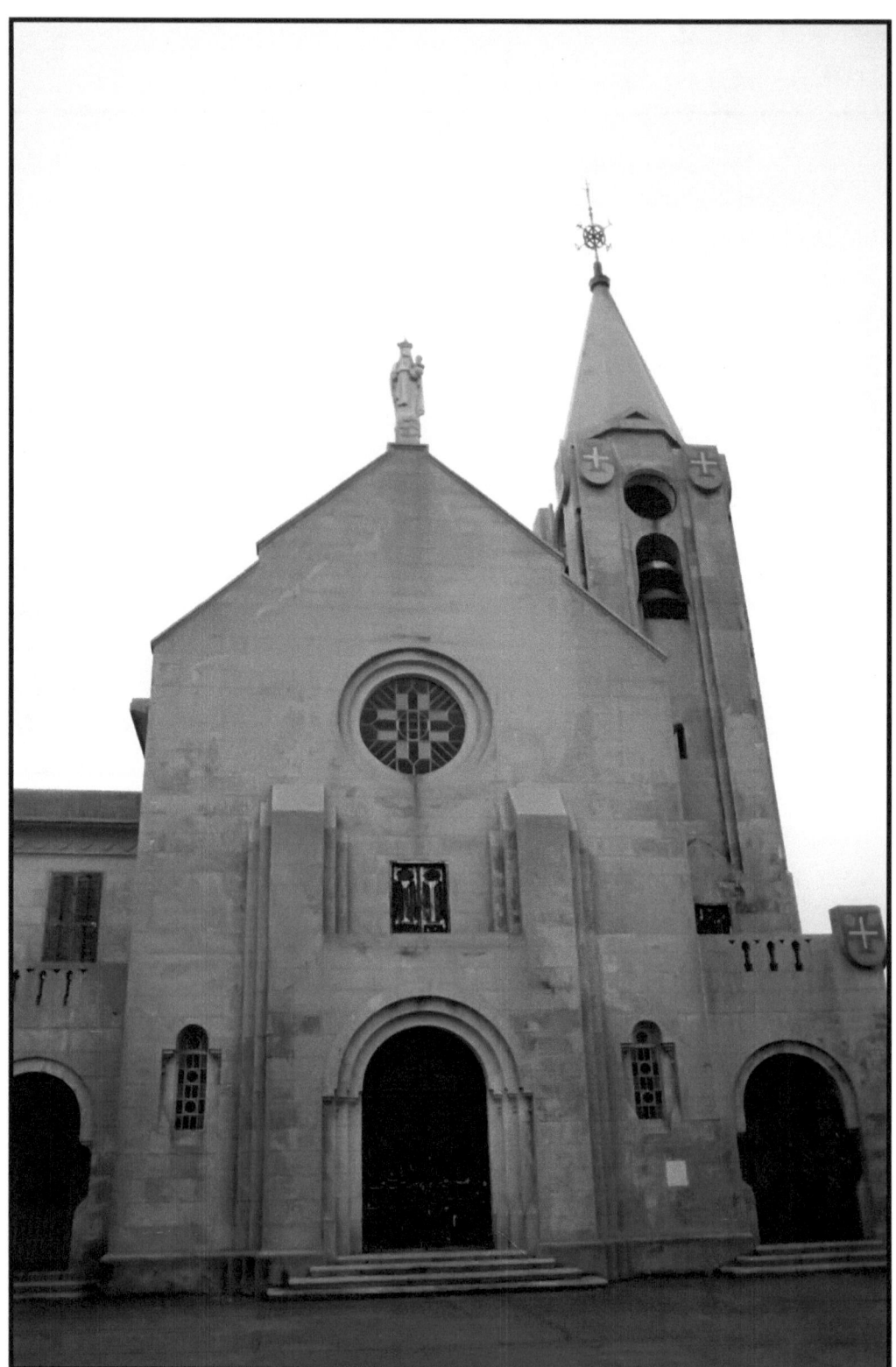

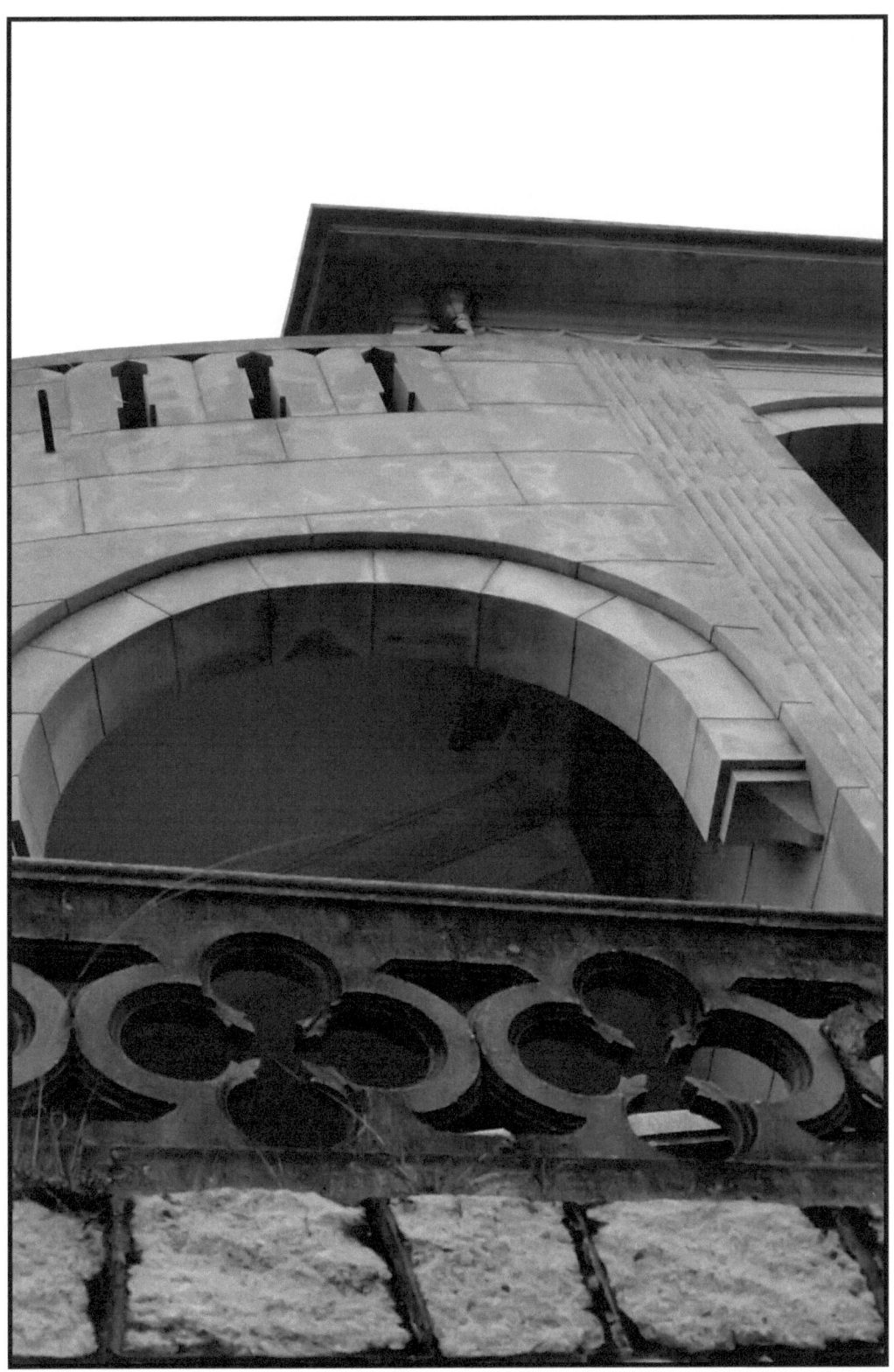

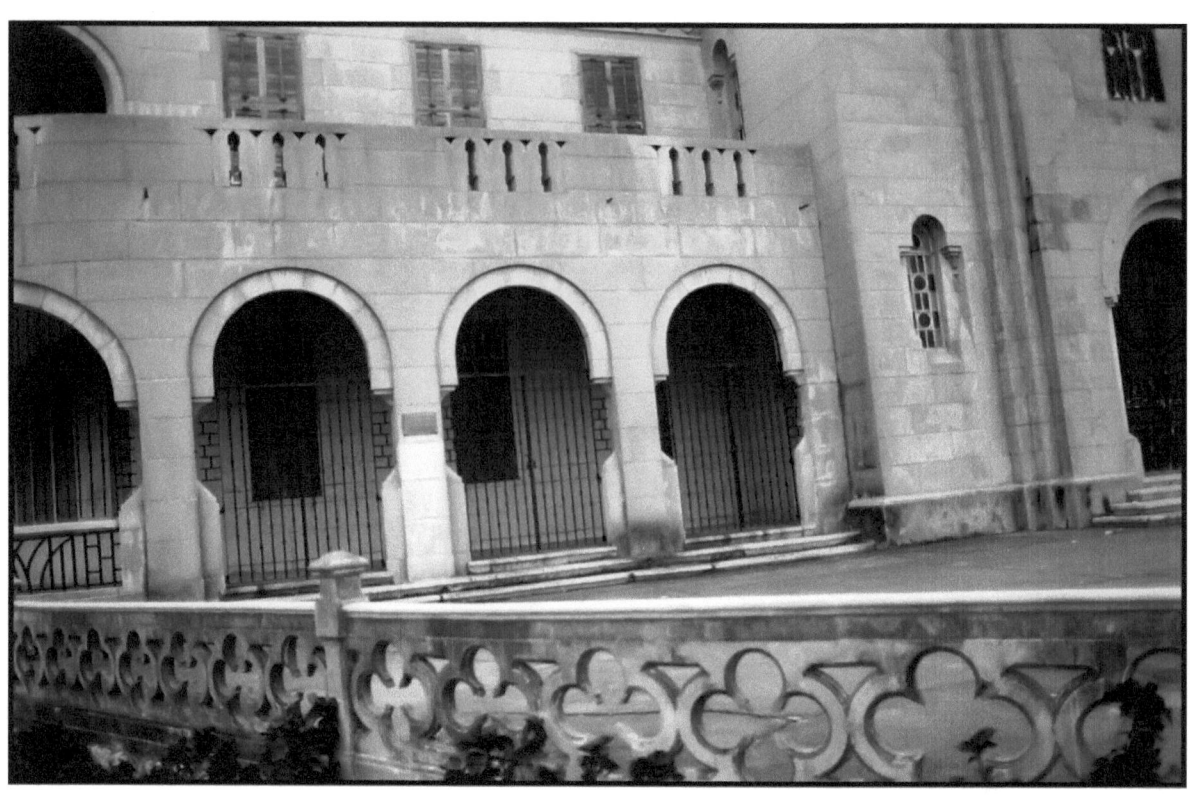

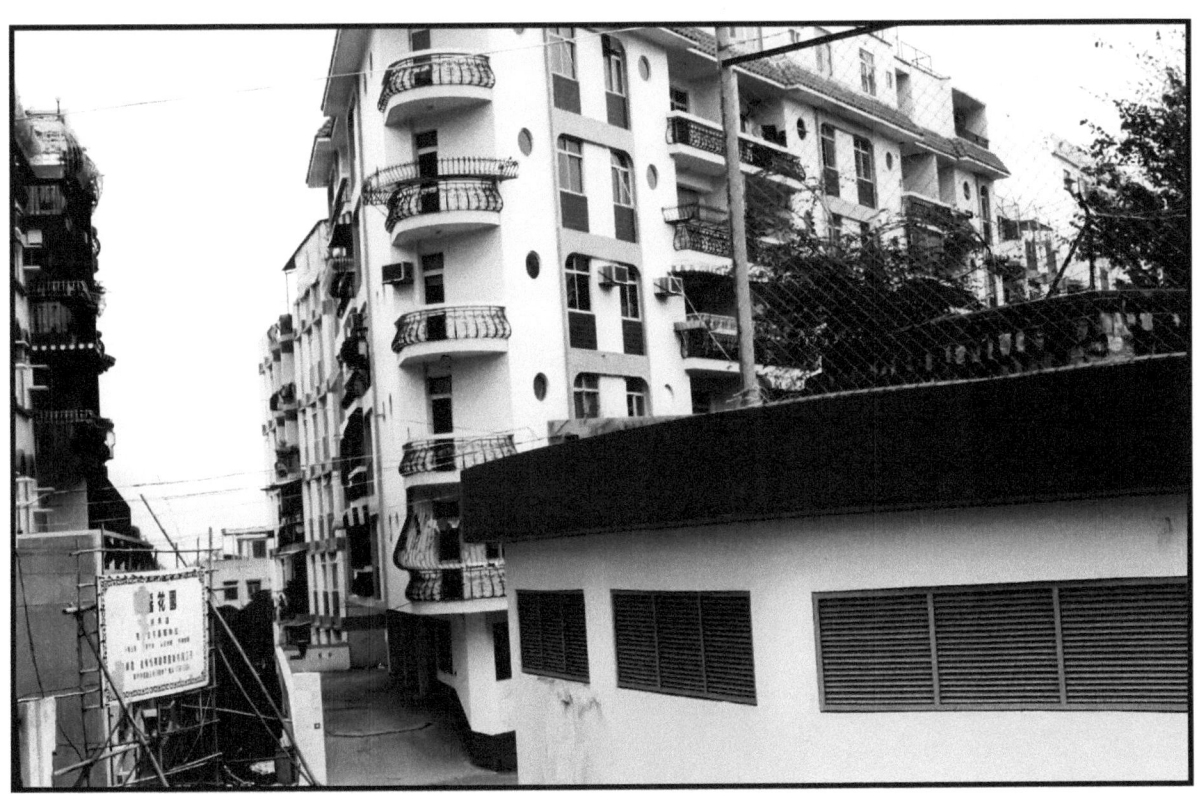

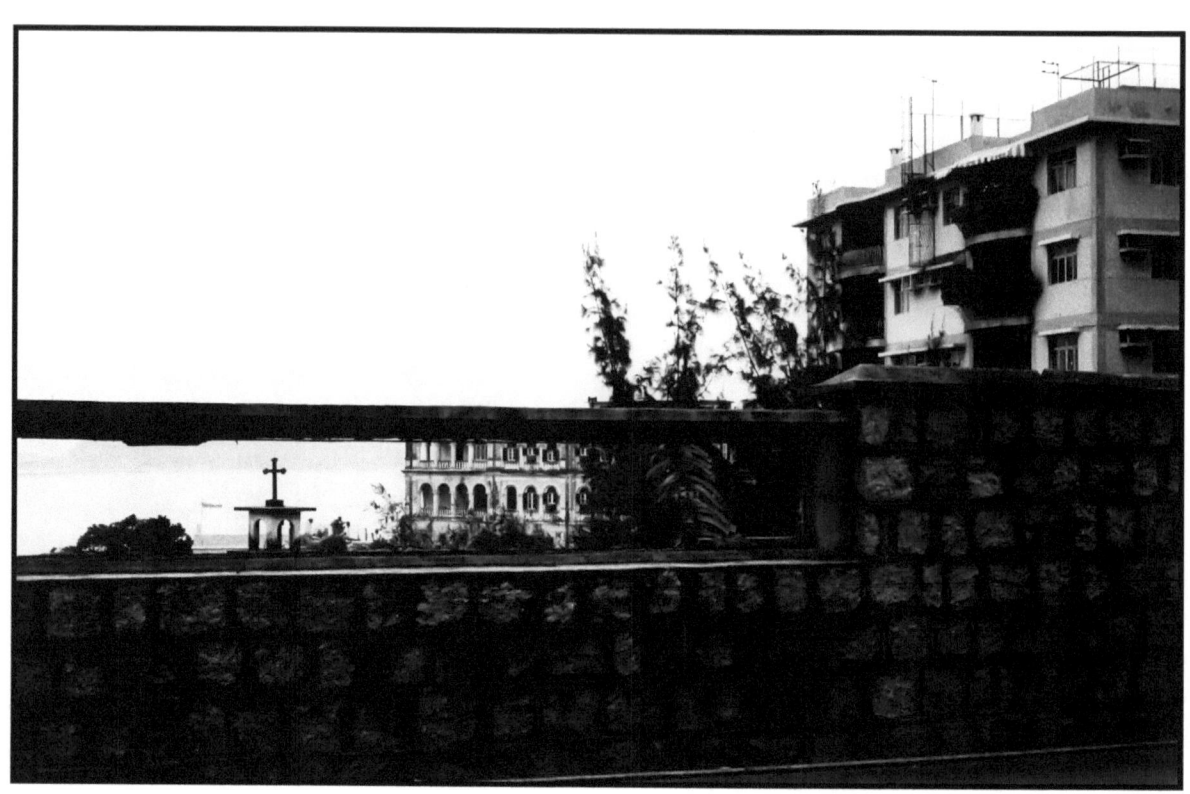

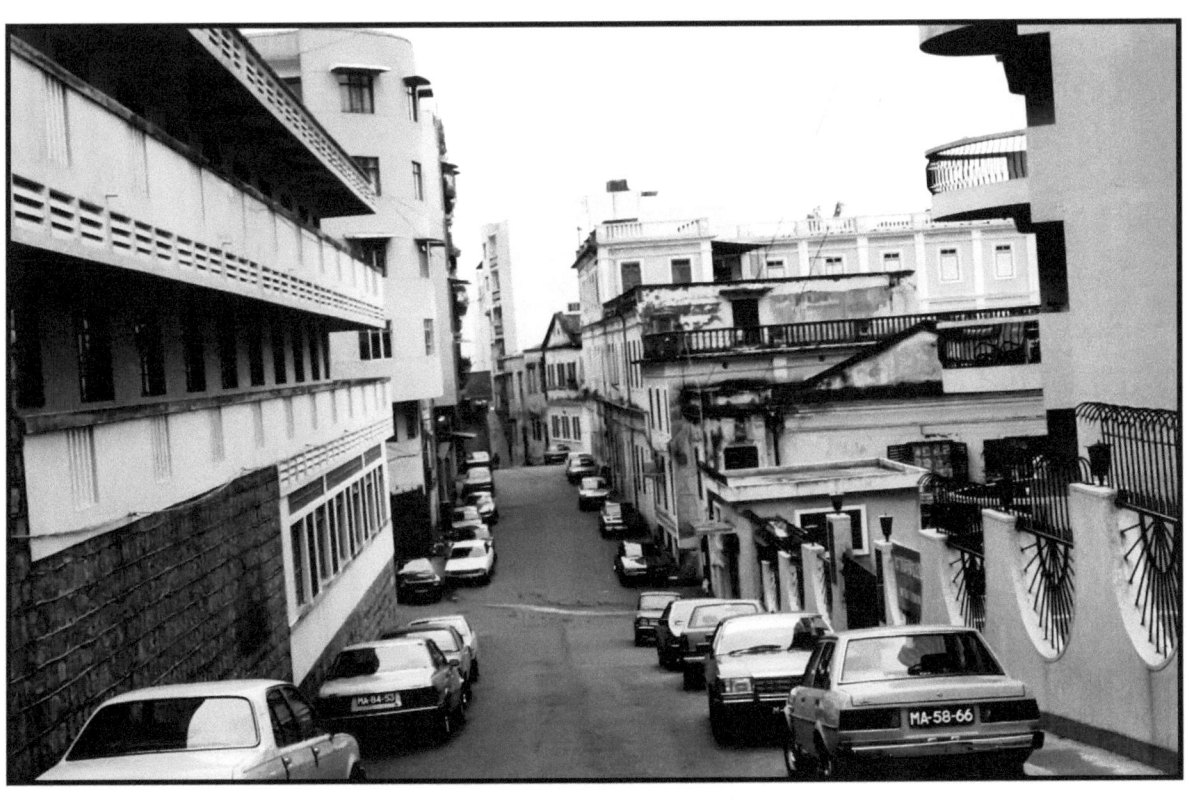

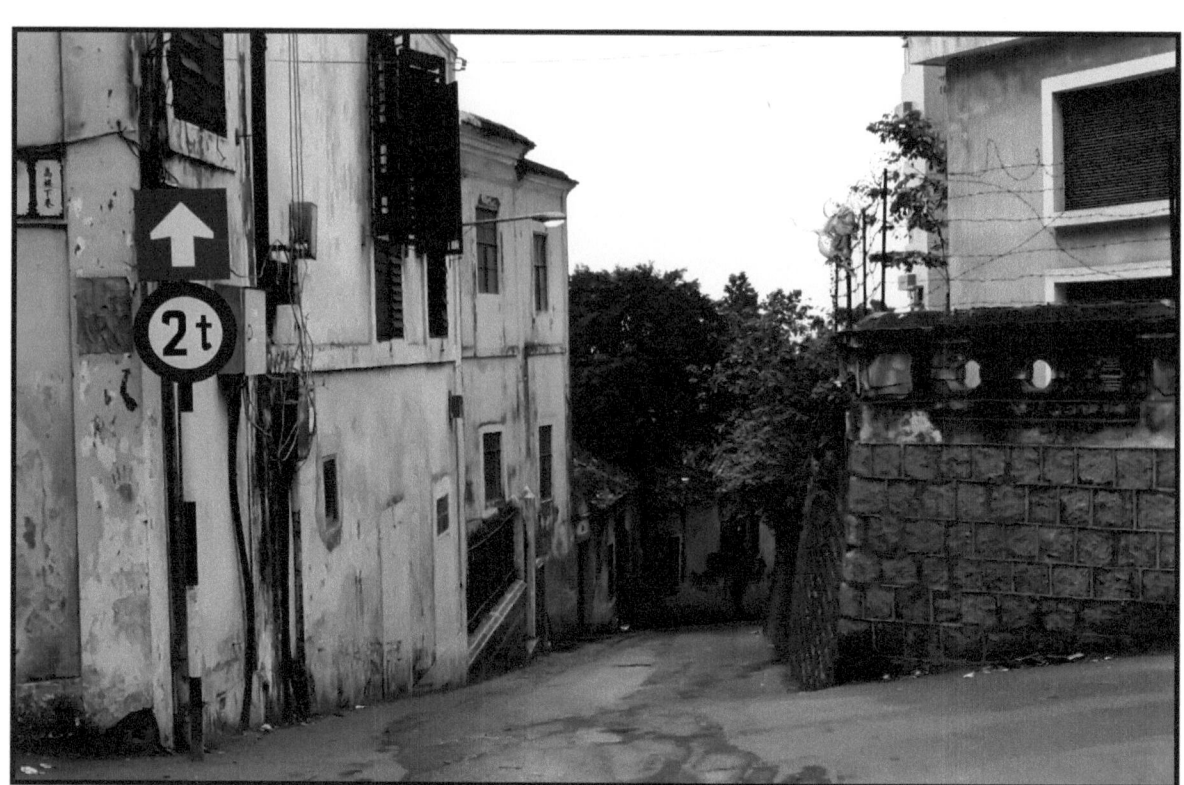

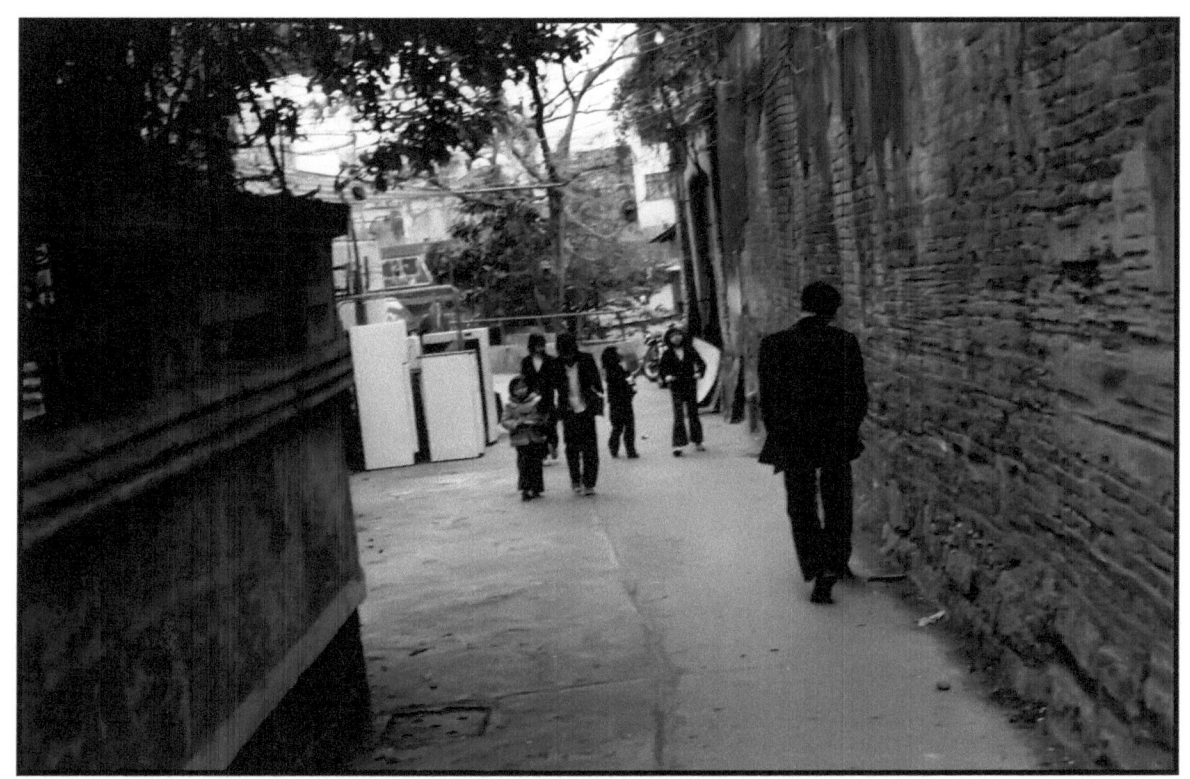

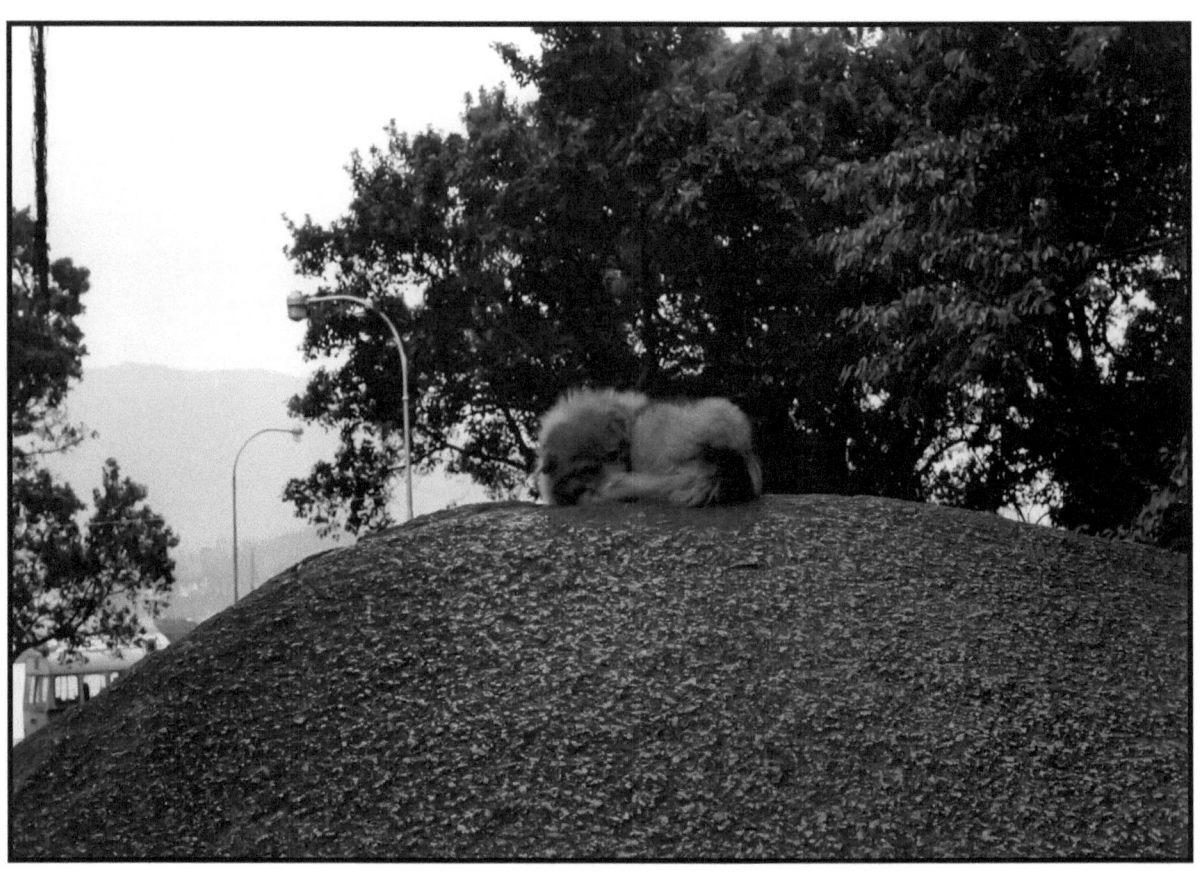

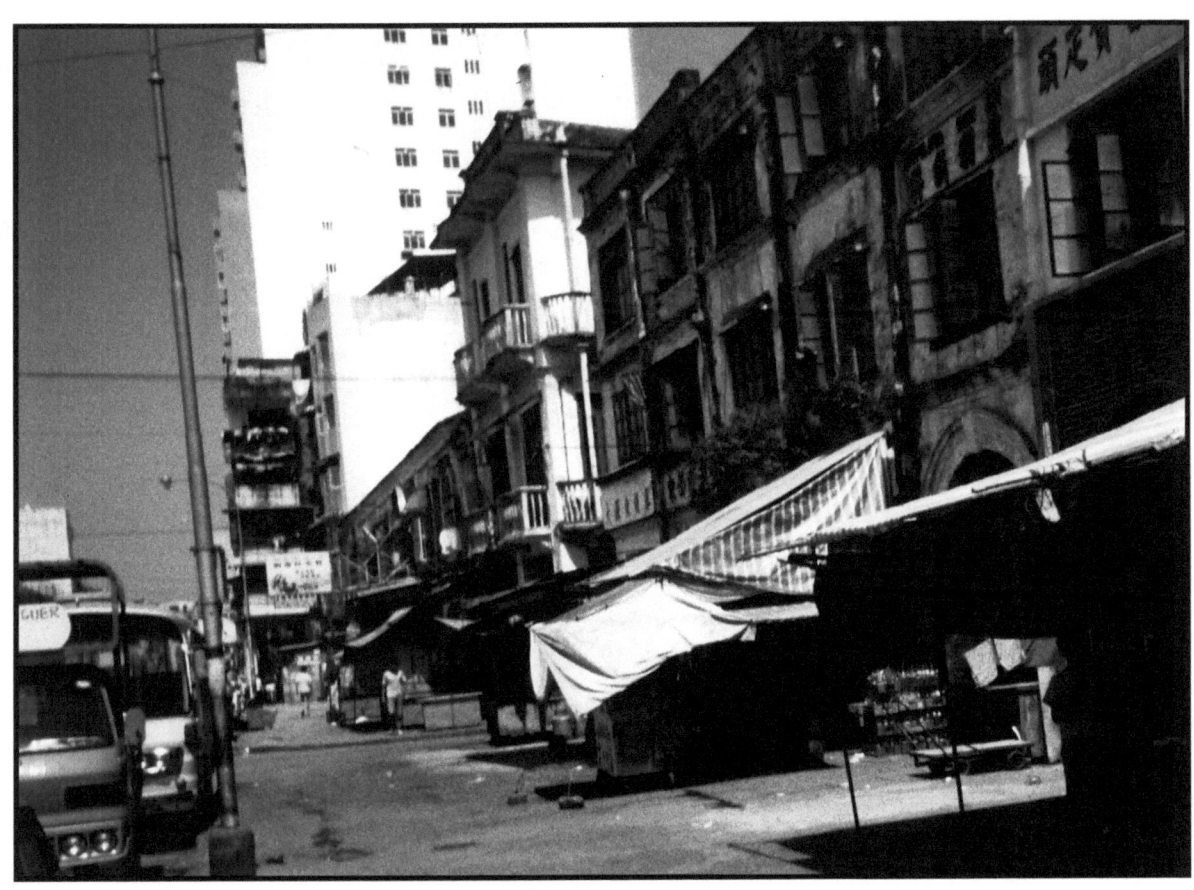

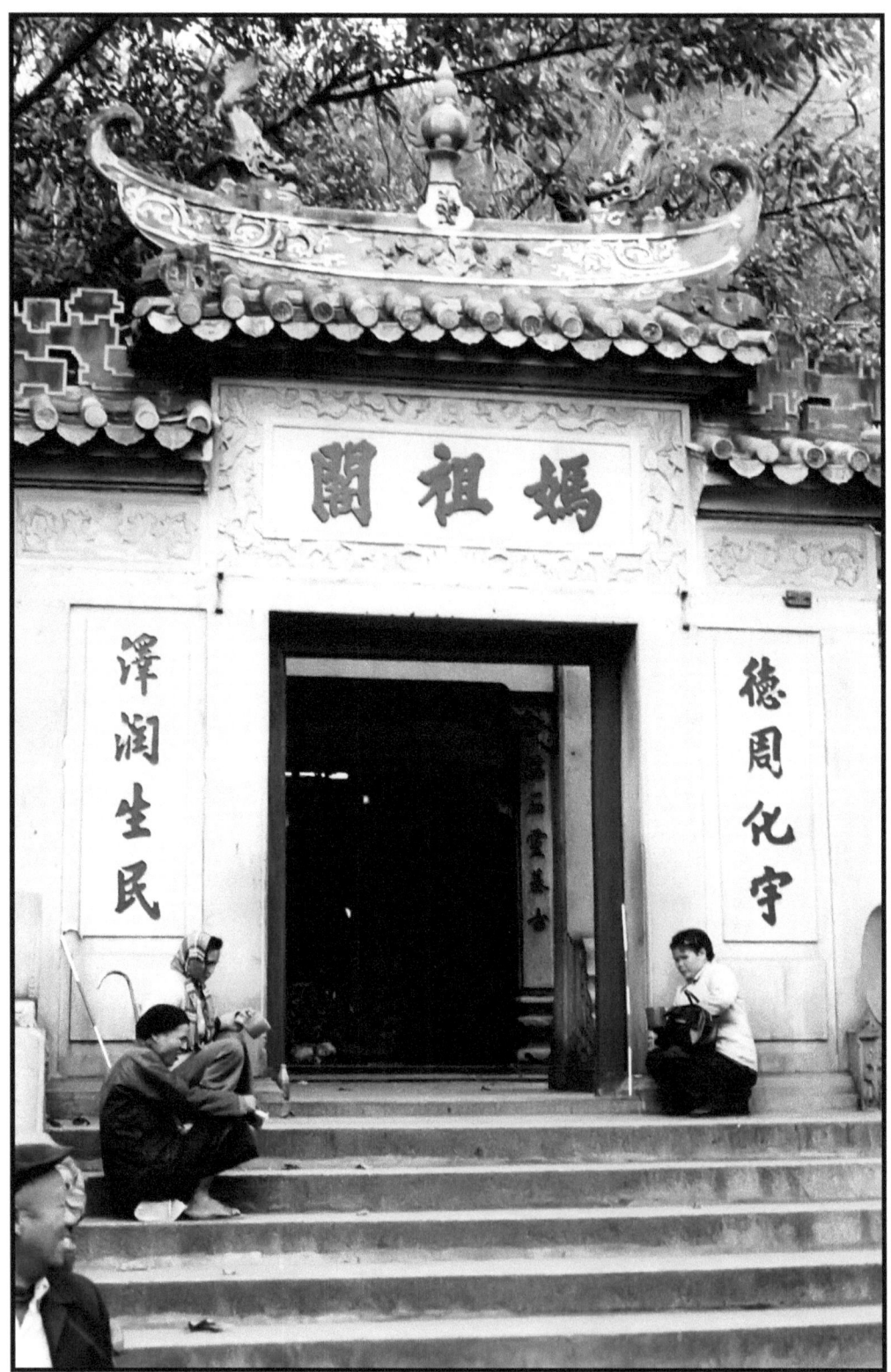

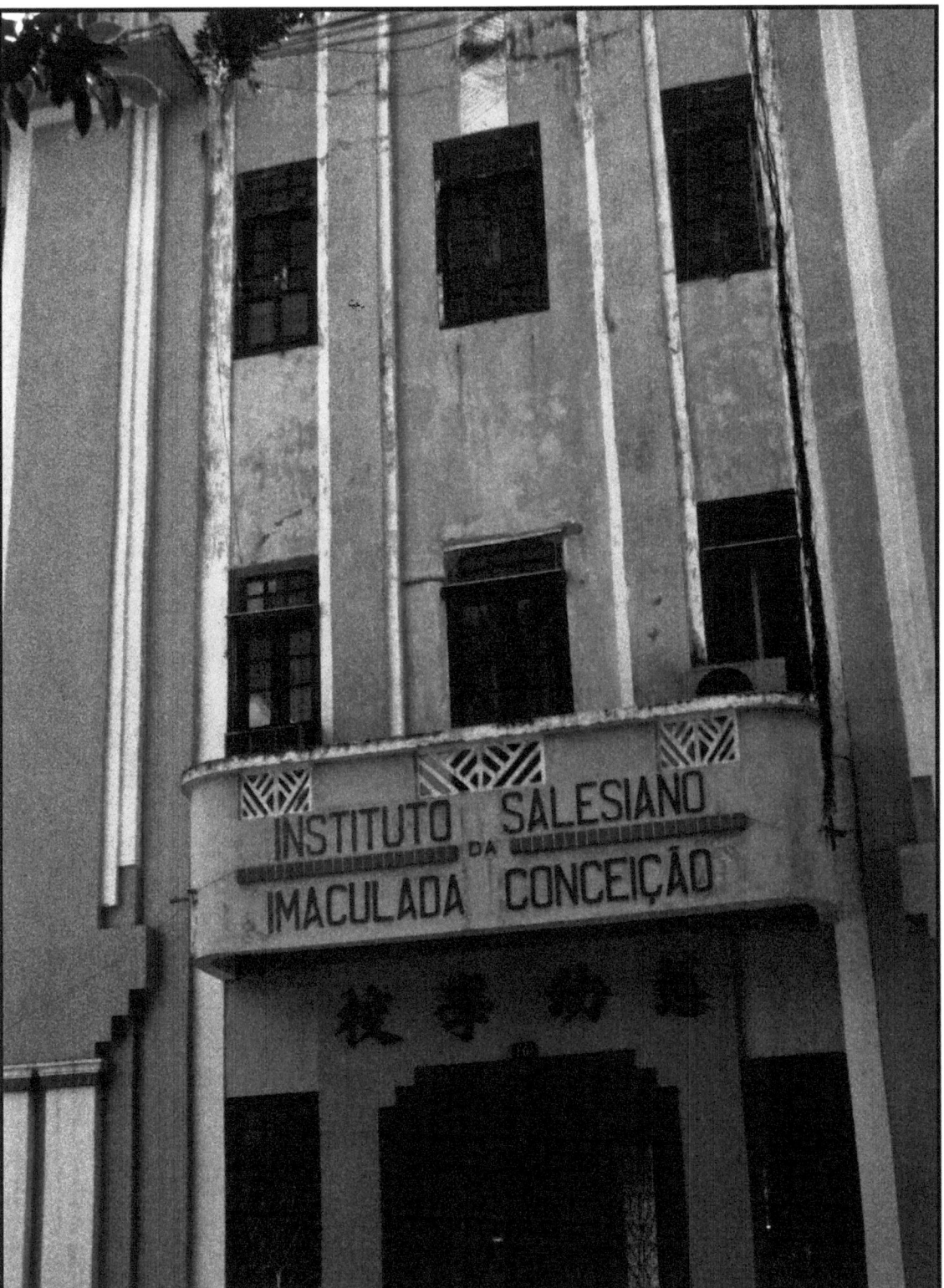

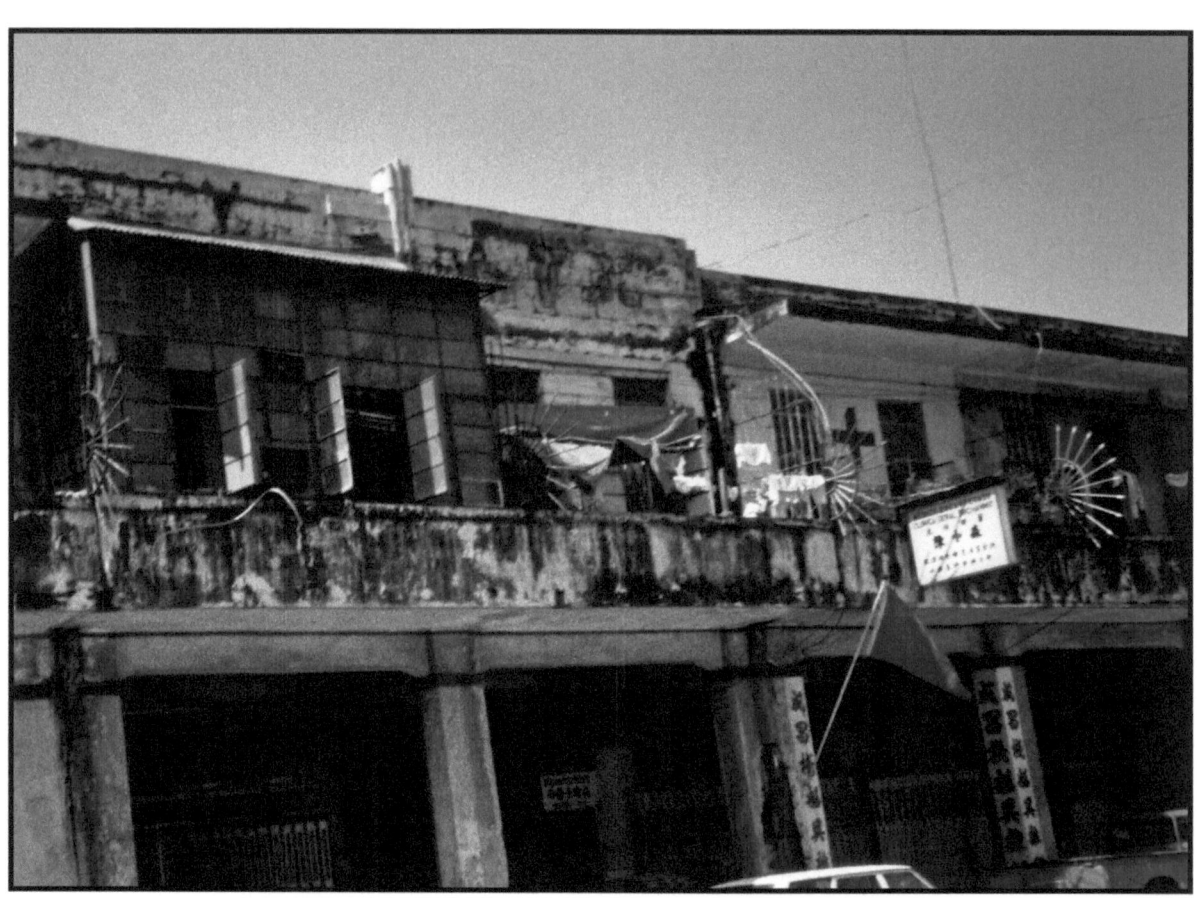

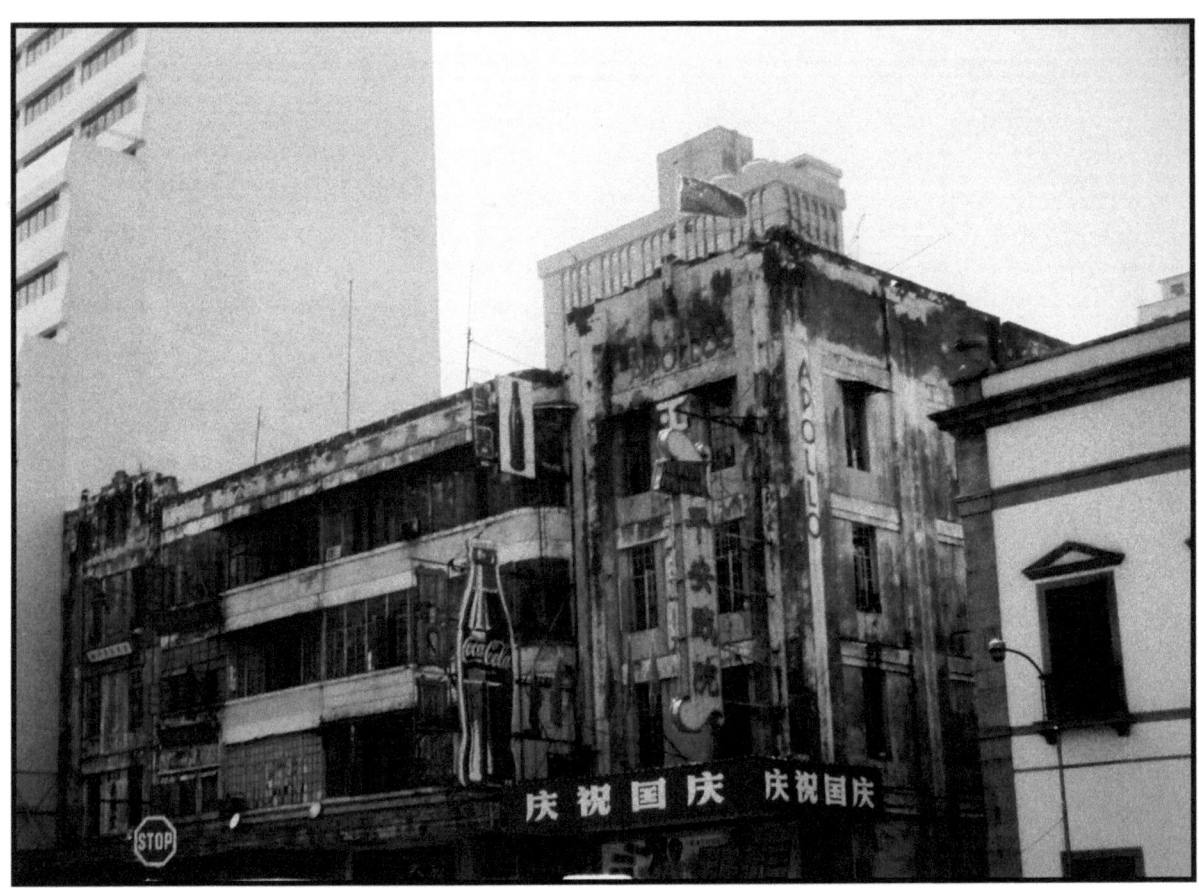

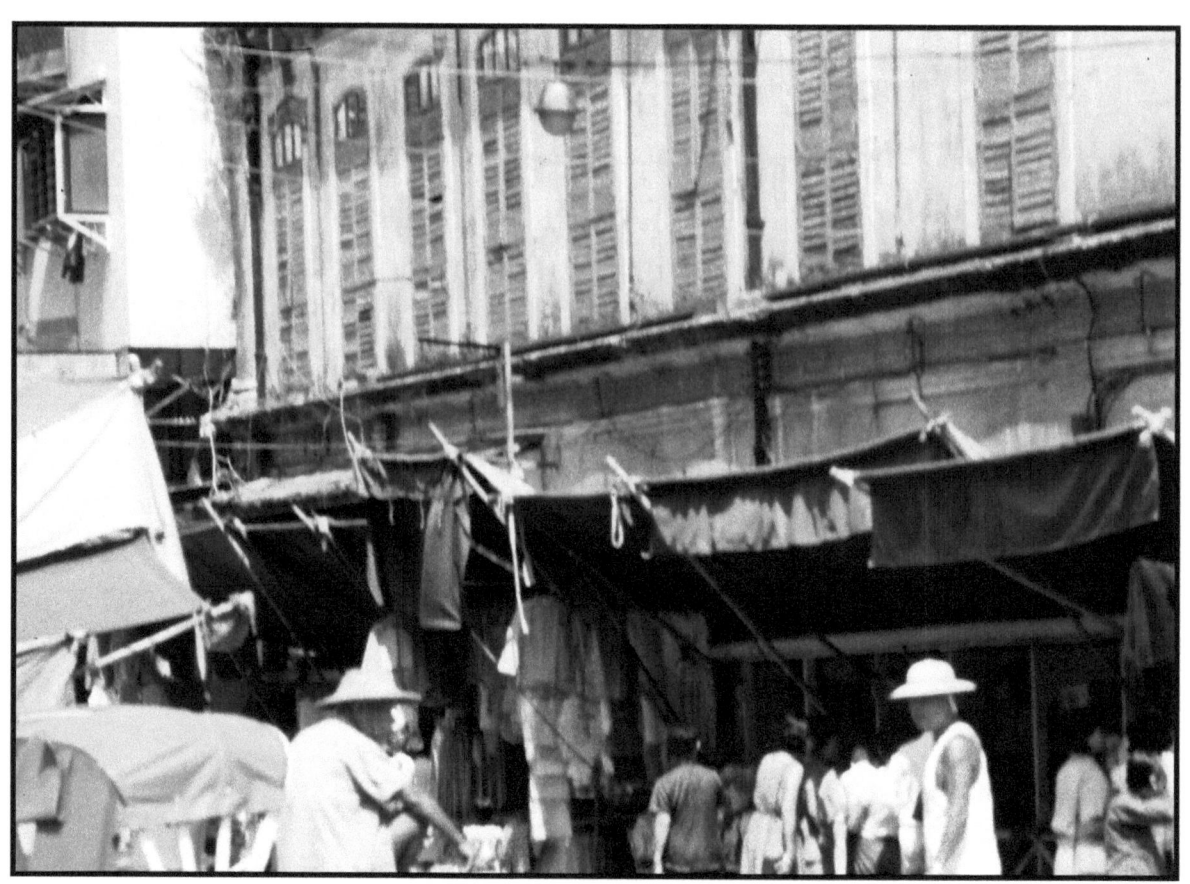

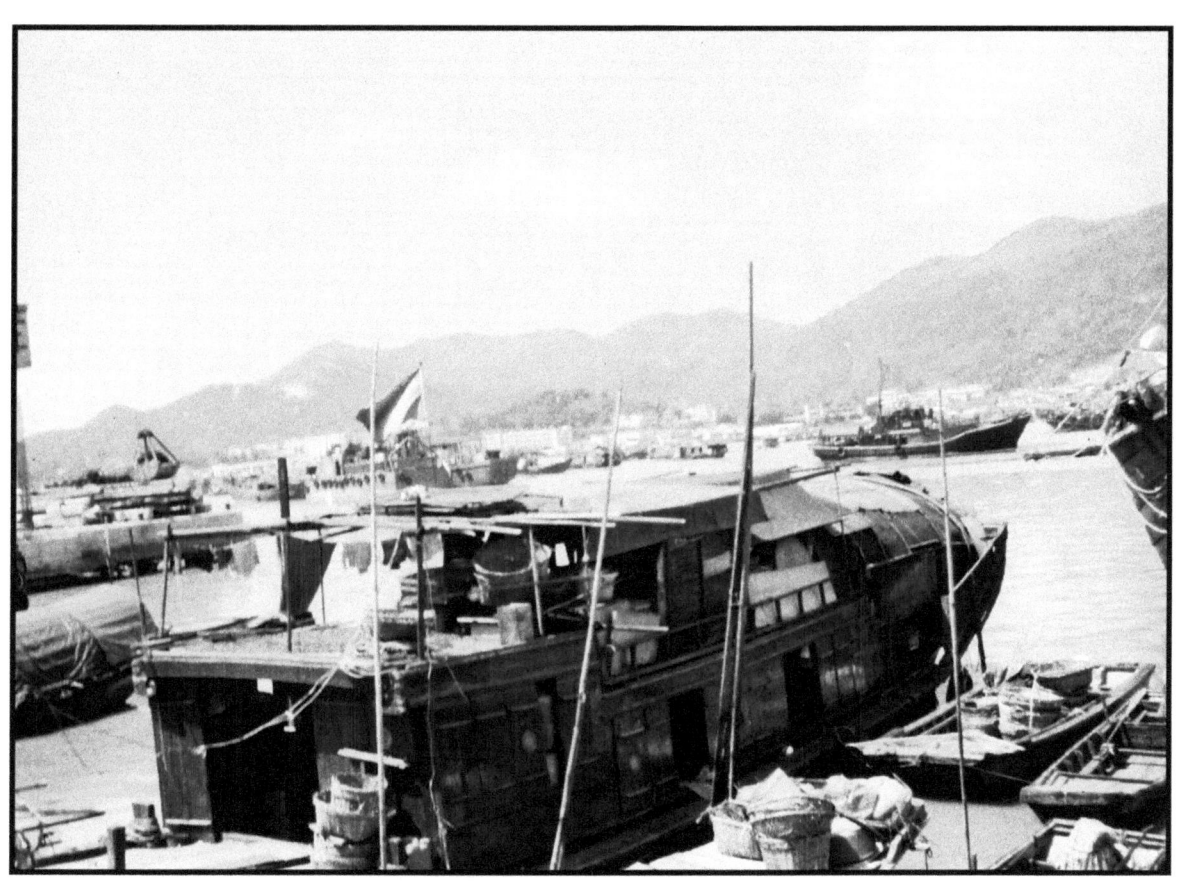

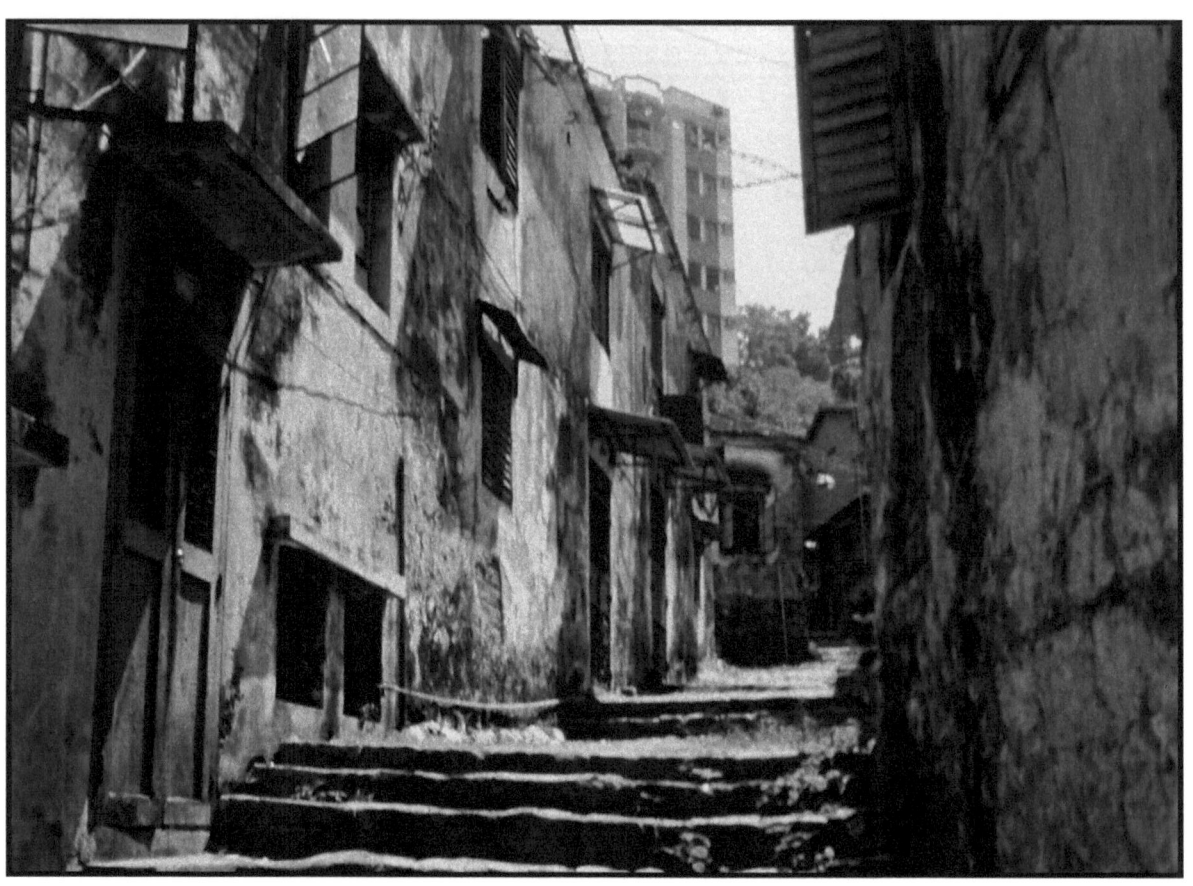

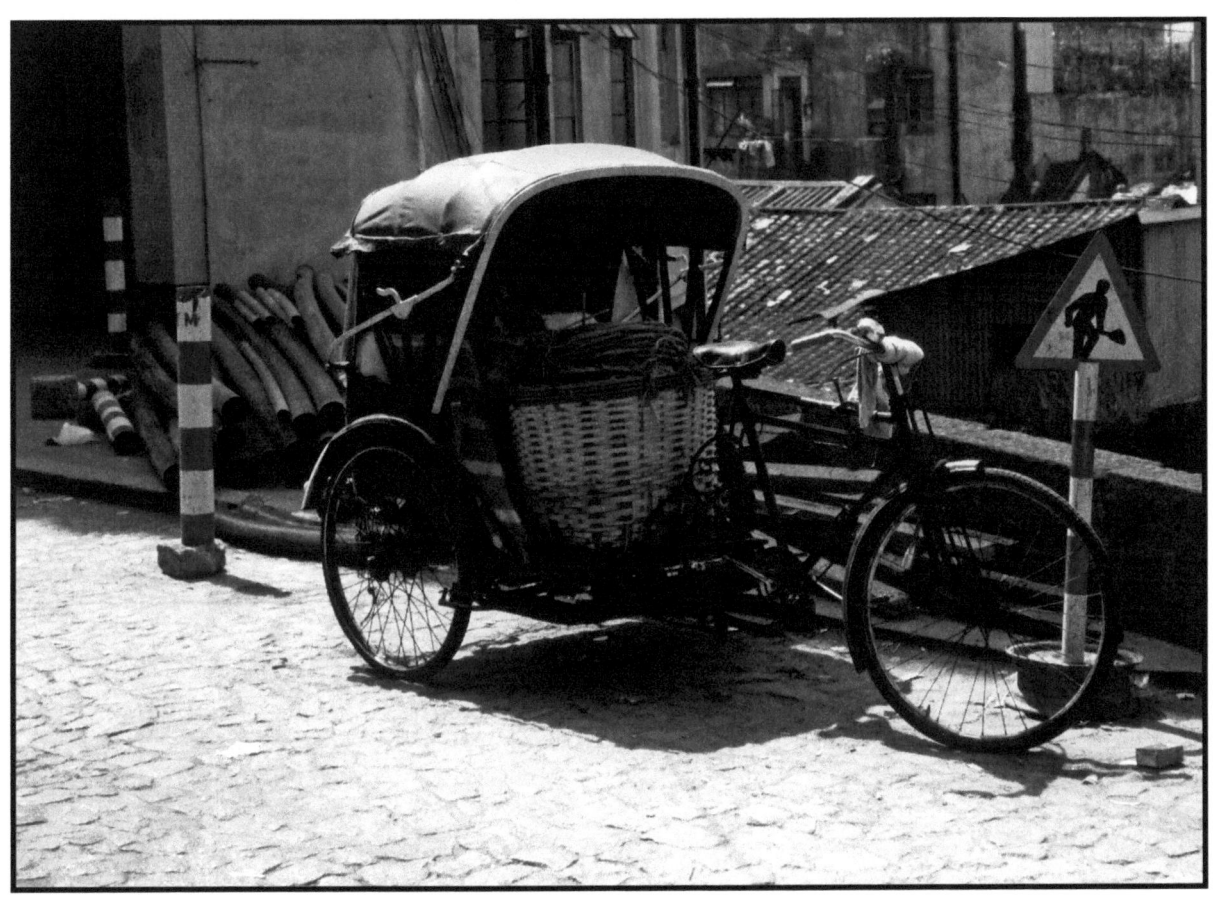

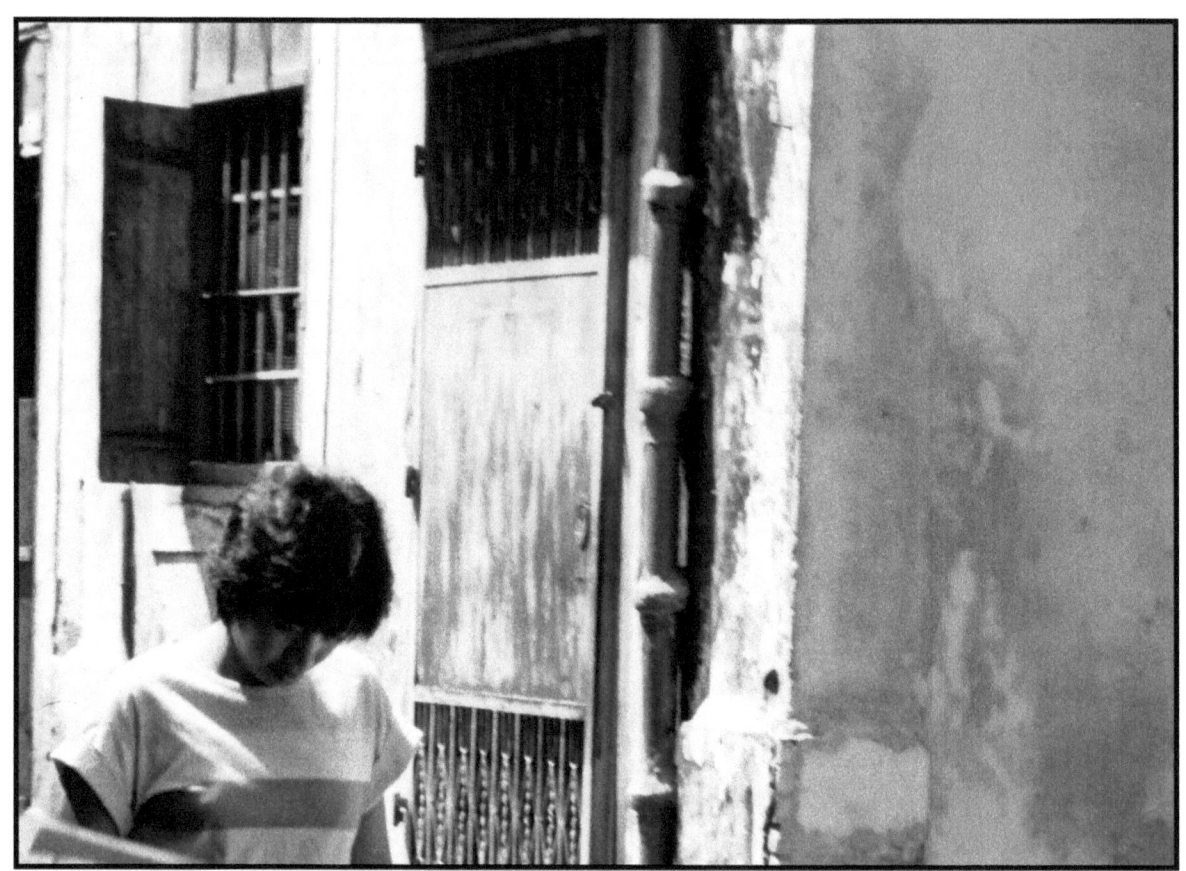

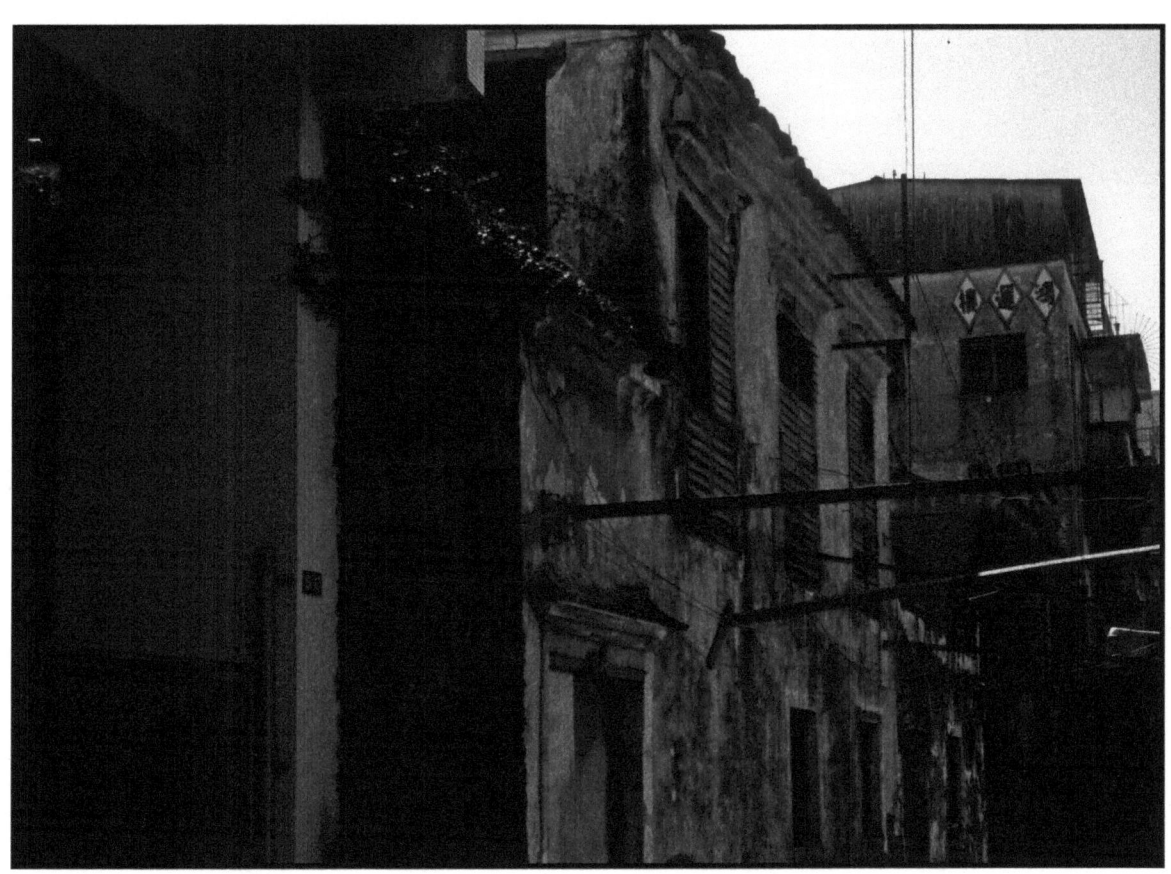

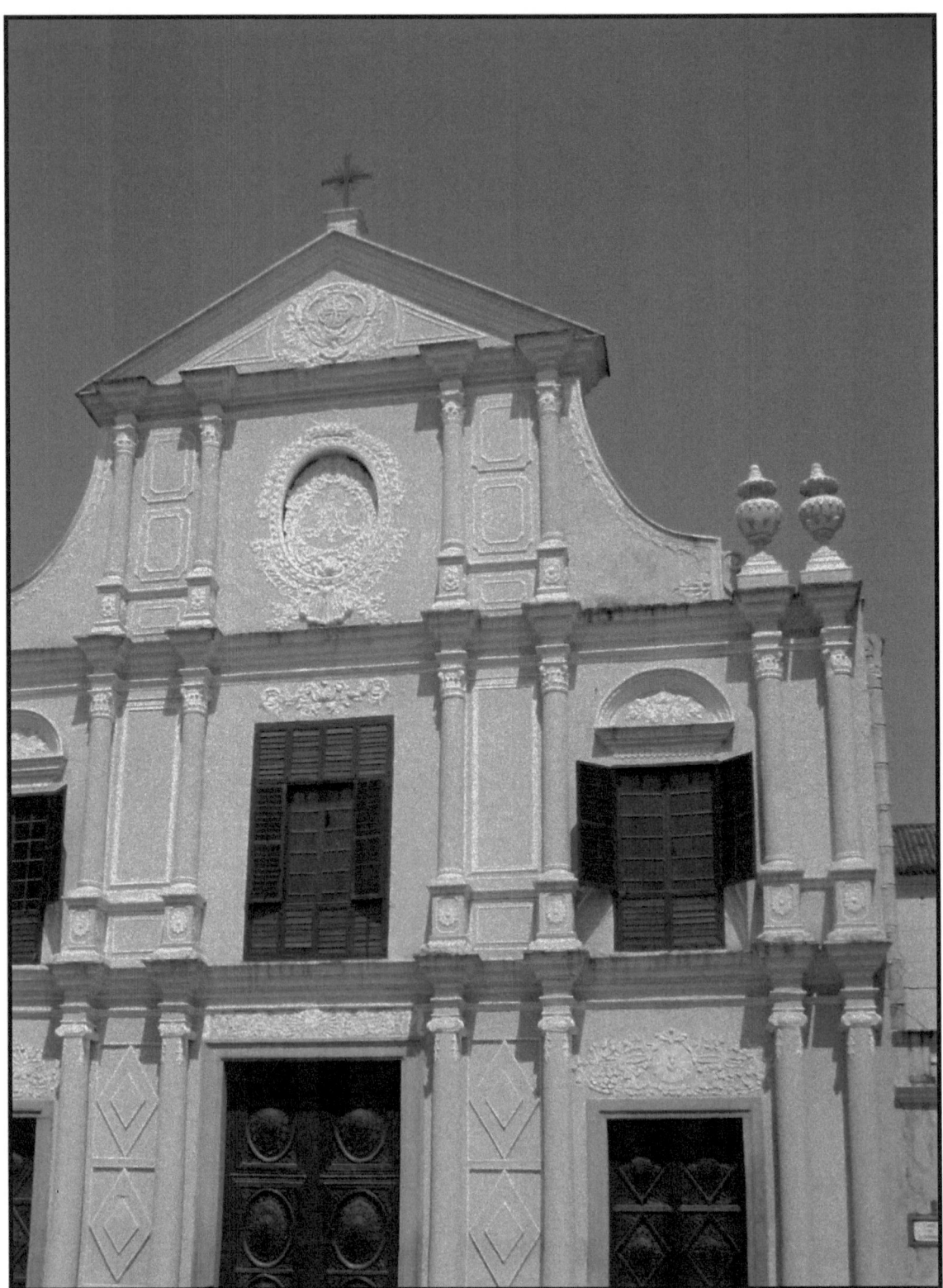

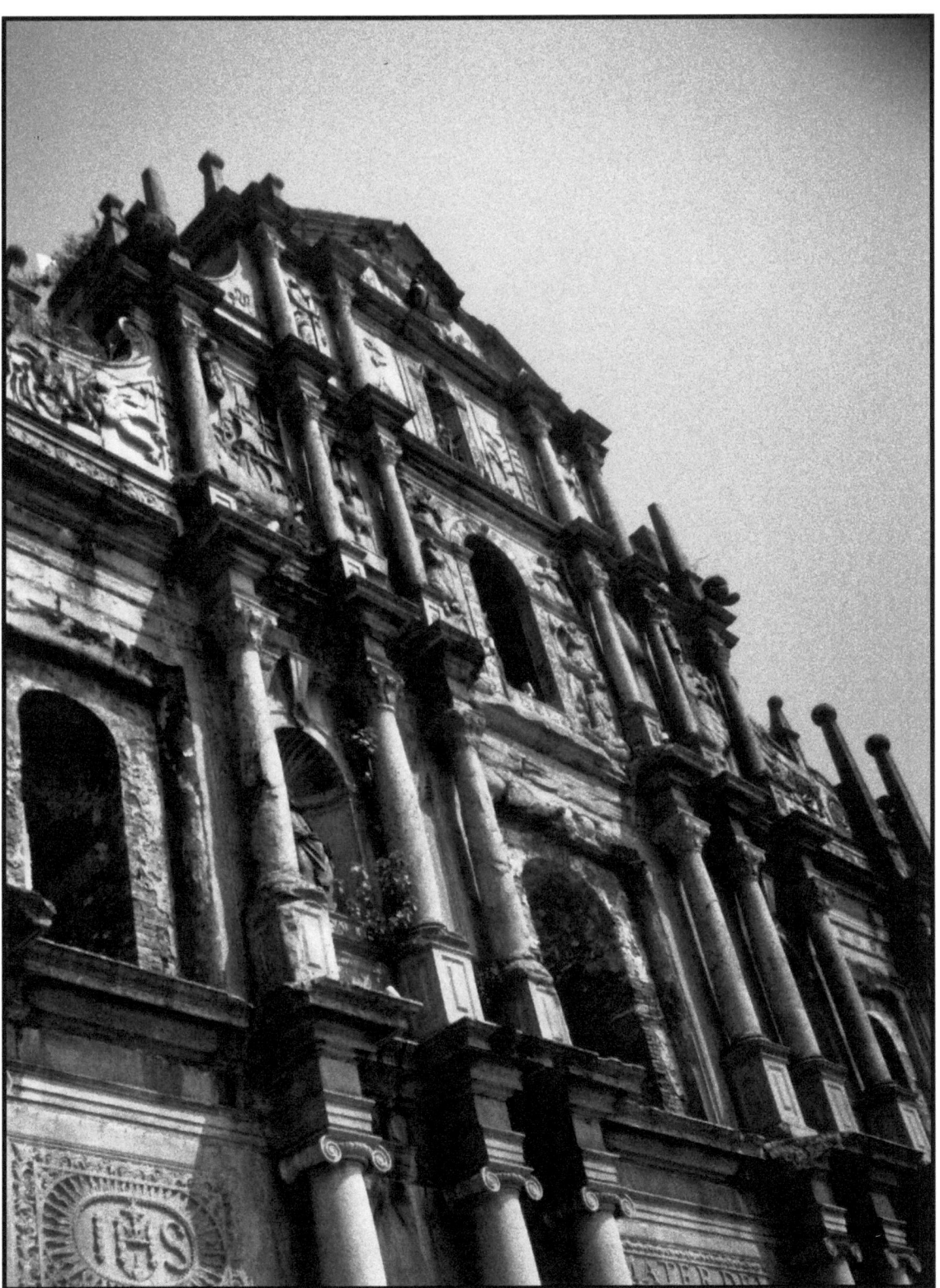

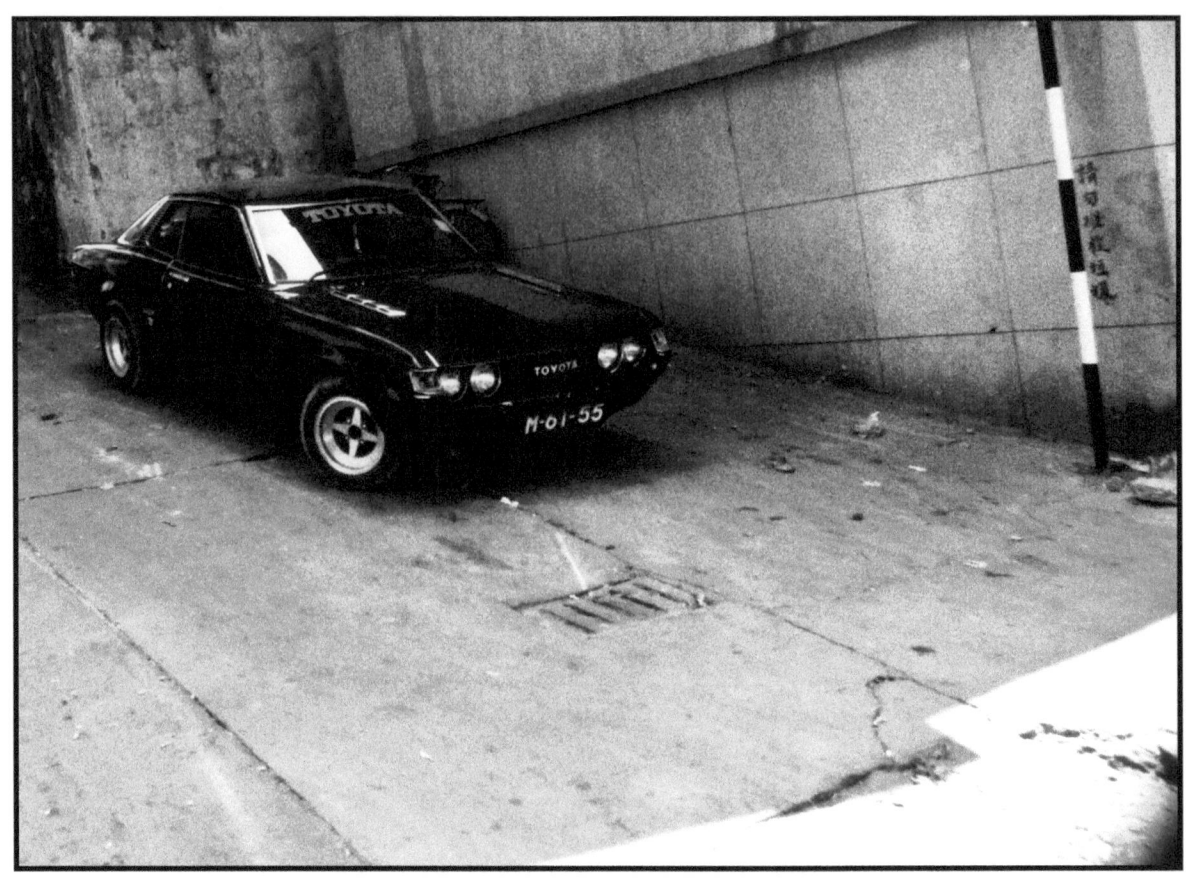

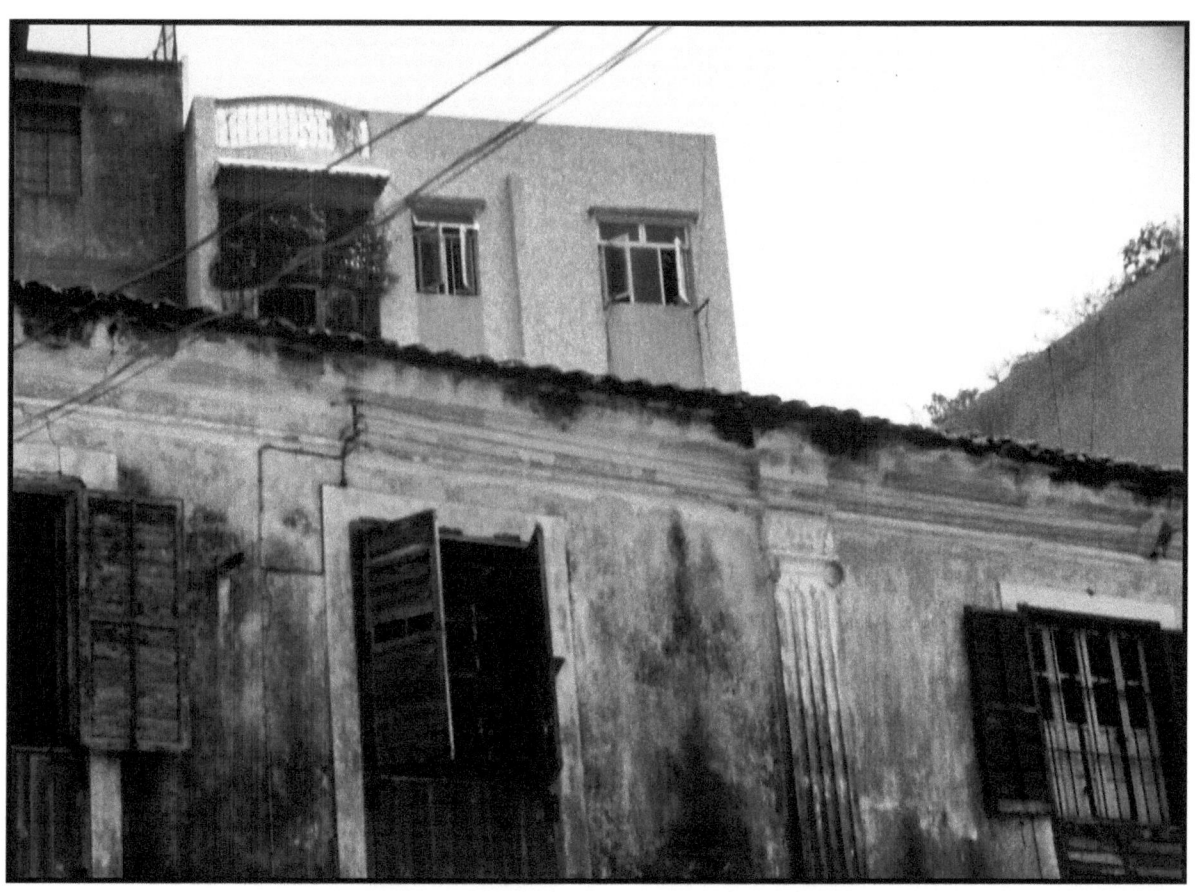

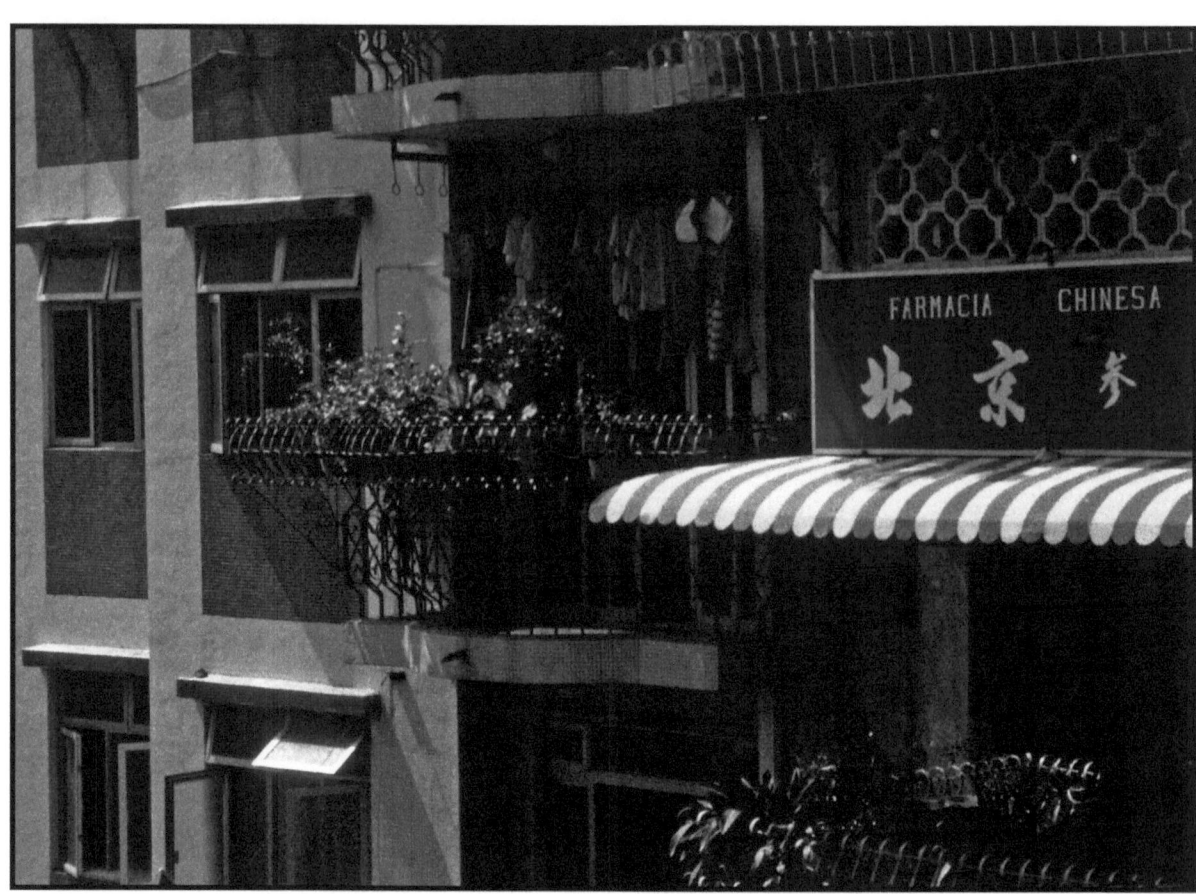

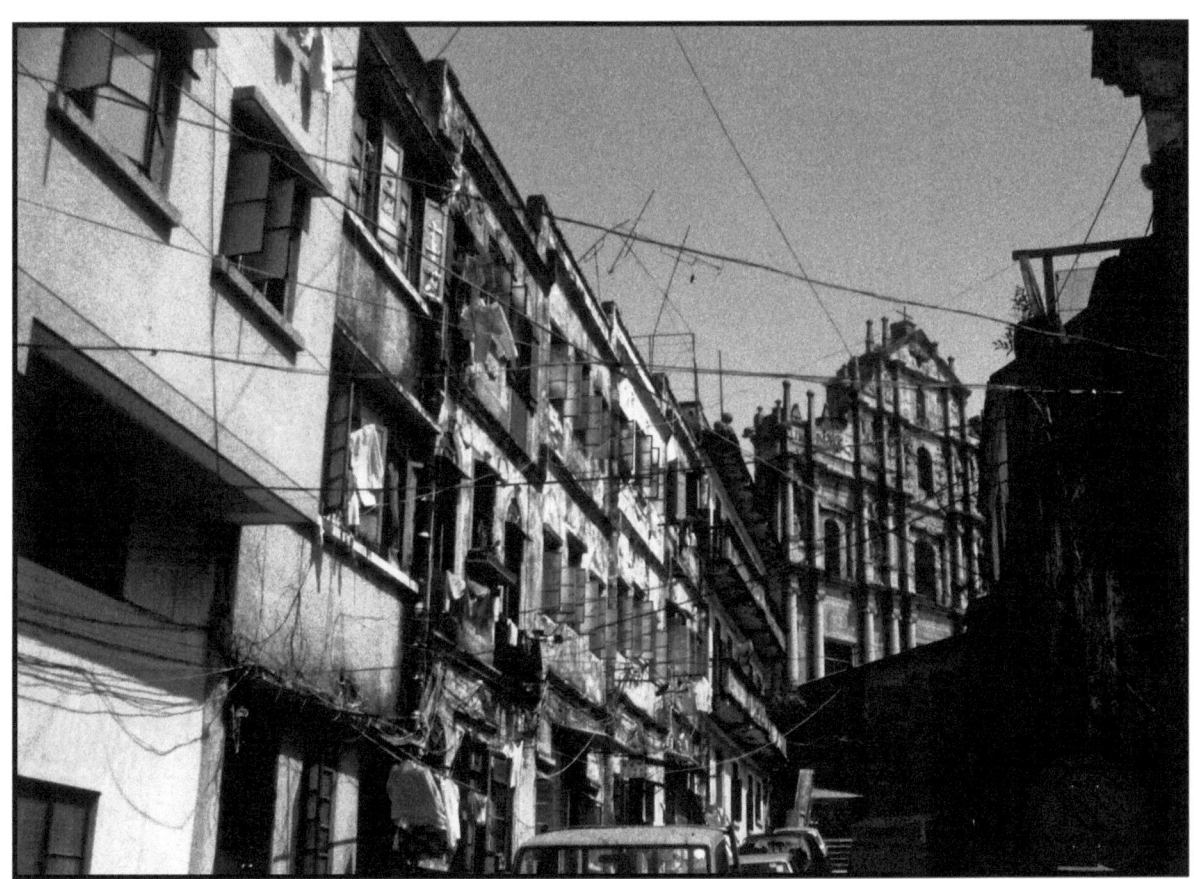

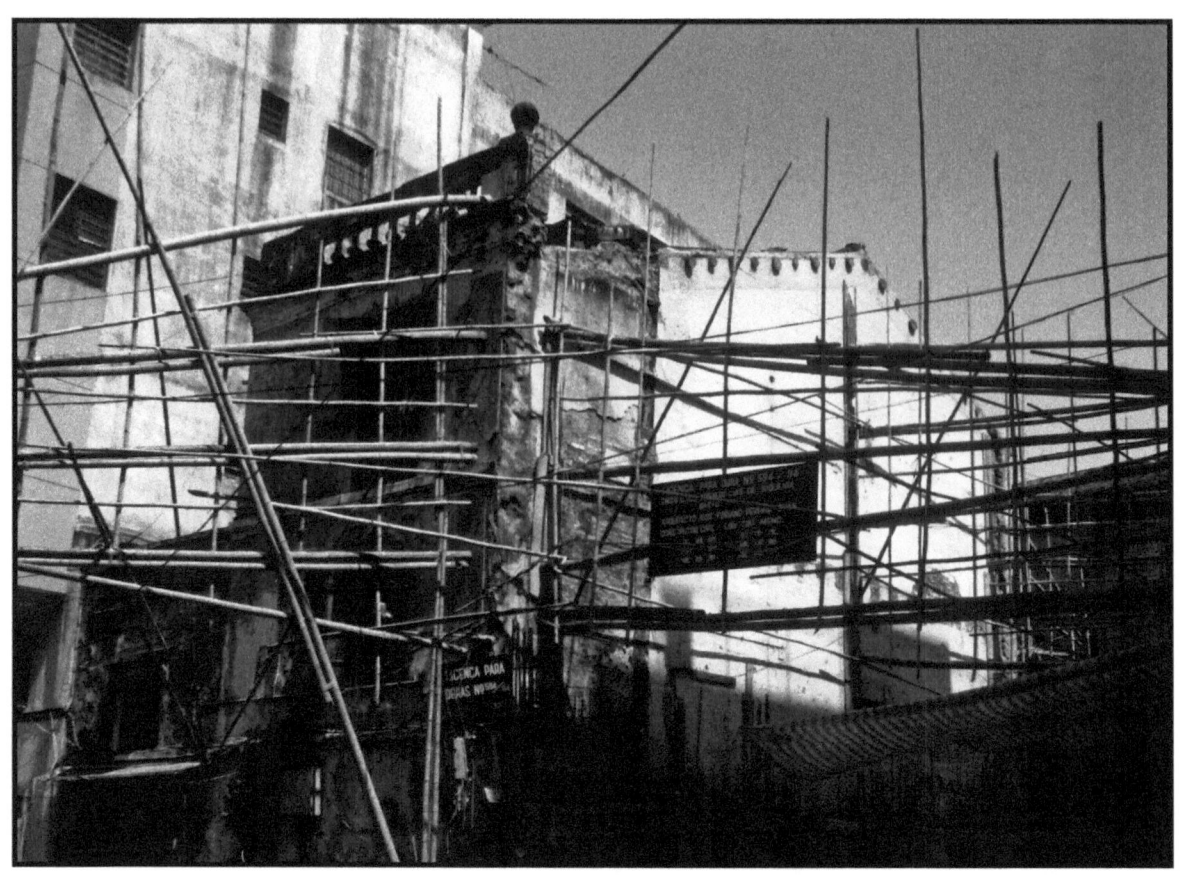

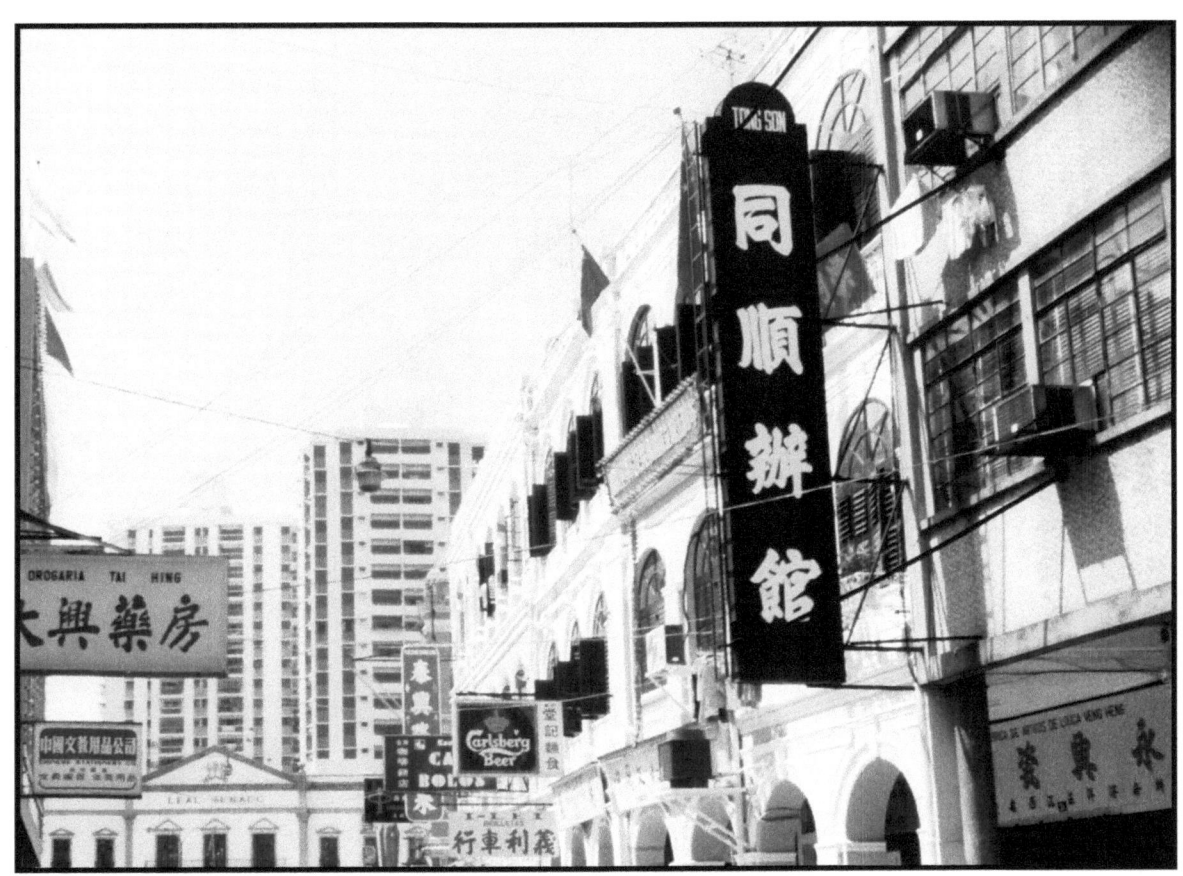

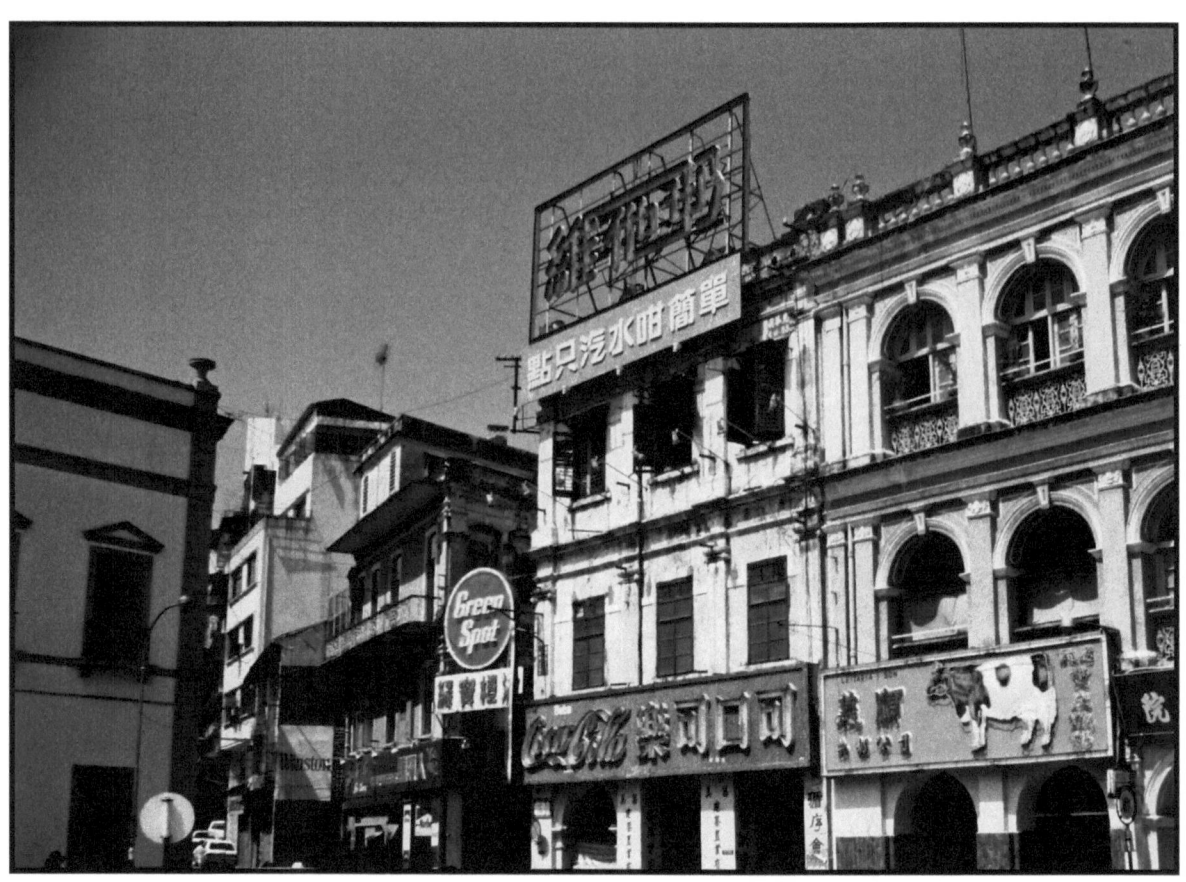

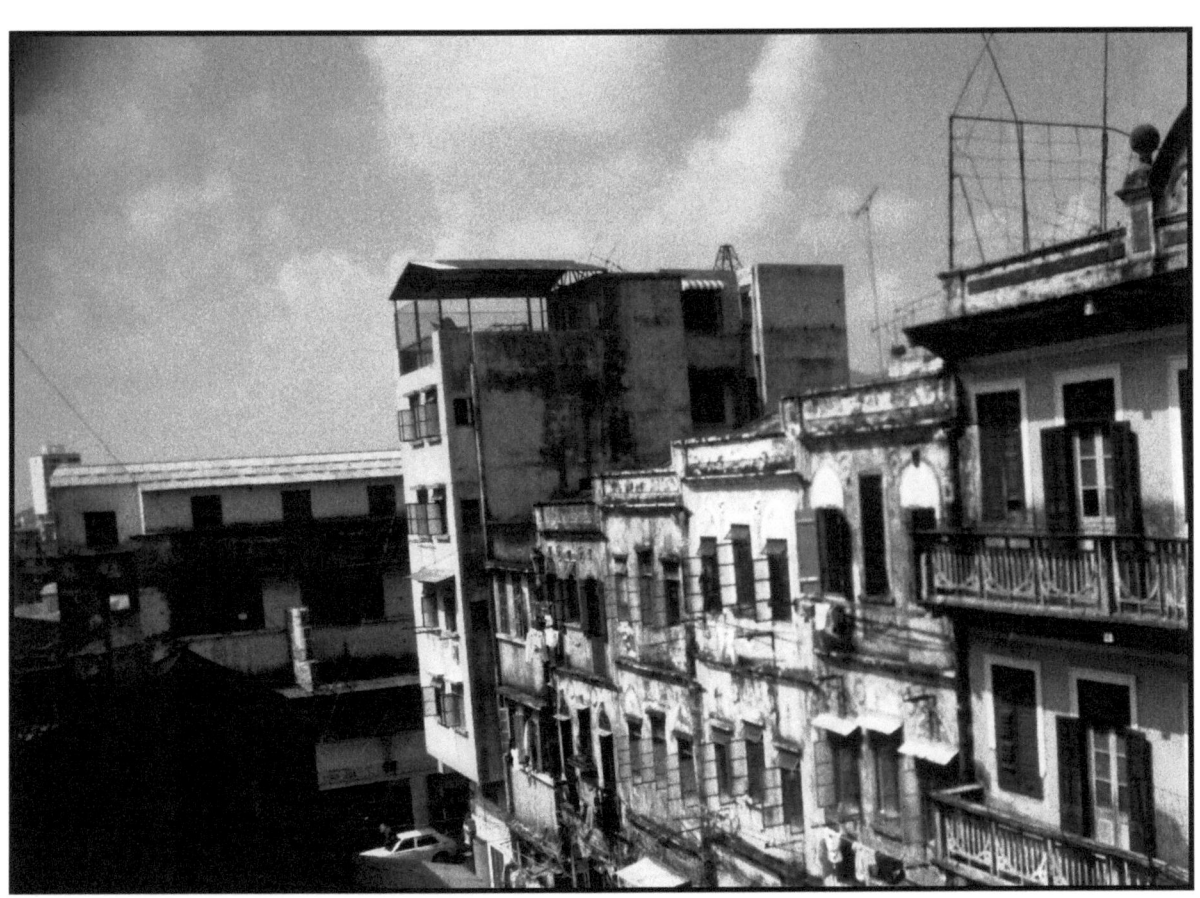

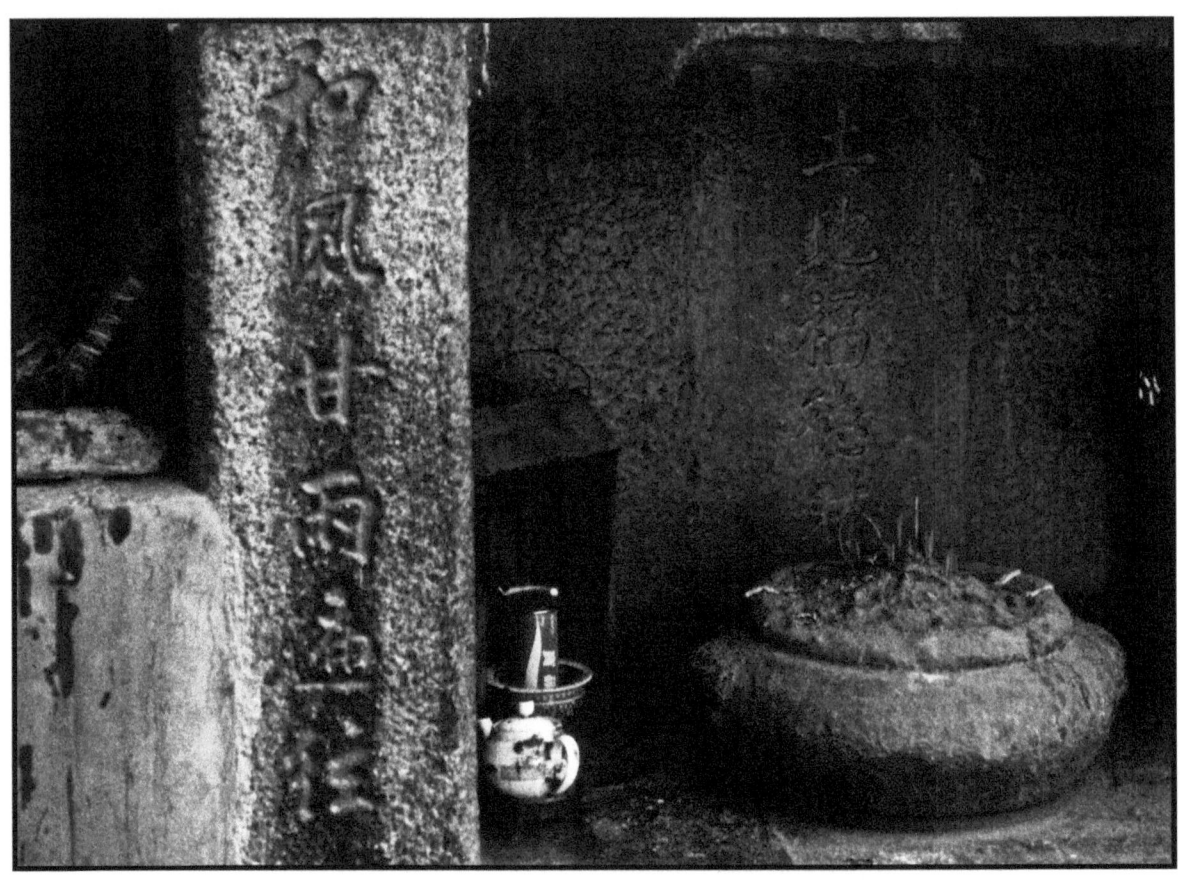

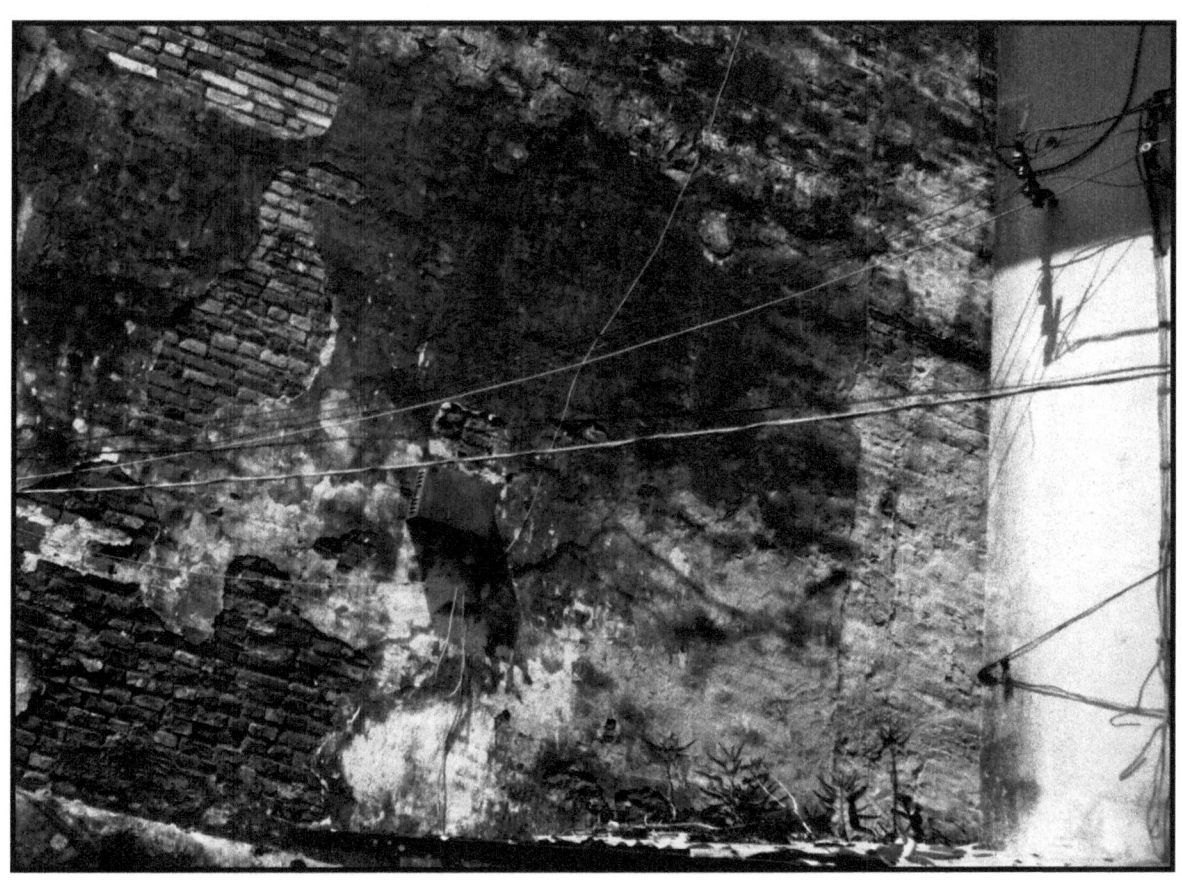

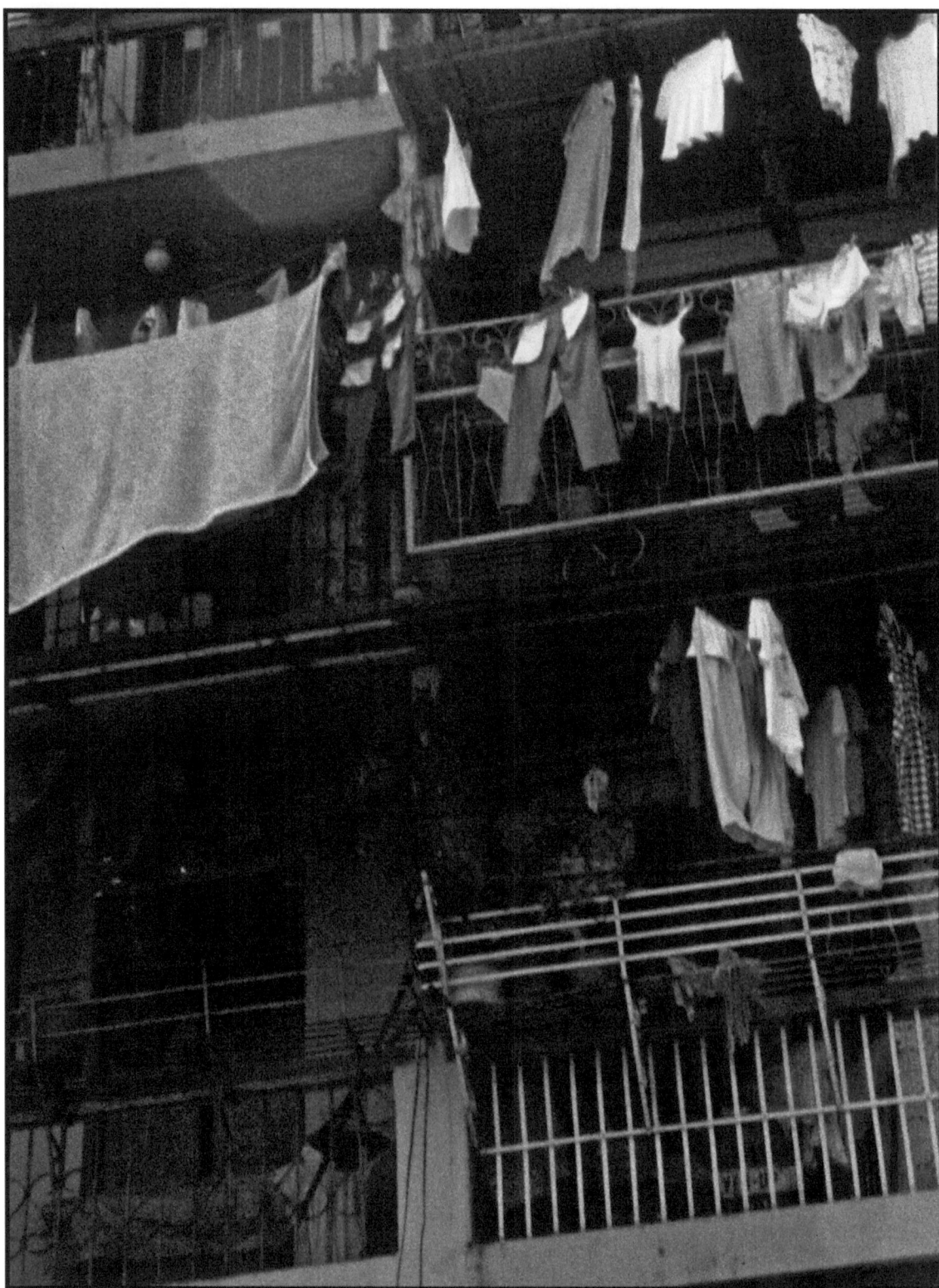

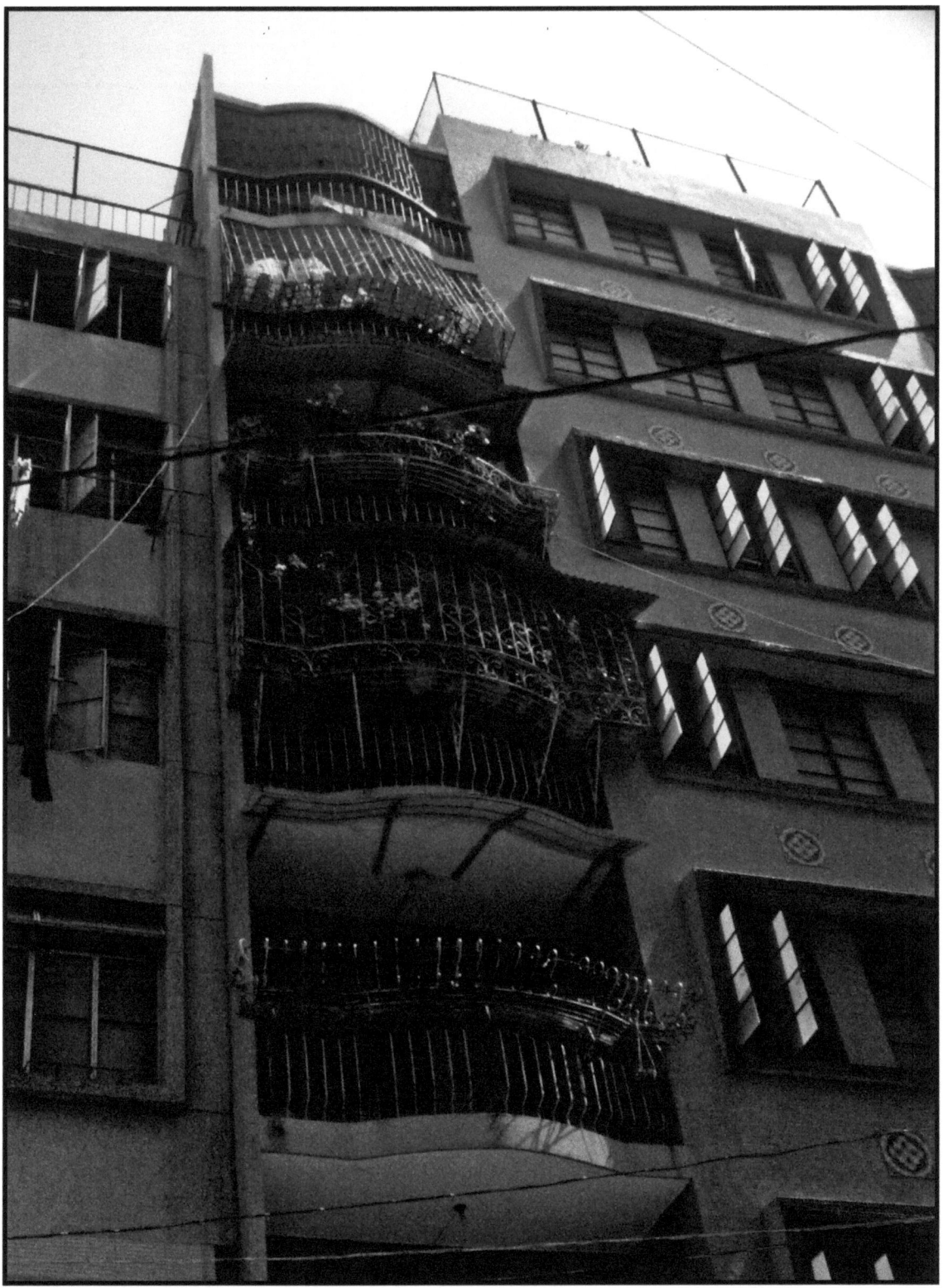

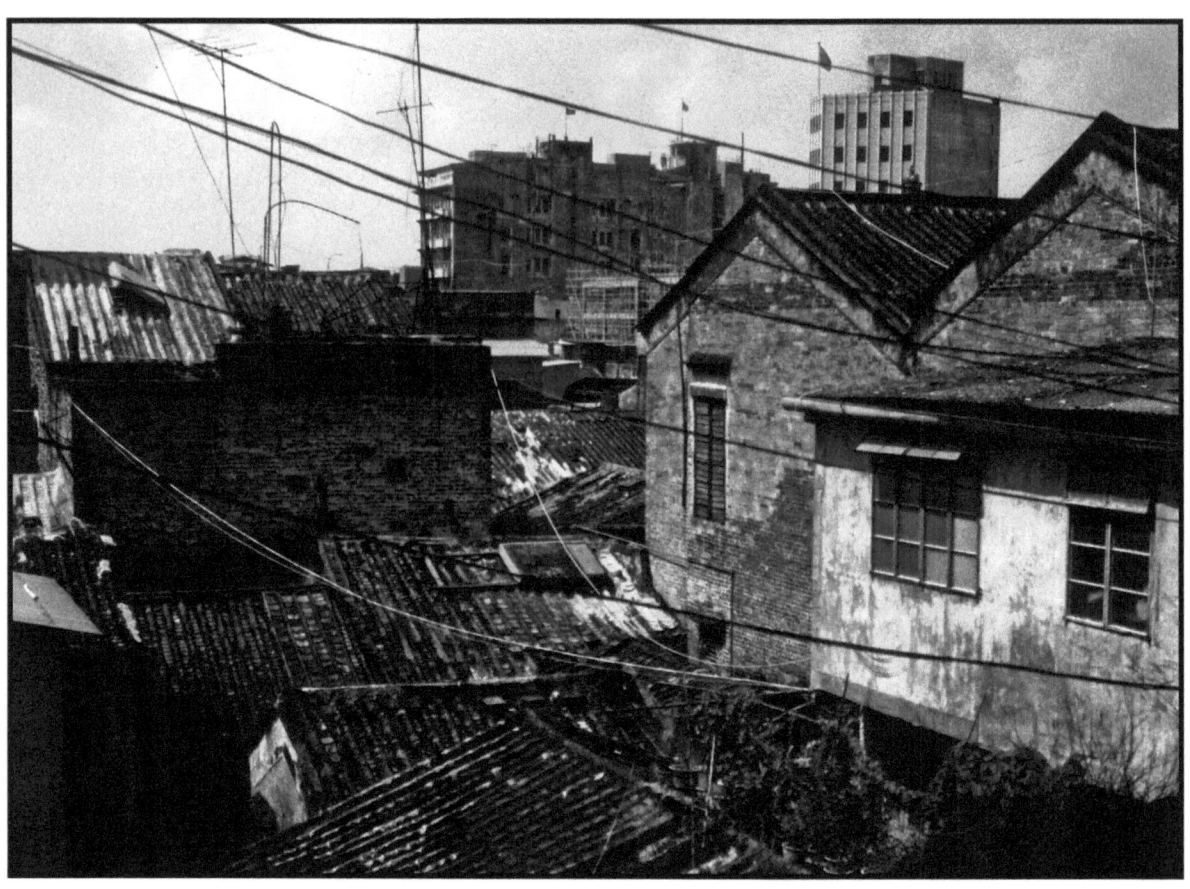

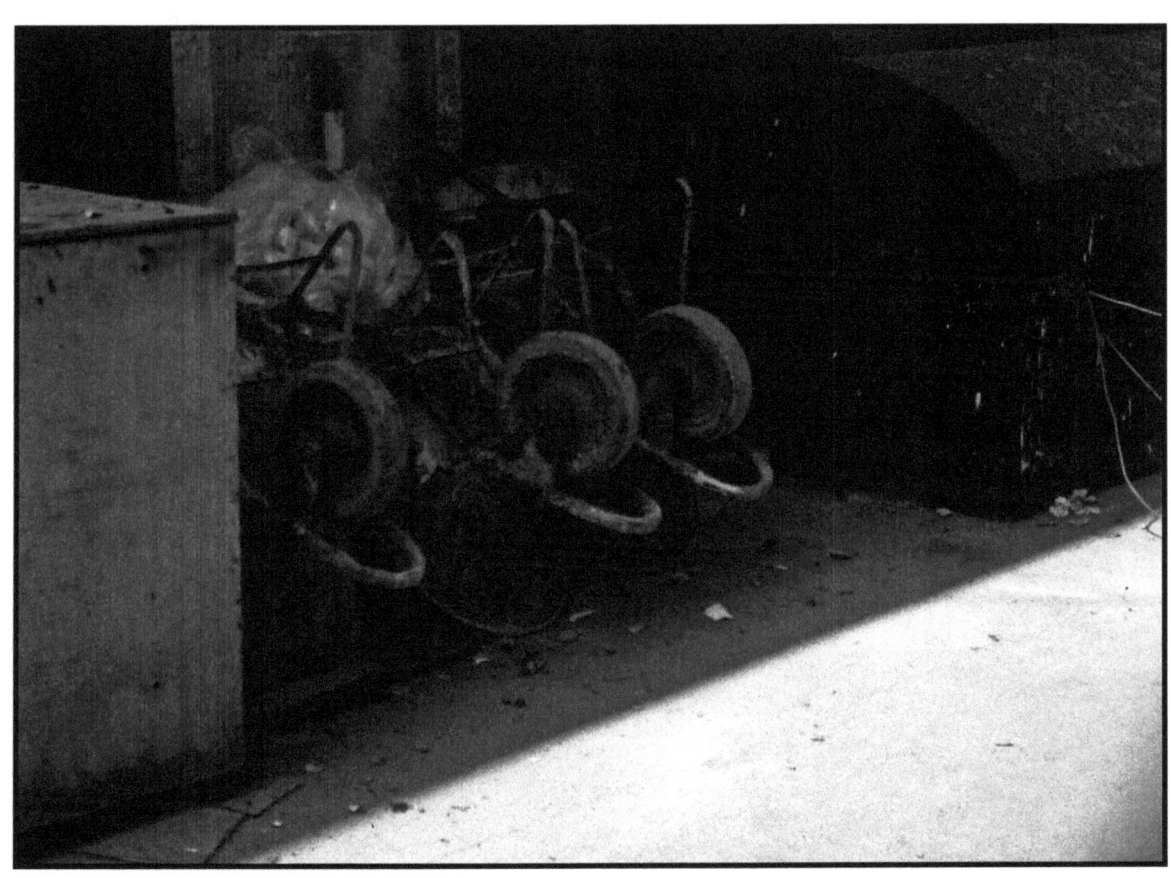

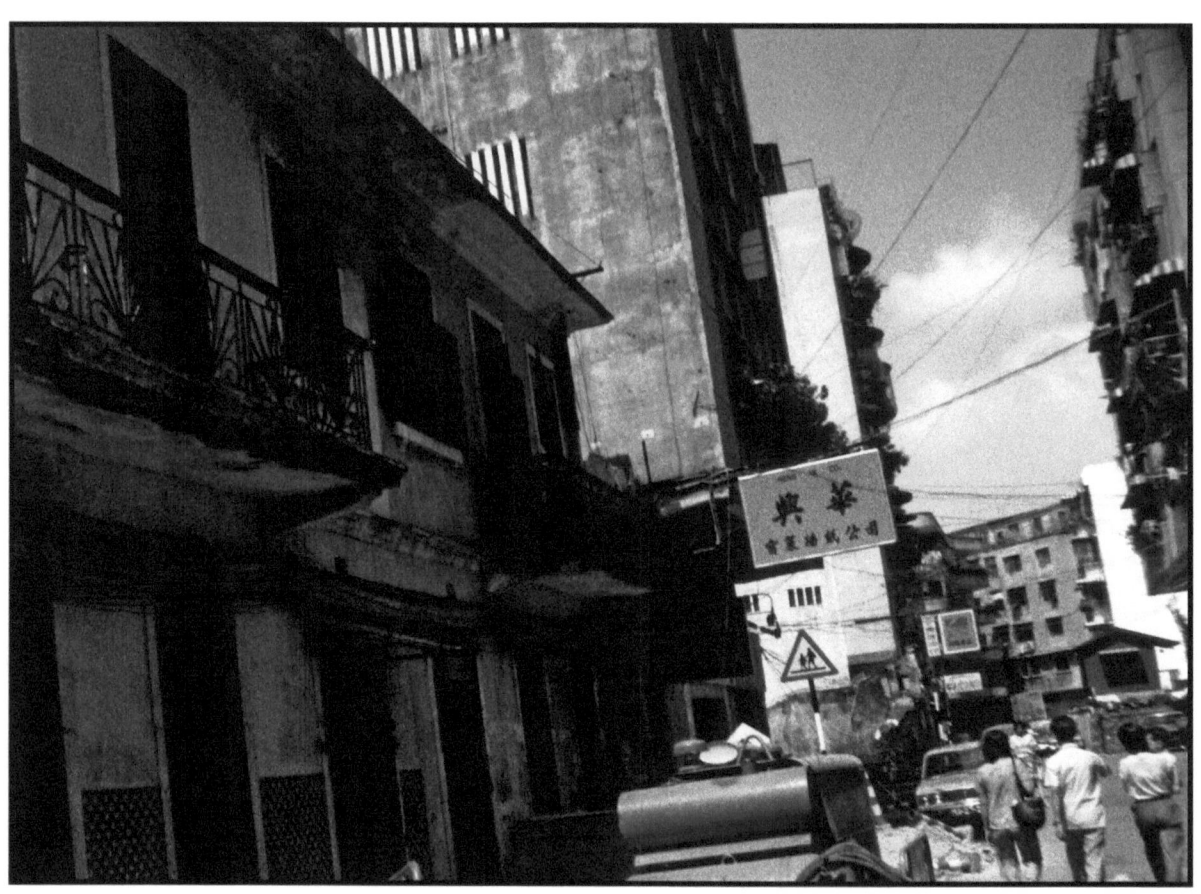

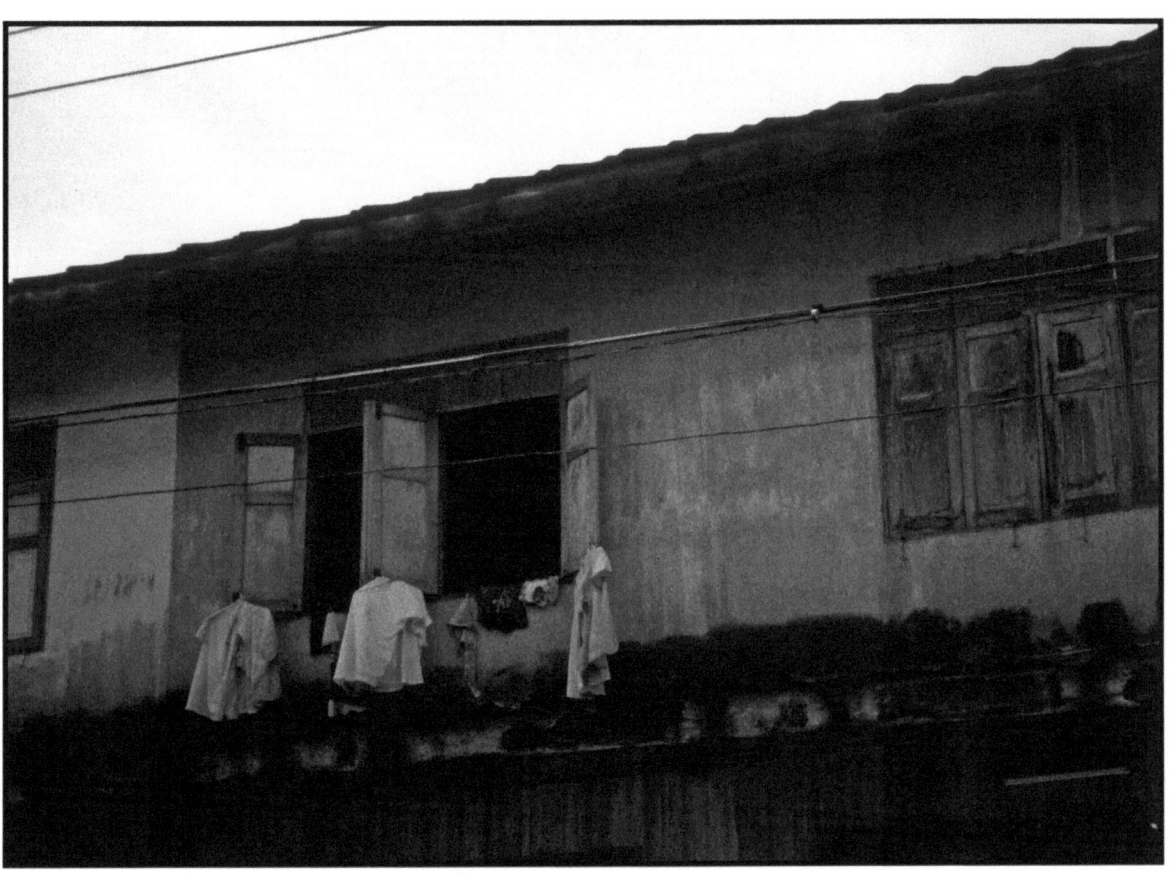

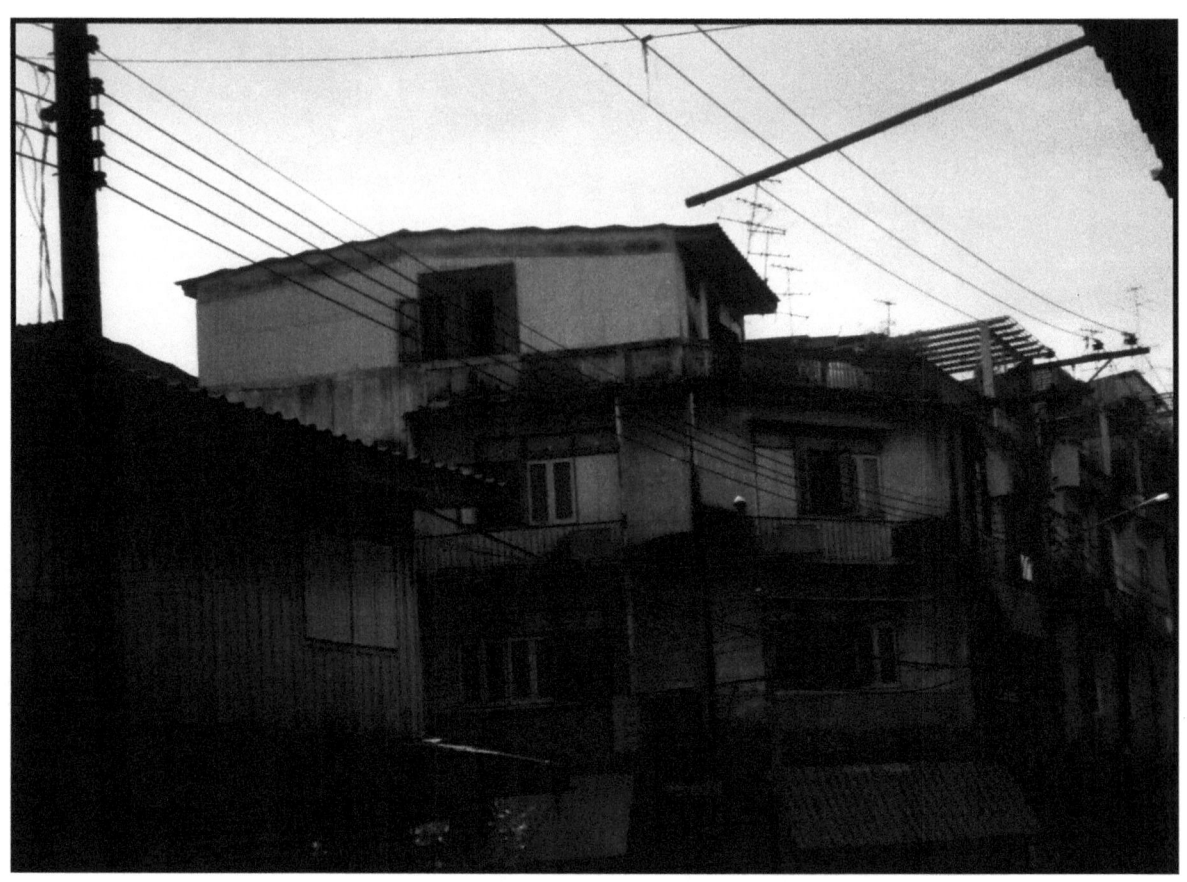

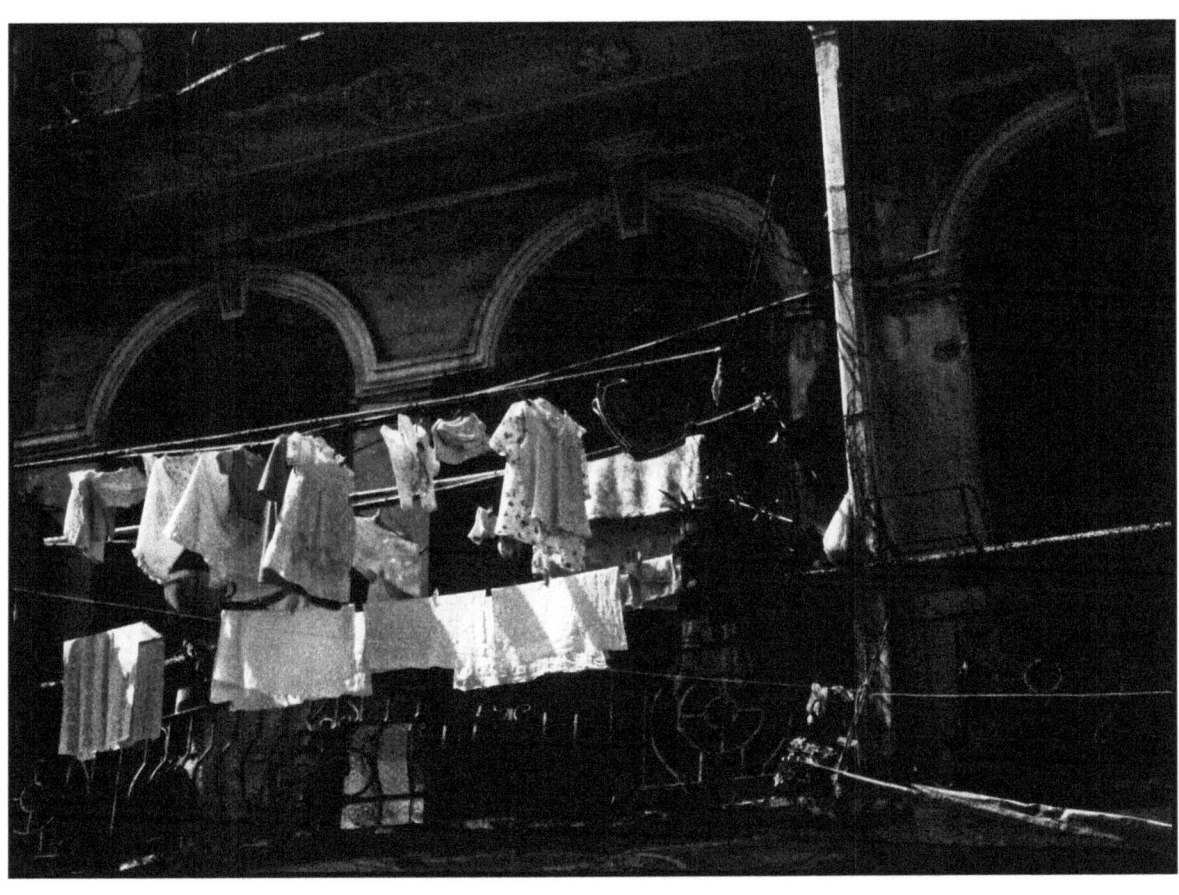

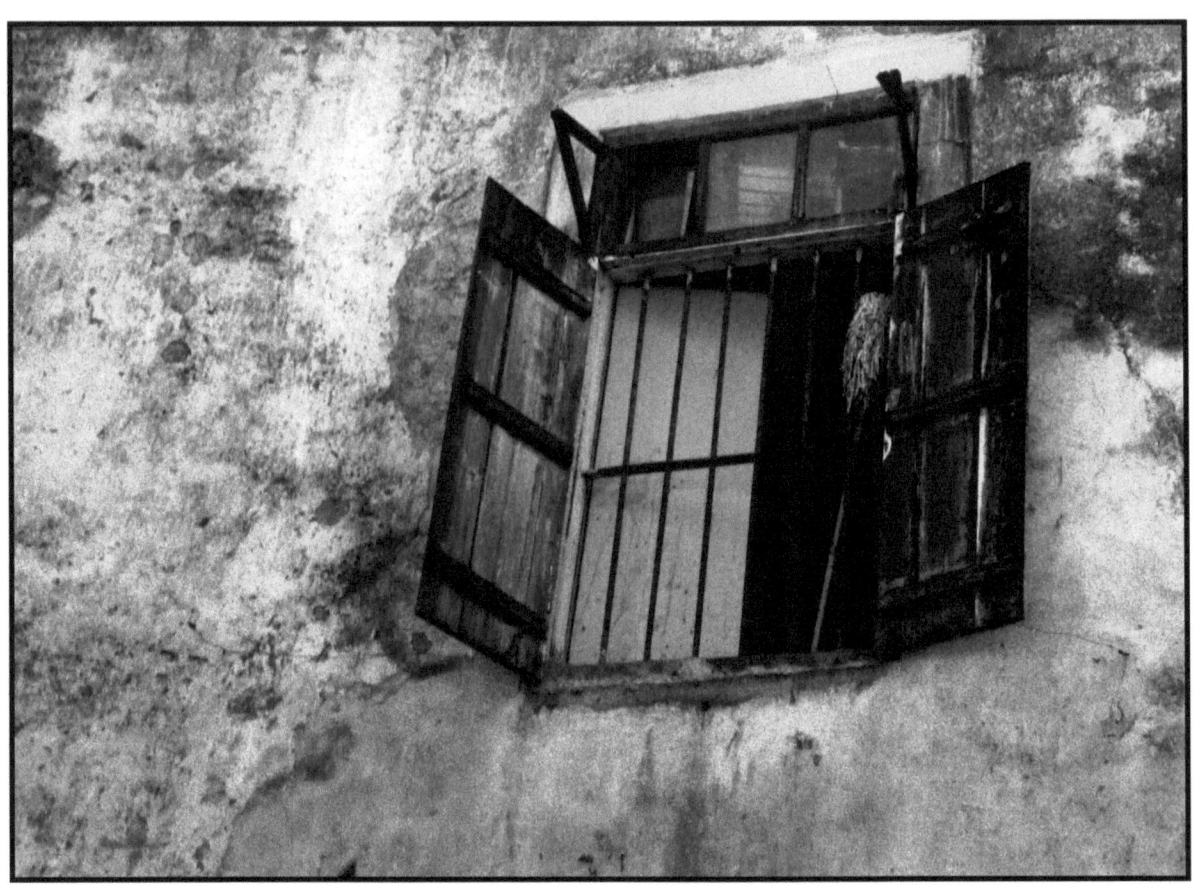

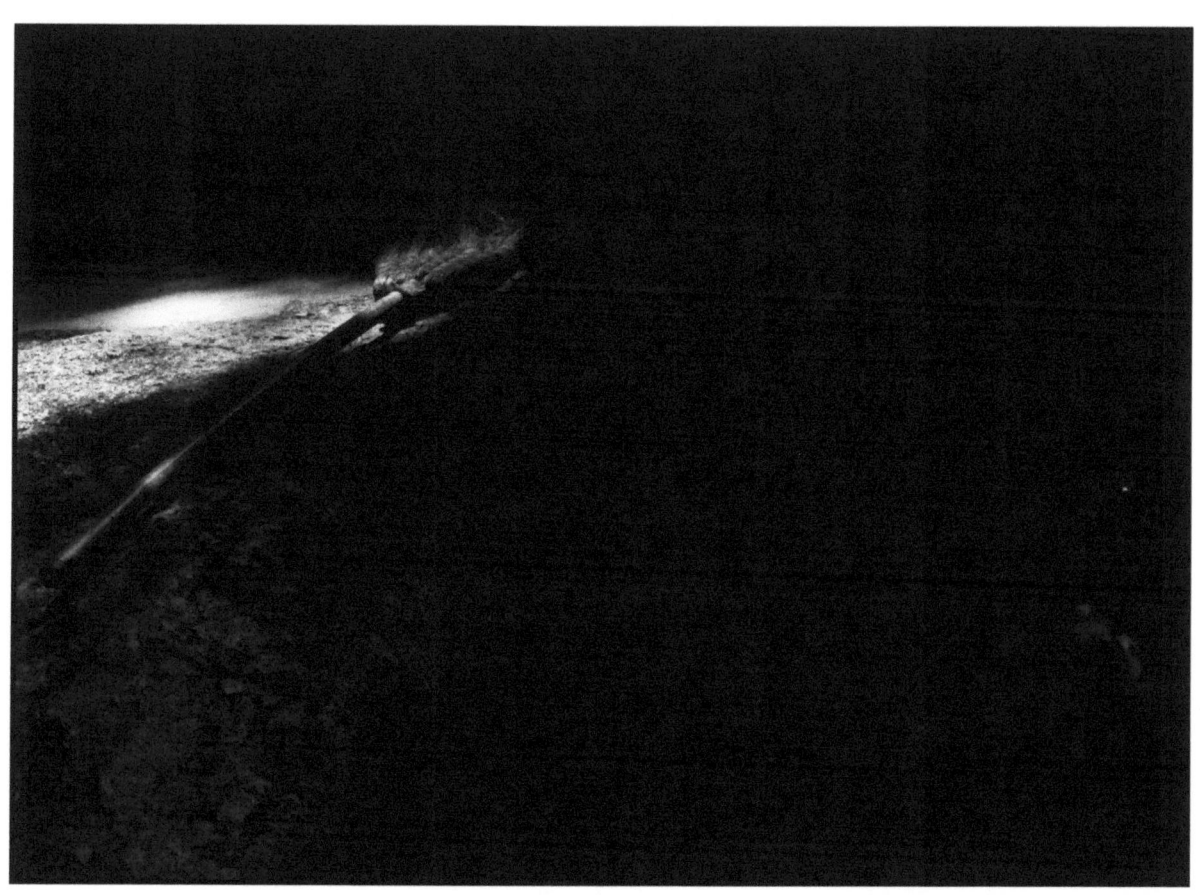

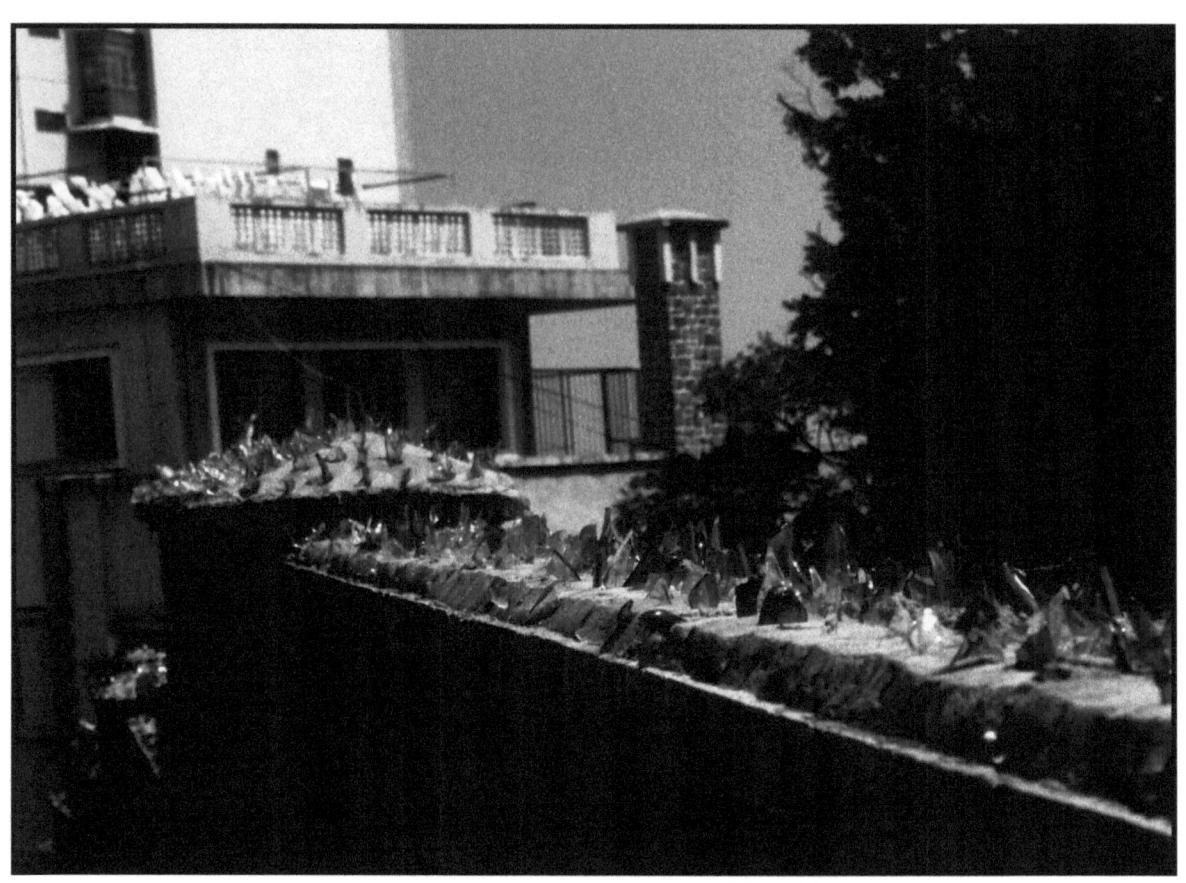

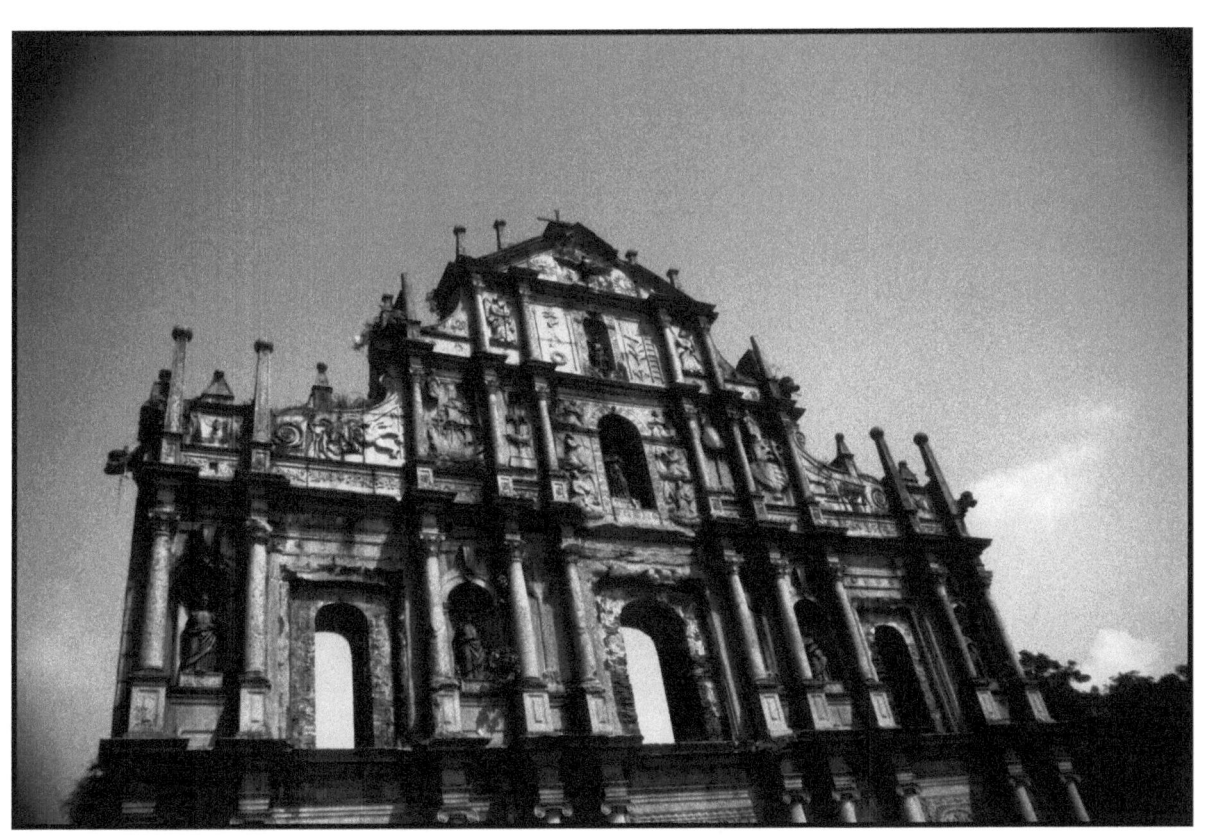

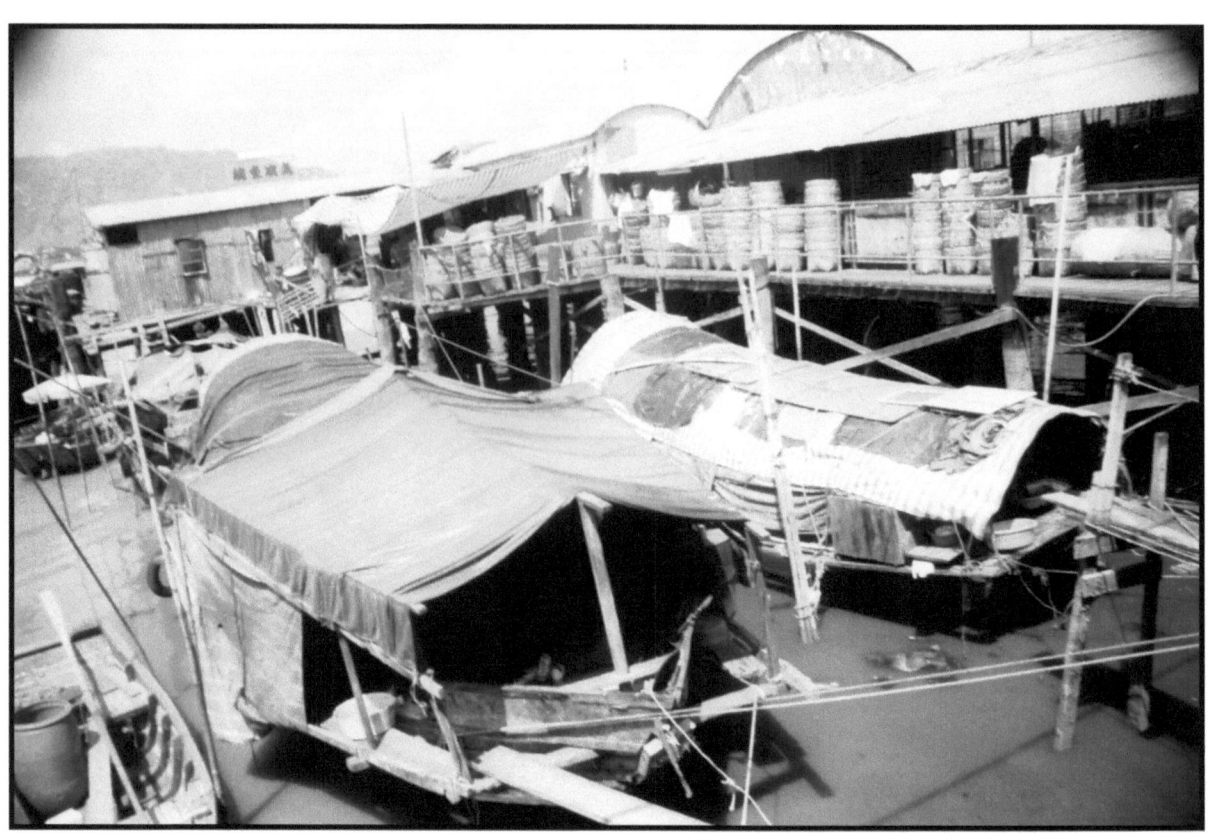

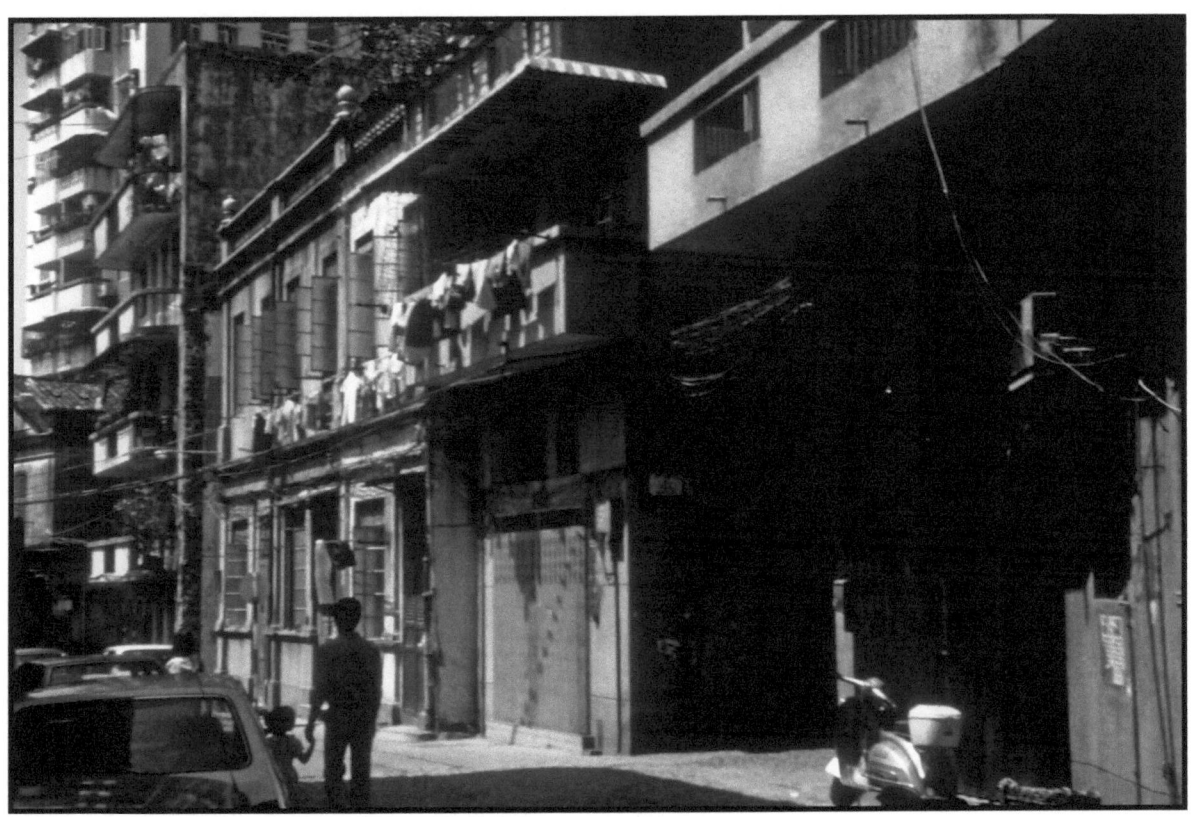

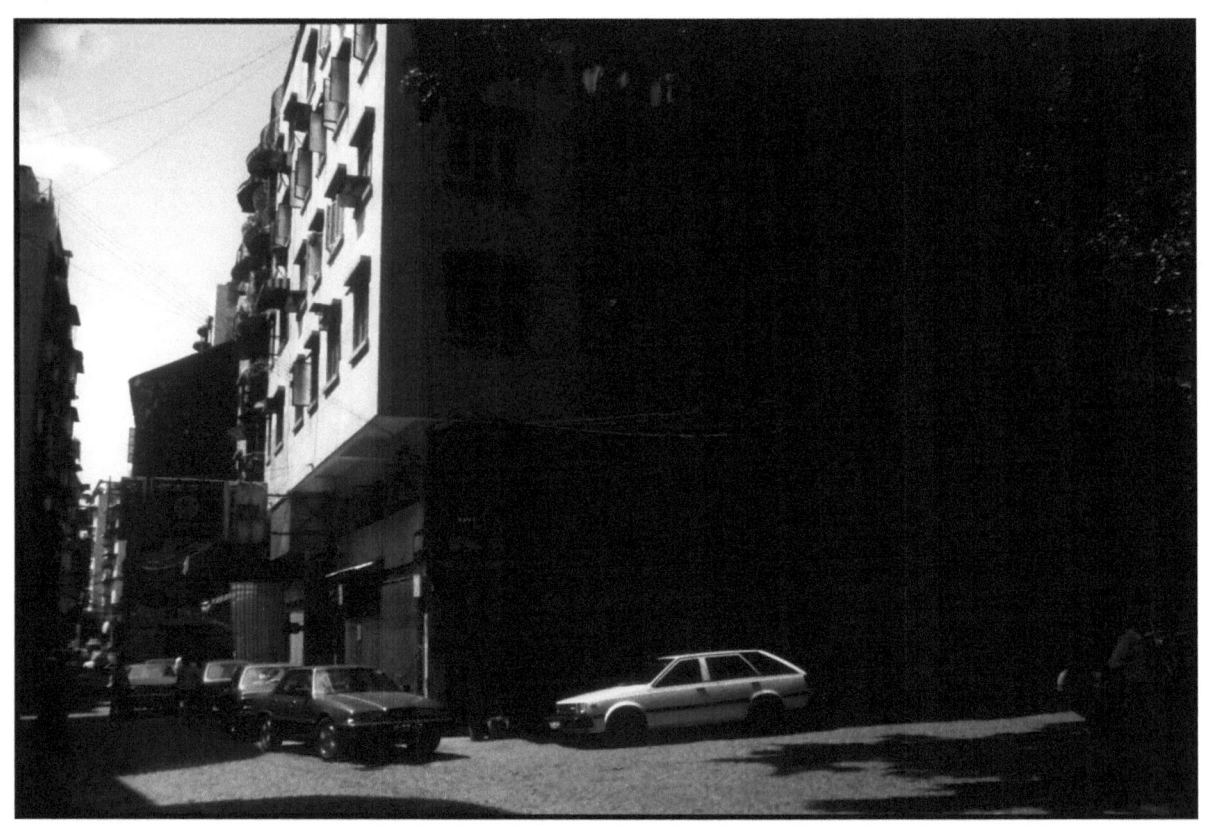

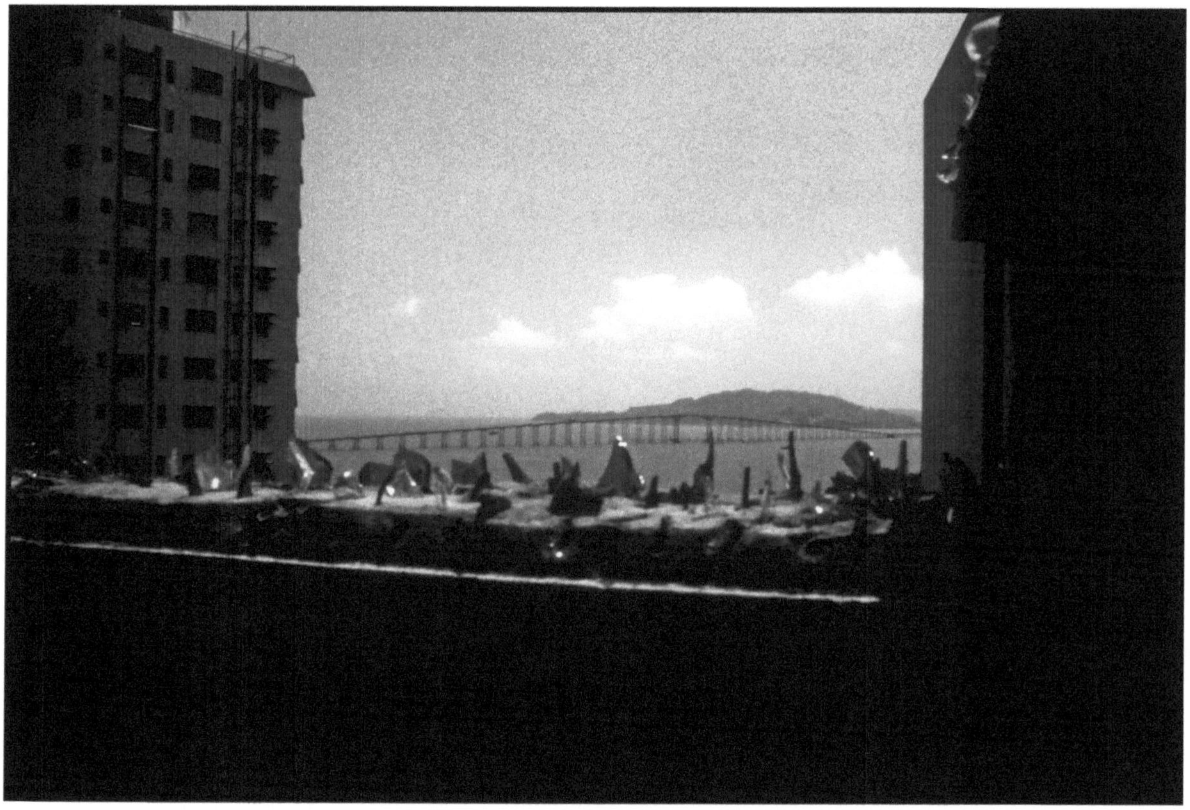

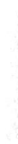

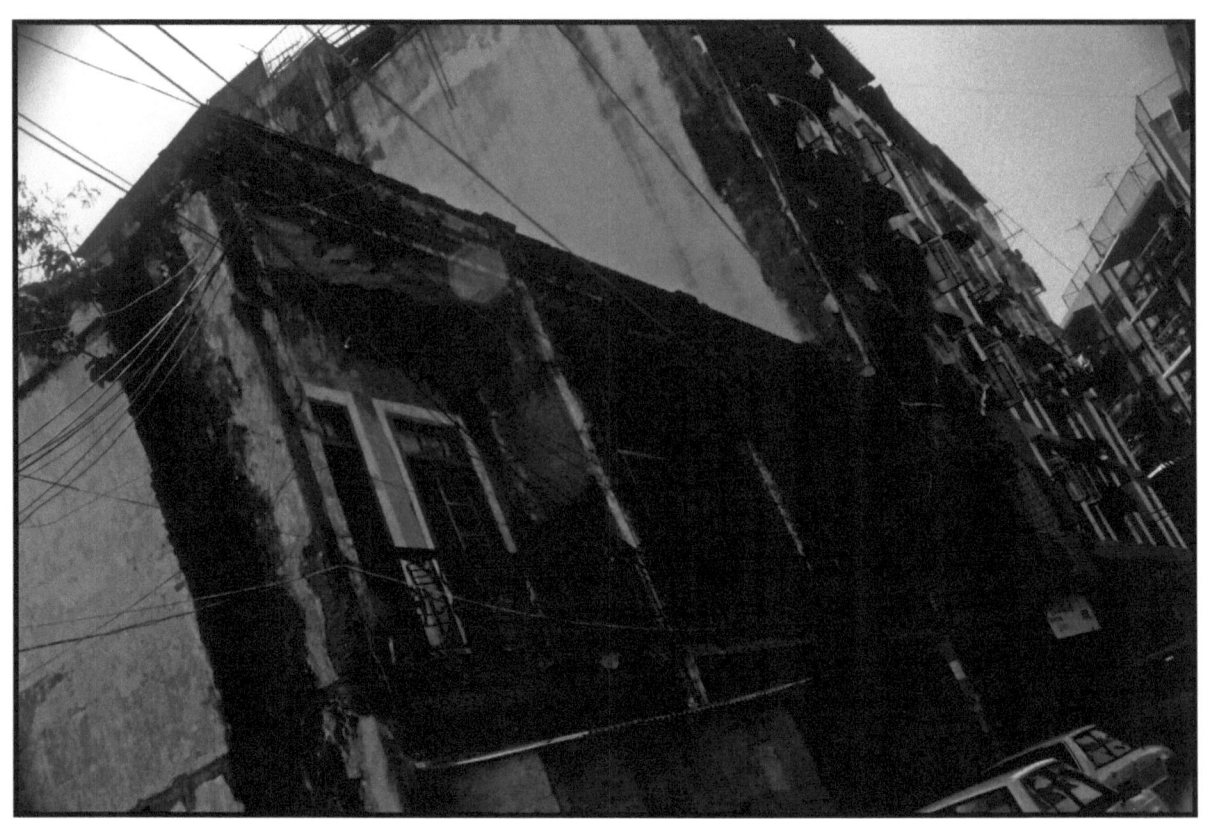

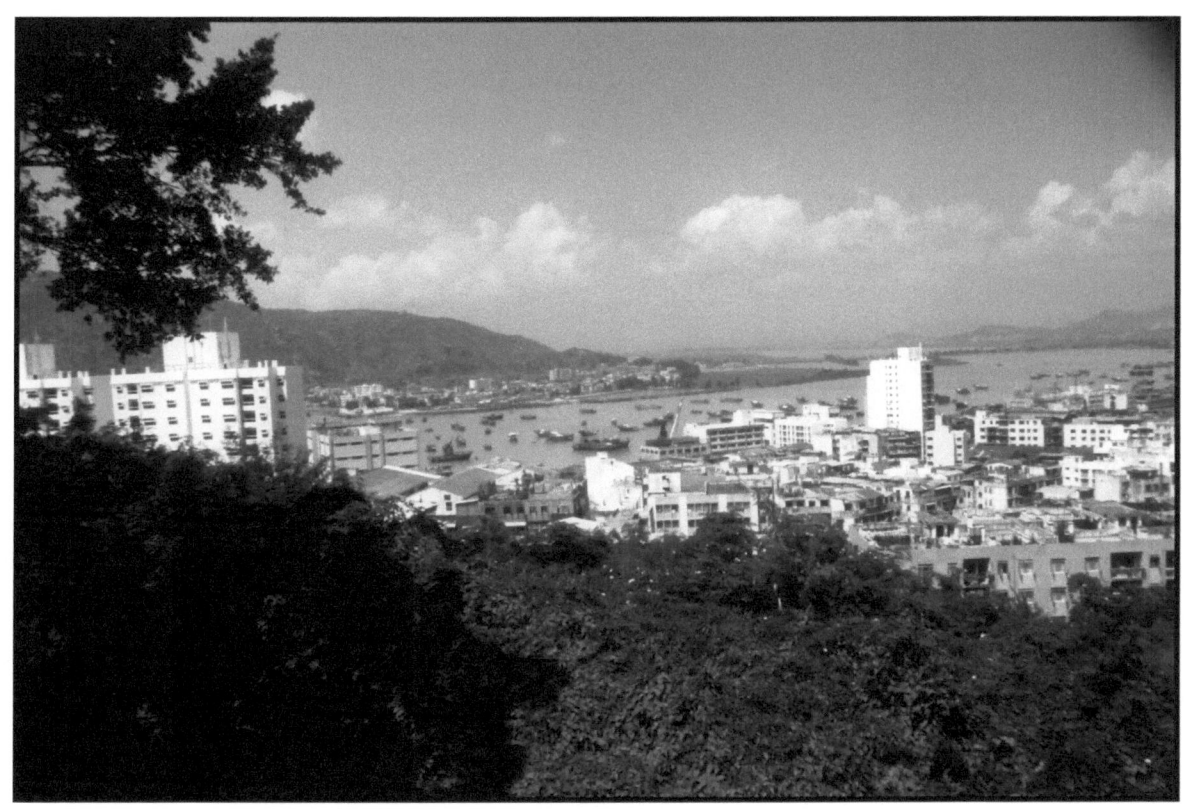

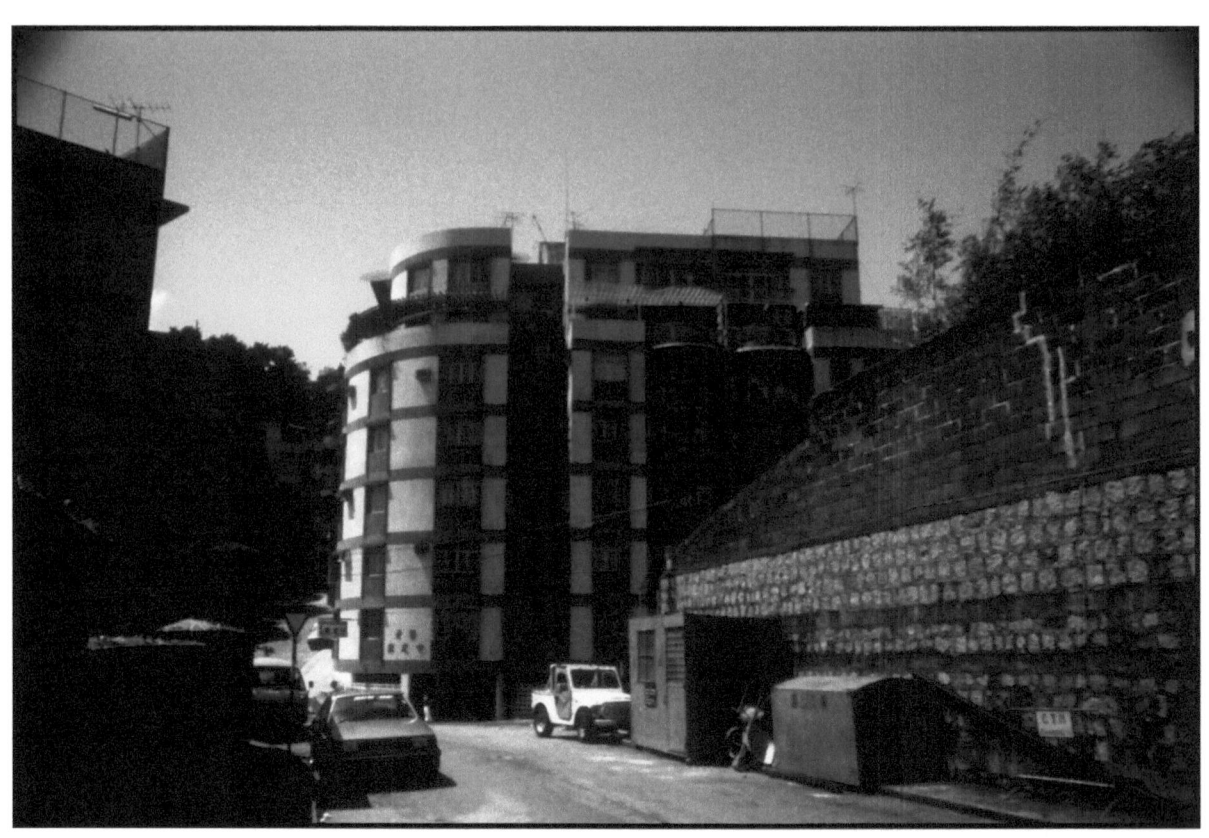

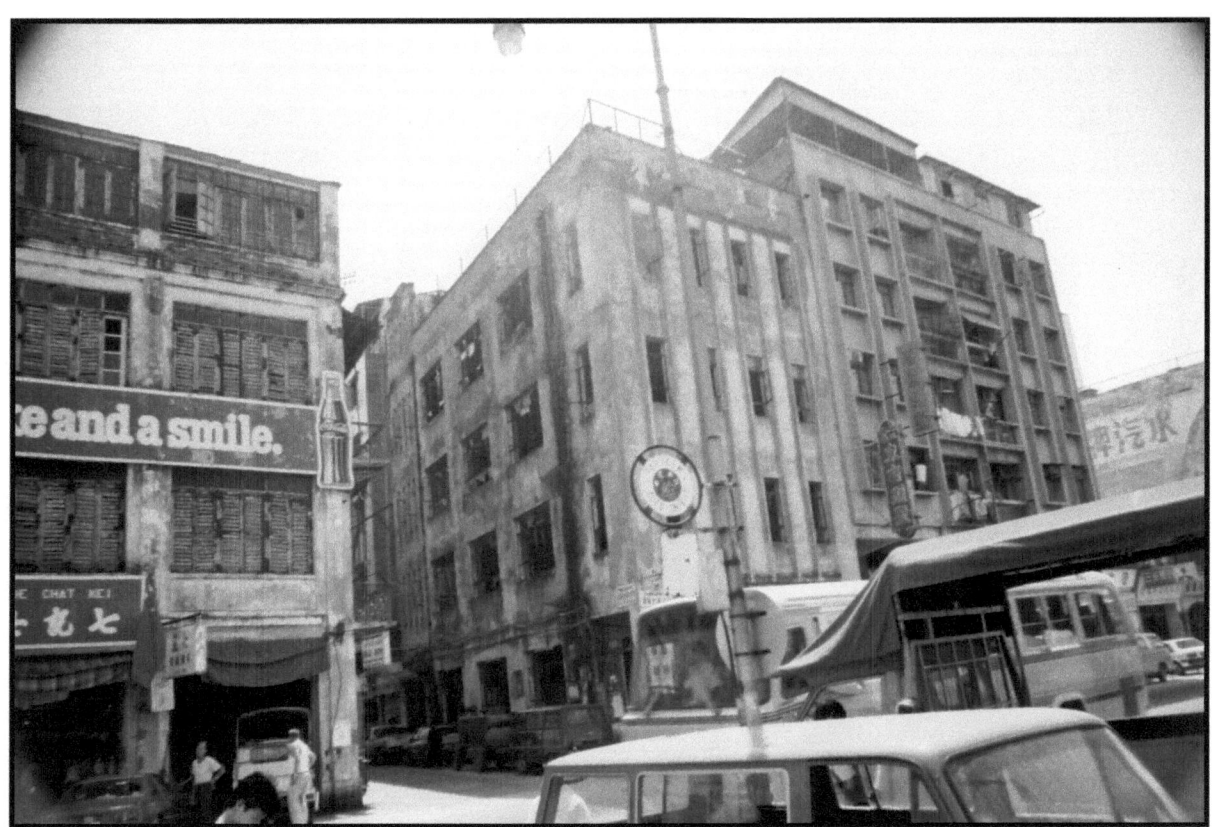

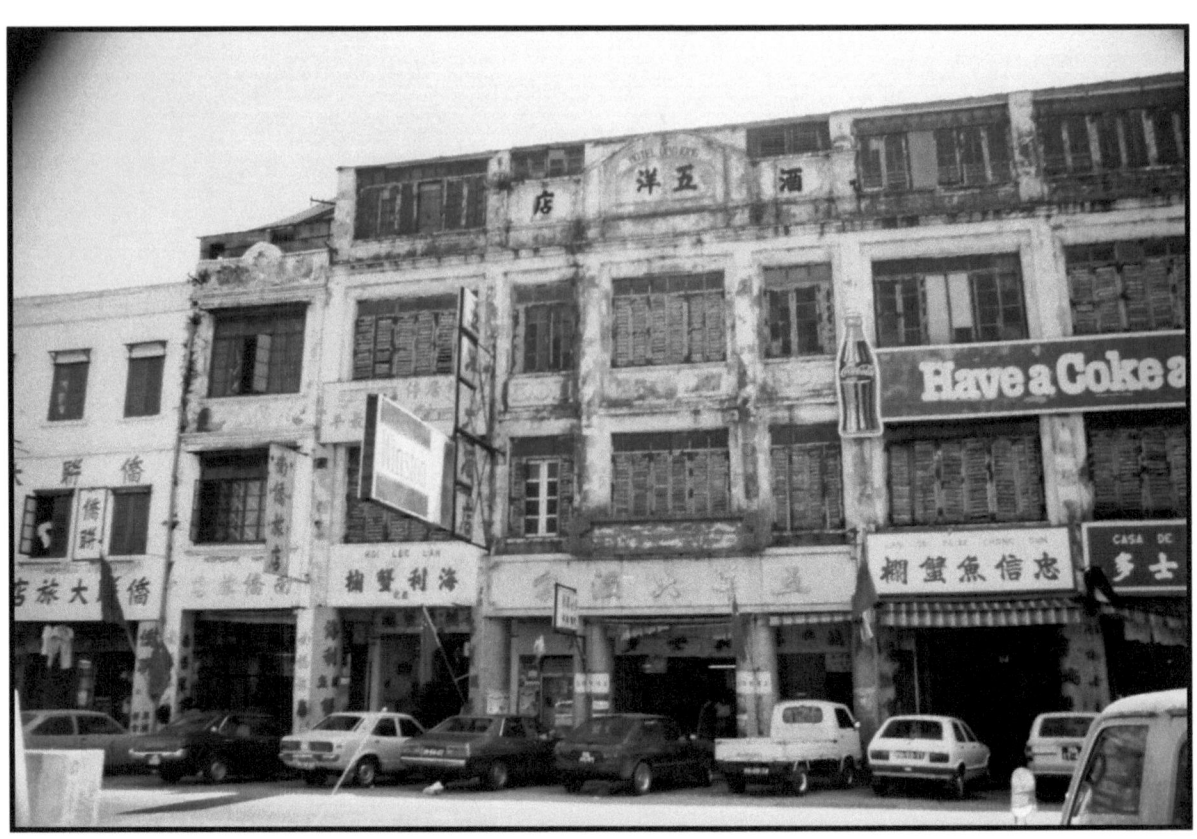

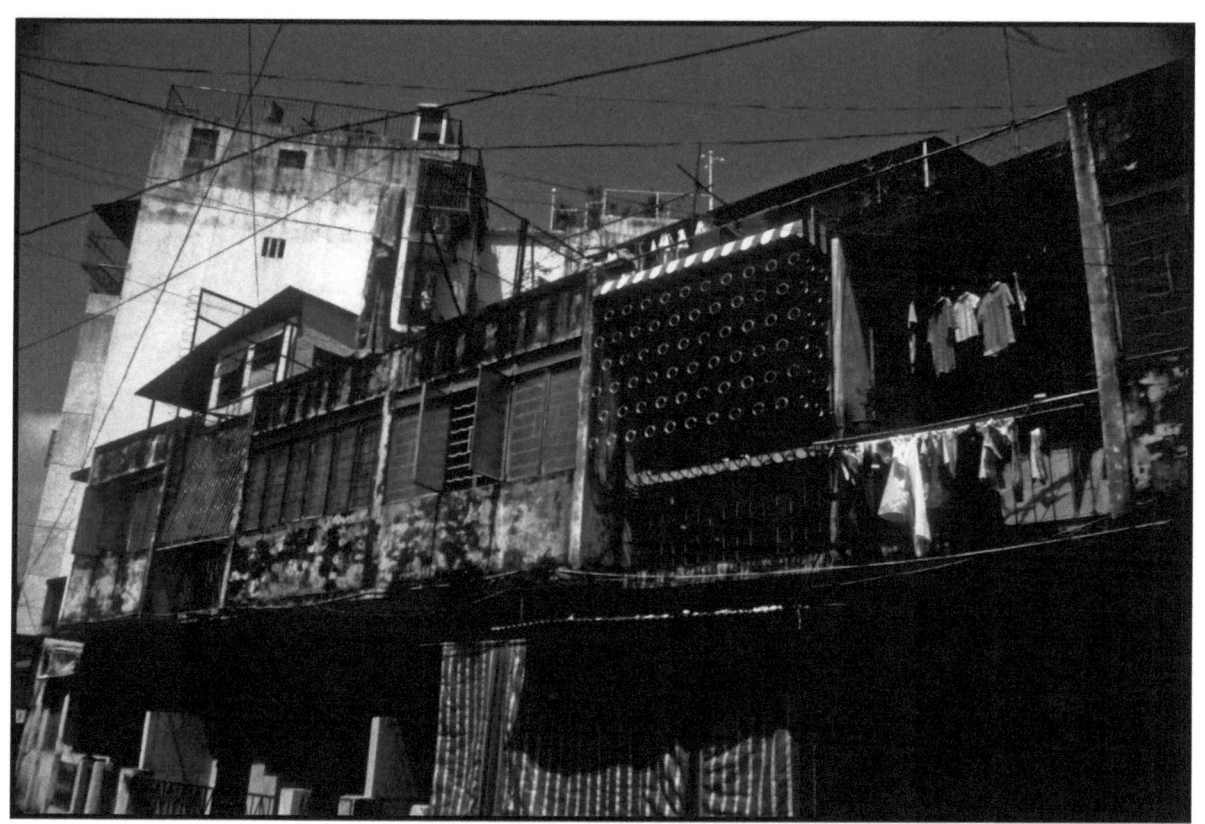

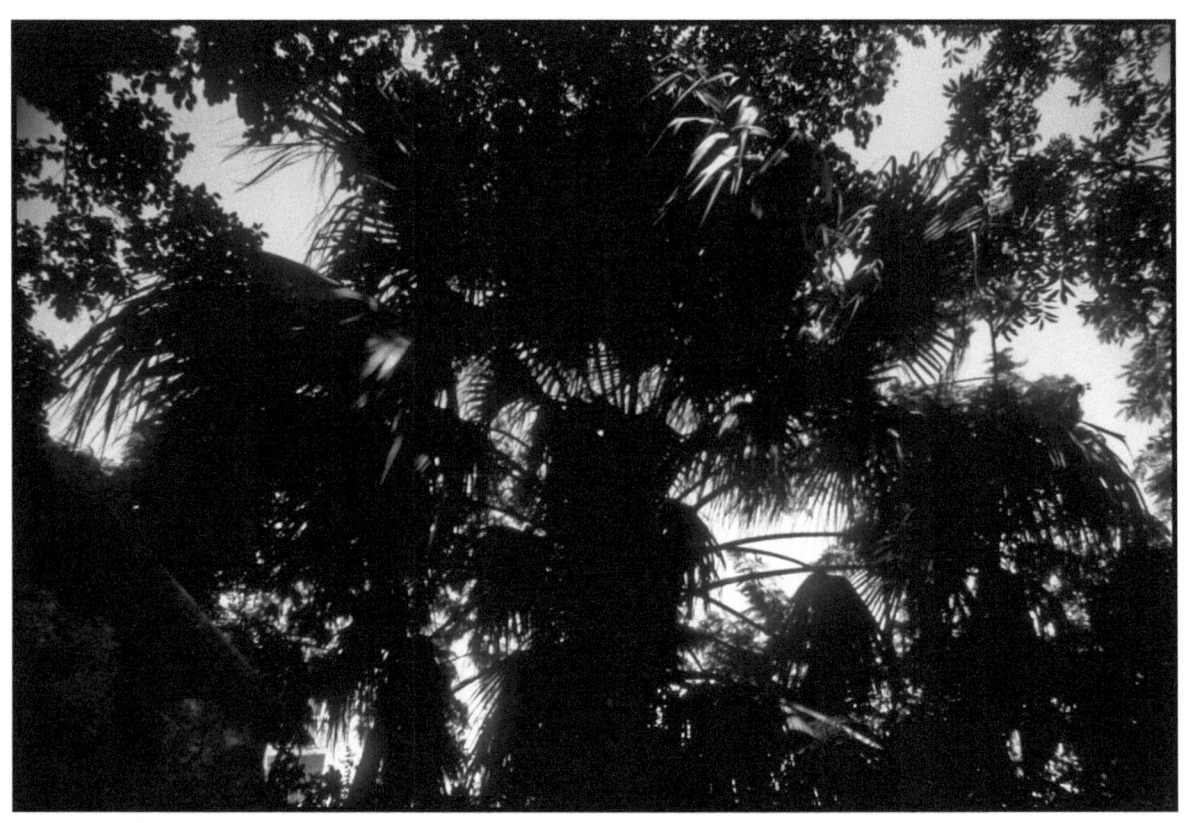

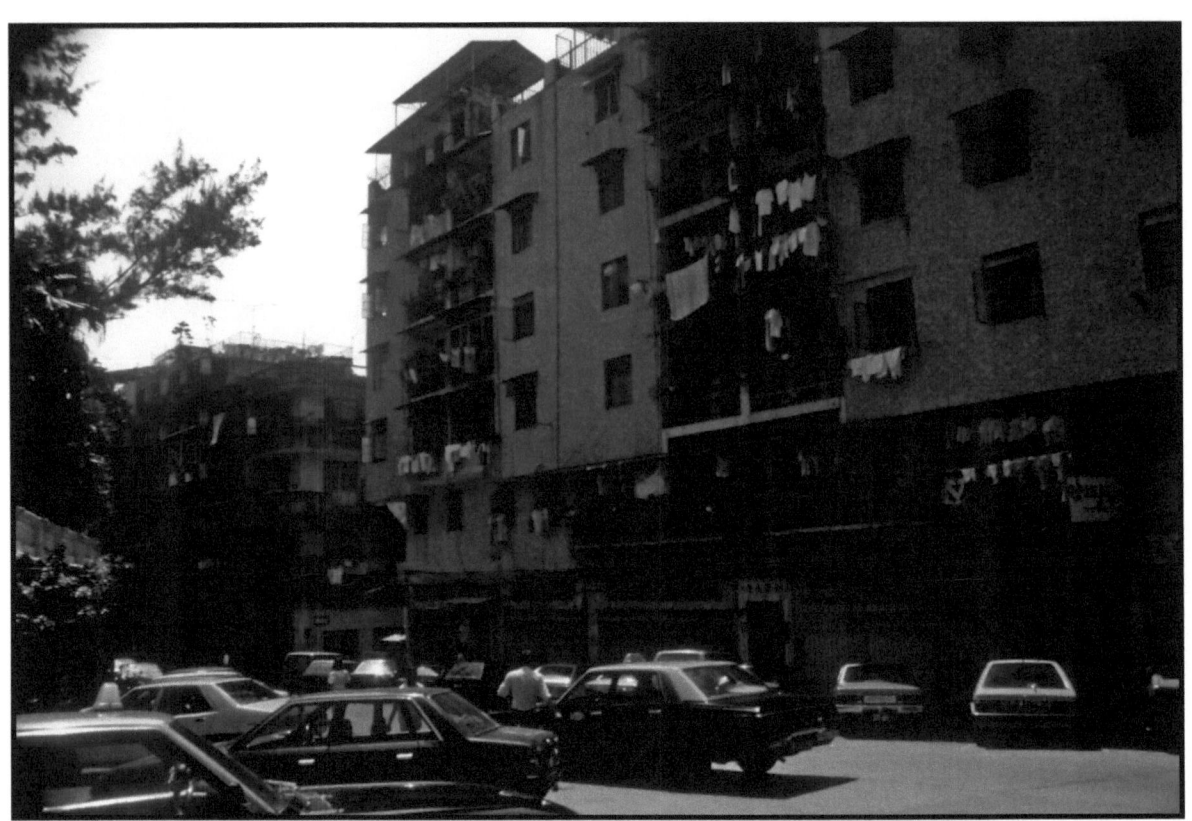

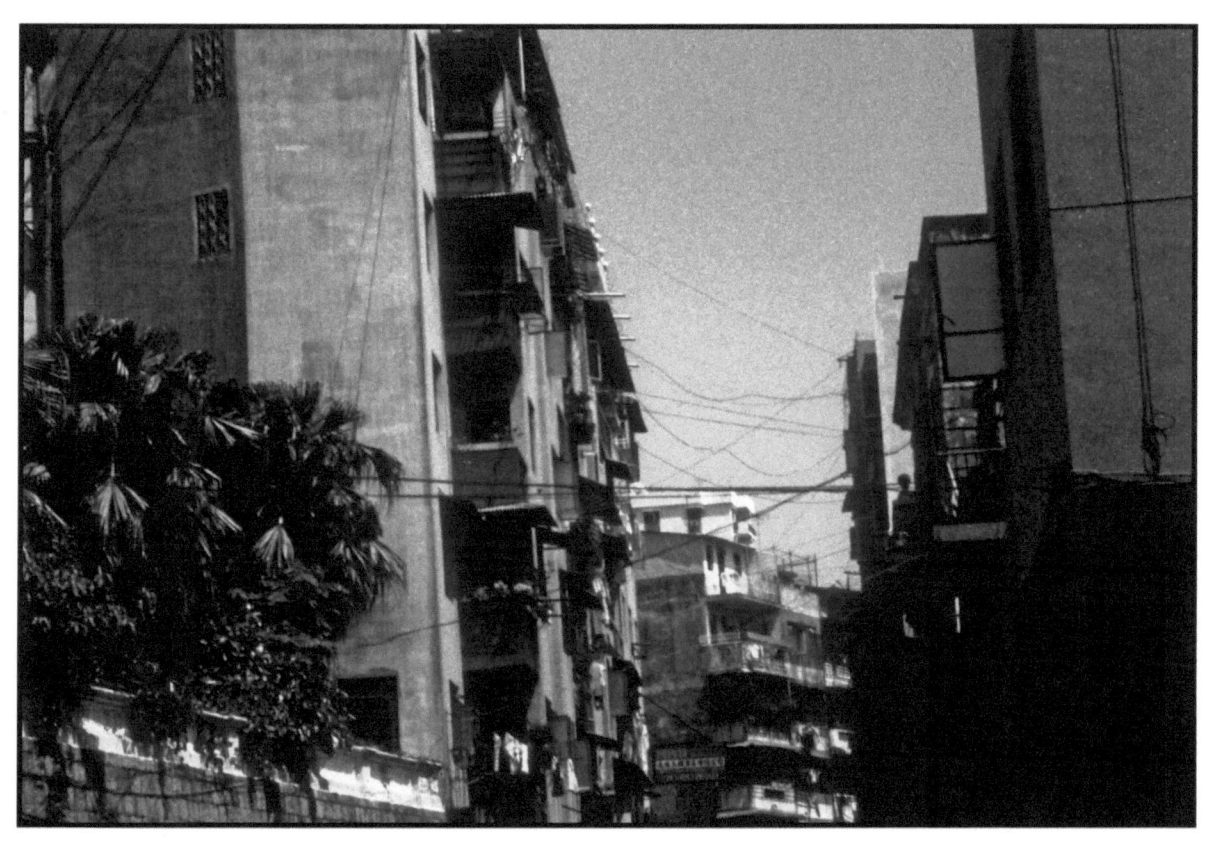

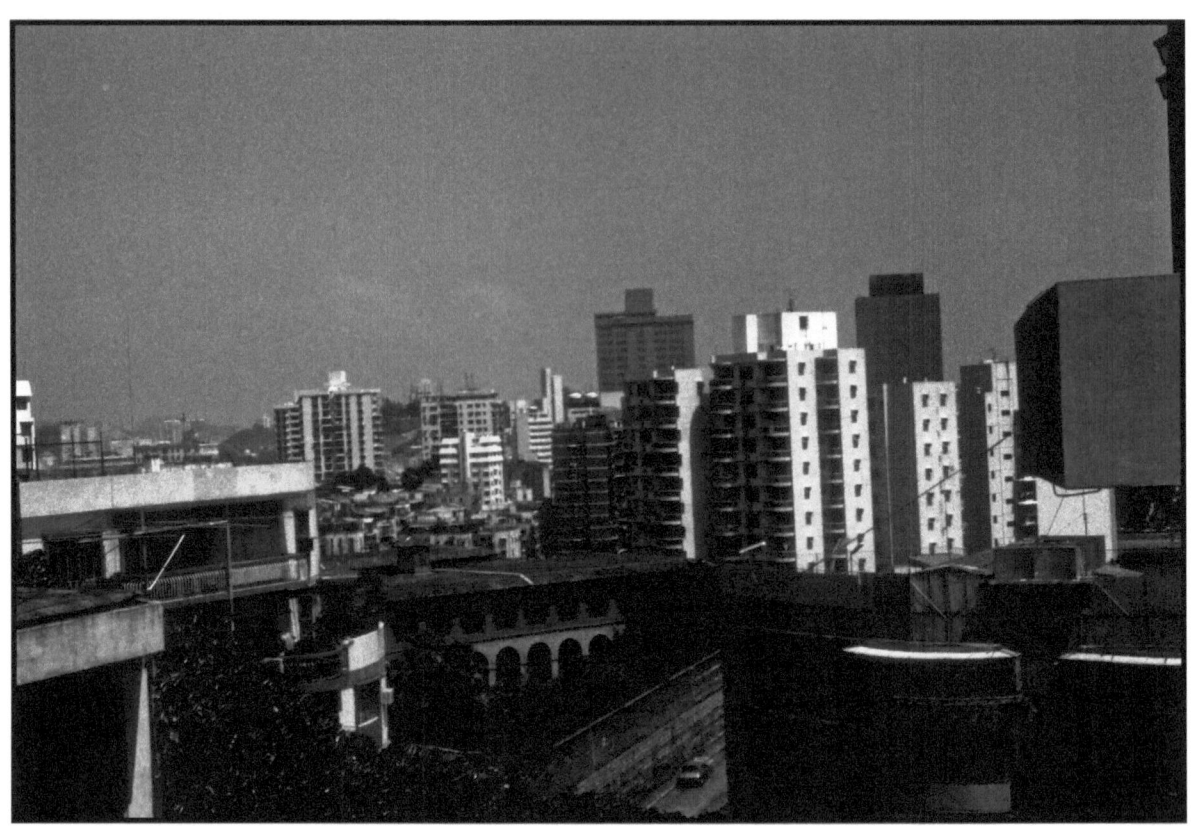

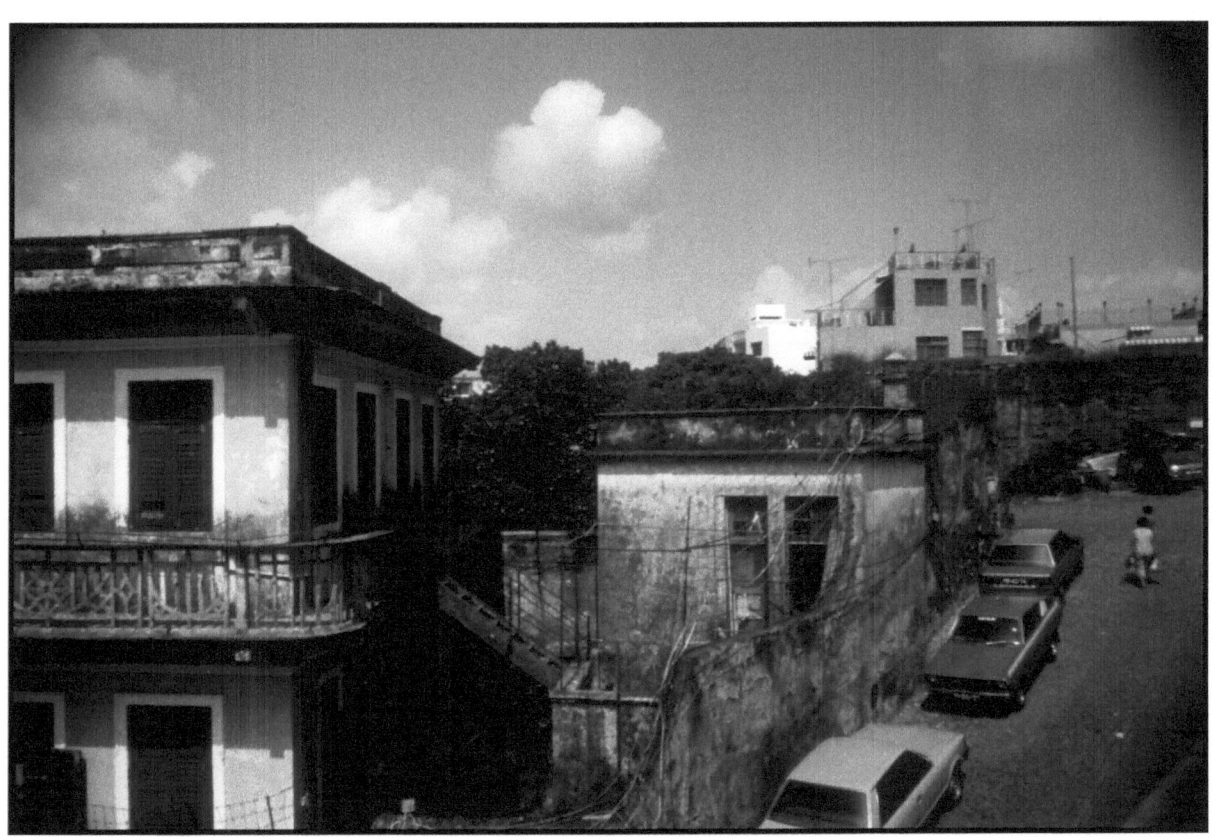

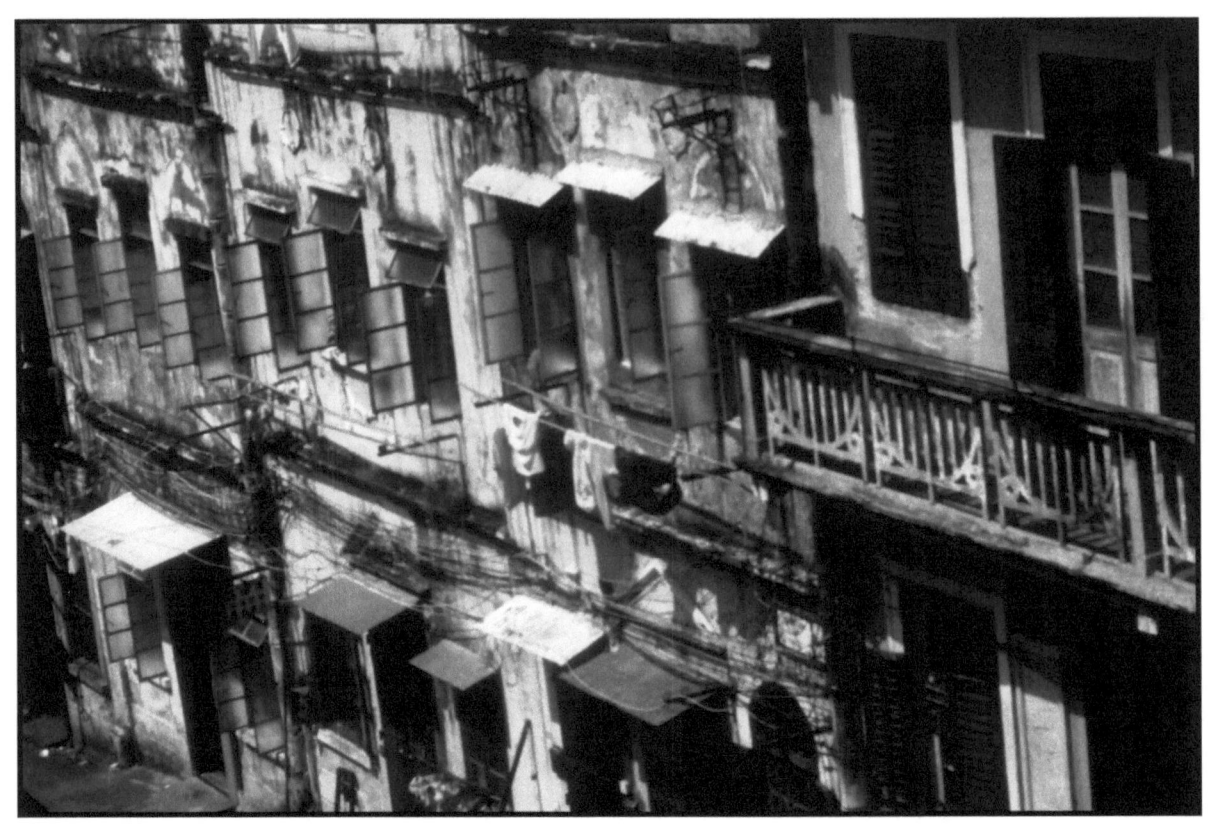

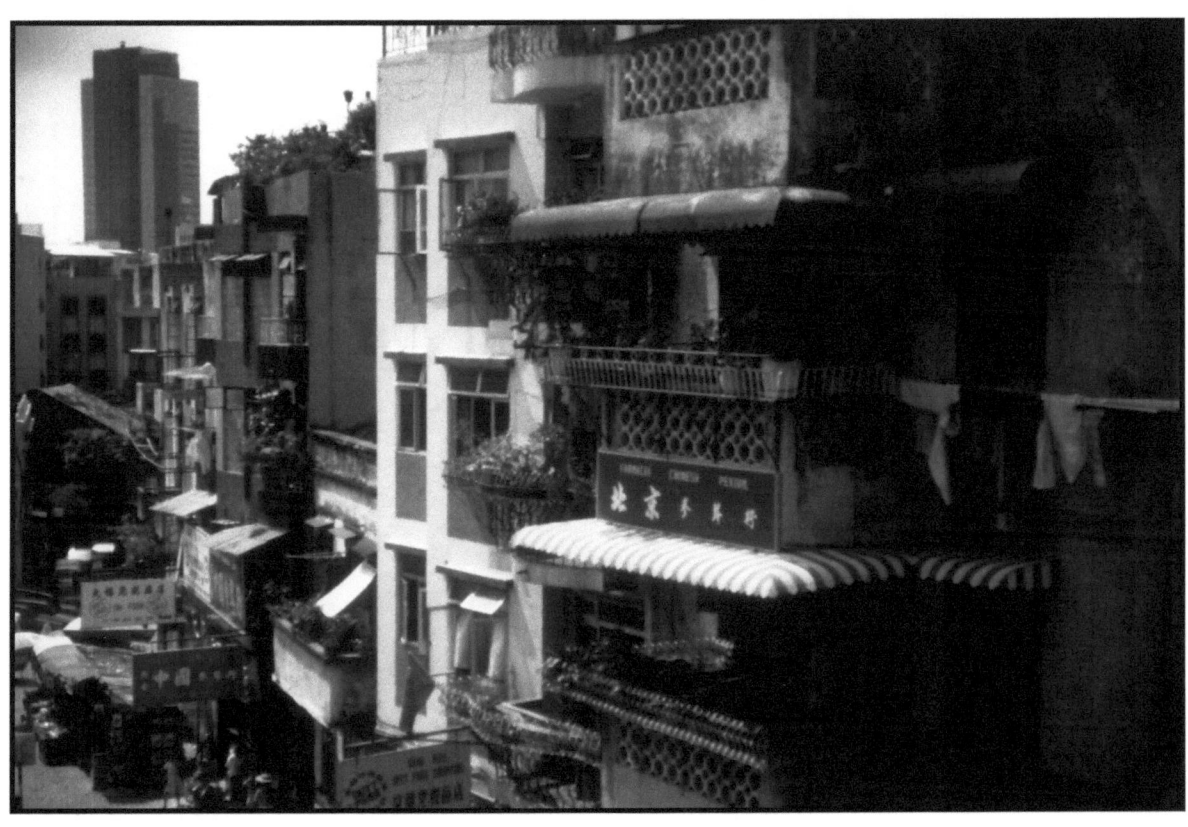

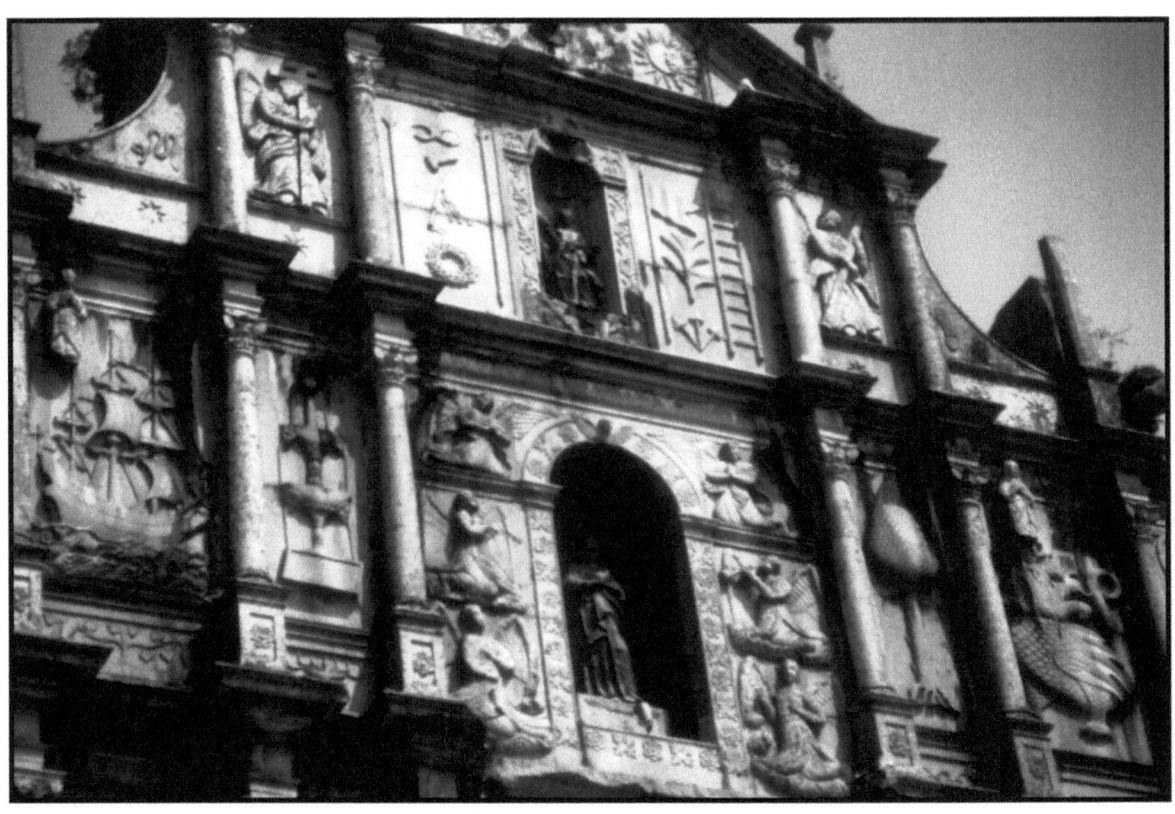

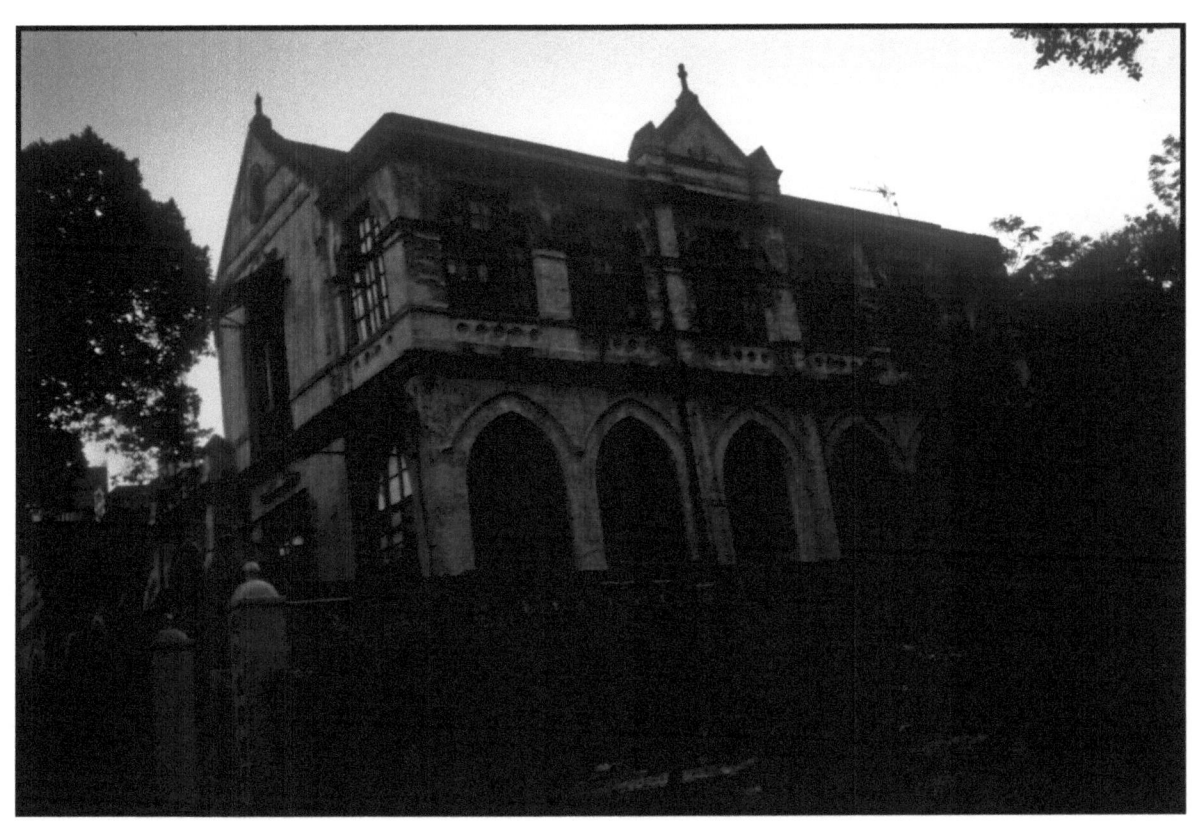

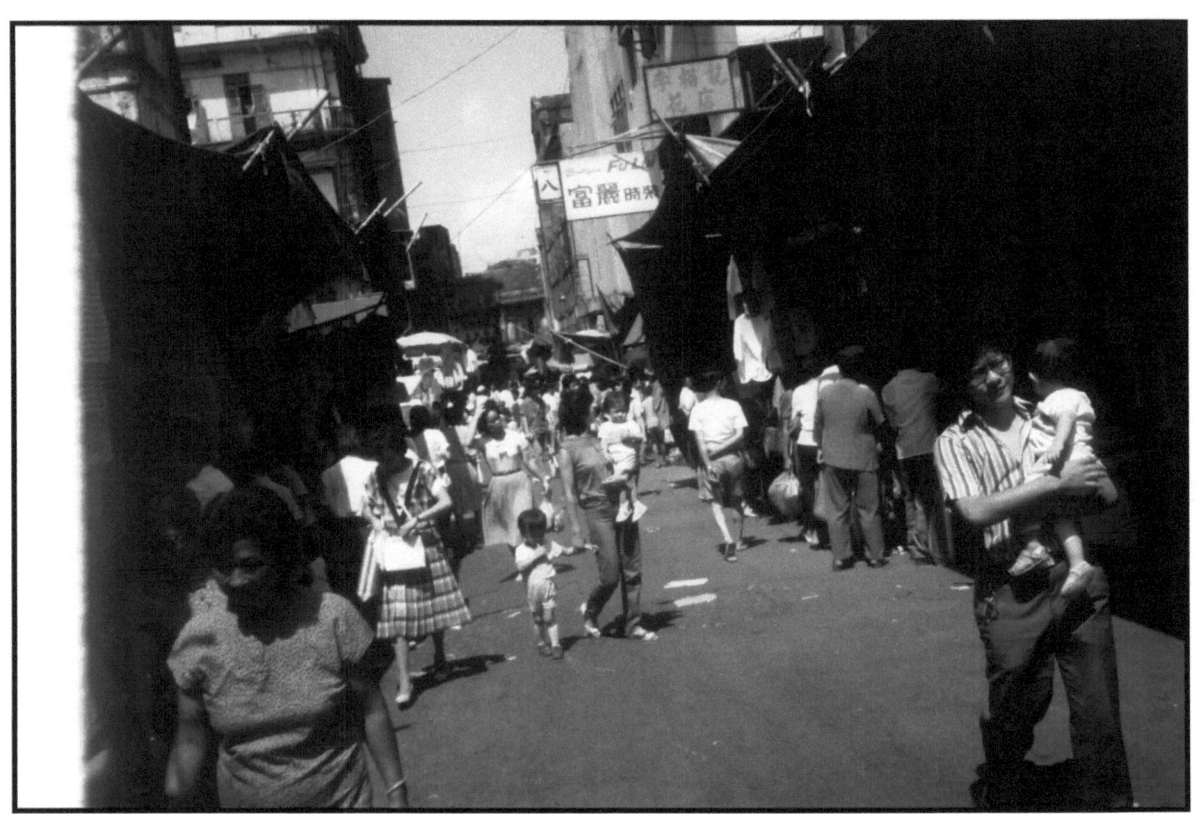

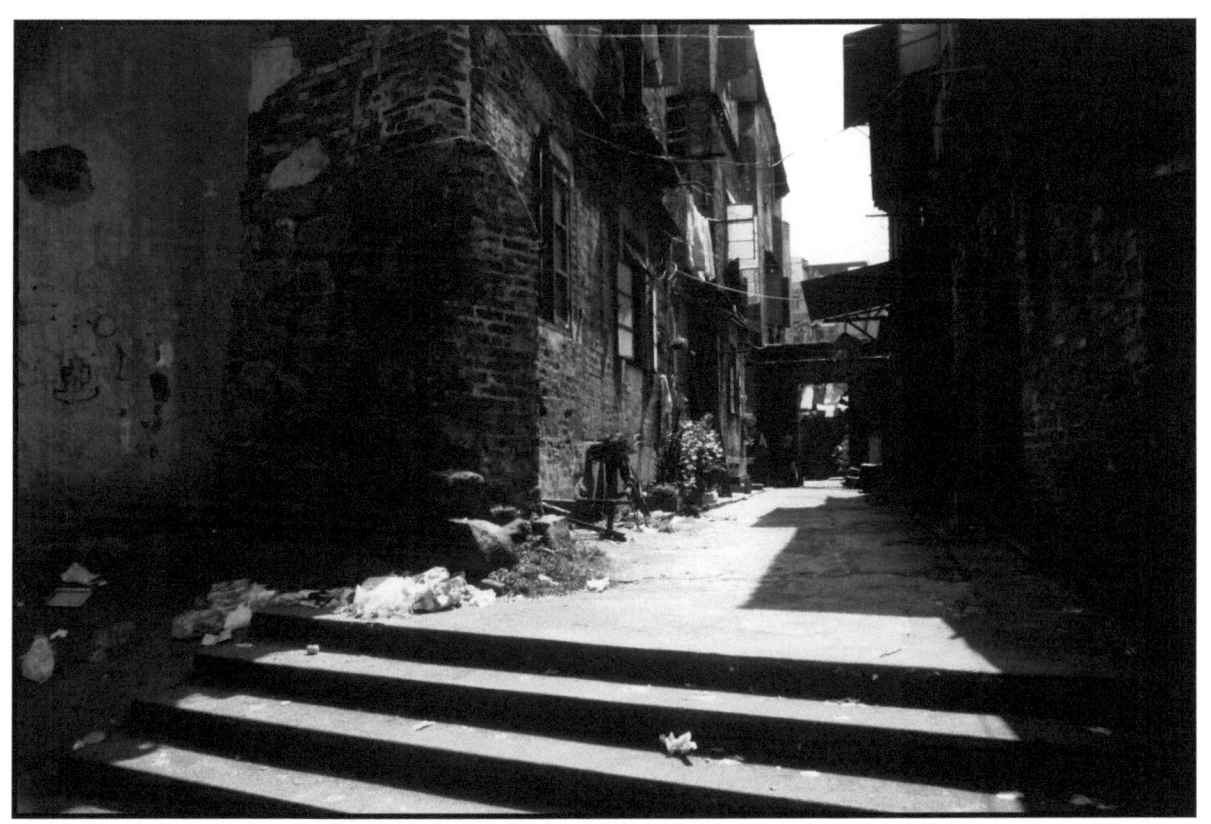

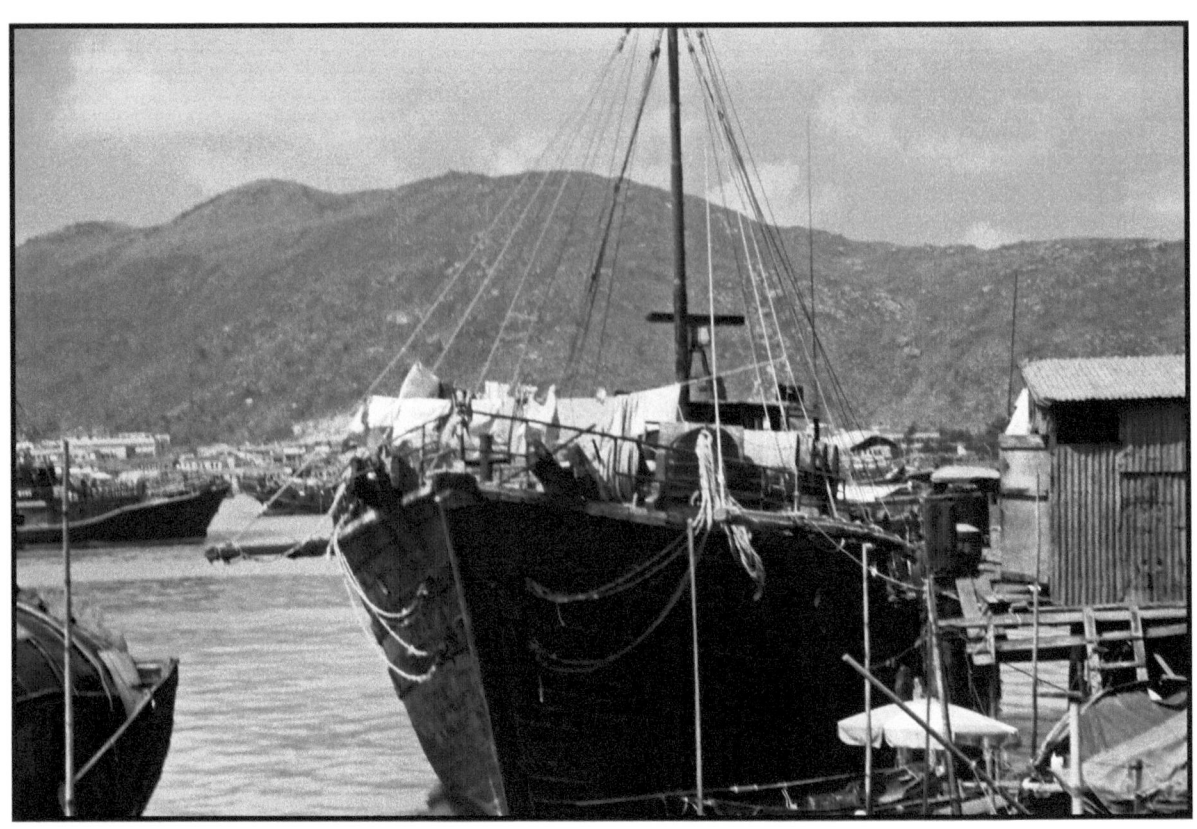

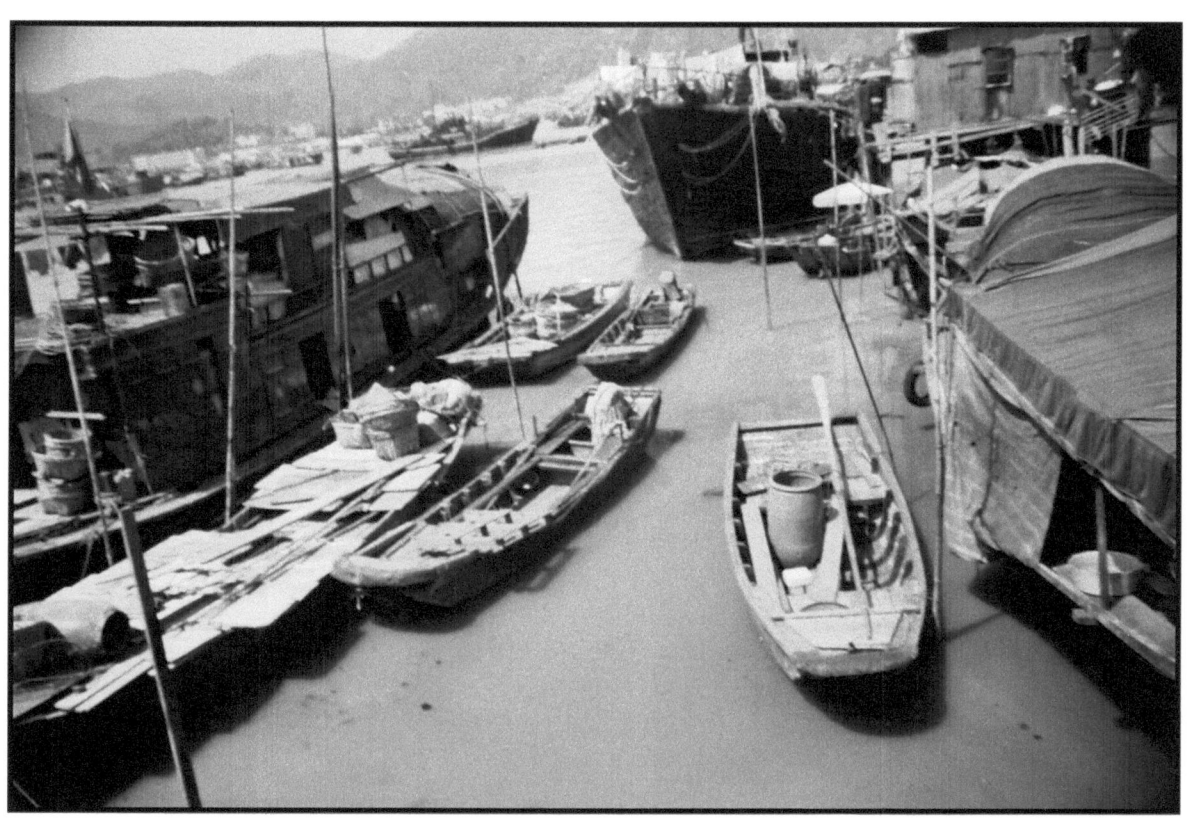

www.ingramcontent.com/pod-product-compliance
Lightning Source LLC
Chambersburg PA
CBHW051147220526
45473CB00003B/688